The Angry Arabs

The Angry Arabs

by
W. F. ABBOUSHI

THE WESTMINSTER PRESS
PHILADELPHIA

BOOK DESIGN BY DOROTHY ALDEN SMITH

Published by The Westminster Press®
Philadelphia, Pennsylvania

PRINTED IN THE UNITED STATES OF AMERICA

Library of Congress Cataloging in Publication Data

Abboushi, W. F., 1931–
    The angry Arabs.

    Includes bibliographical references.
    1. Jewish-Arab relations.   2. Arab countries.
I. Title.
DS119.7.A597   956   73–16128
ISBN 0–664–20991–2

To Arabs and Jews
Who Wish to Live in Peace
as One People
and
To the Palestinian Refugees
Who Endured Much Suffering

Contents

Table of Maps

Foreword

Few conflicts of the twentieth century have engendered the rancor, bitterness, hatred, and intransigence of the Middle East Arab-Israeli dispute. For a quarter of a century it has gone on and it does not abate. Some have even gone so far as to speak of it as the first stages of a modern hundred years' war. Given the present factors, this could actually be so. Because of this, those of us who are not direct combatants but who have an interest in the stability of the area certainly must ask ourselves why this is so, why this failure to resolve so serious an issue, and why literally no progress toward a solution after a quarter of a century and three violent outbreaks.

Professor Abboushi, himself an Arab and also an American, has articulated the complicated sociopolitical contexts from the Arab point of view. This study provides the reader with an understanding of the issues from the Arab point of view— something hard to come by in nonpolemical form in the English language. Professor Abboushi is not always kind to Arab actions and leadership; he does not whitewash either his fellow Muslims or his fellow Arabs. His study is a representative presentation of the general Arab point of view, but at the same time it shows an understanding of the actions of Western Christian nations and peoples.

This is a scholarly work, meeting the classic expectations of scholarship. Professor Abboushi draws upon the appropriate sources, and, given his plainly stated purpose (the exposition

11

of the Arab point of view in the matter), he has set forth a logically valid exposition of their meaning. Fortunately, he avoids tortuous interpretations of sources and data. Most persons without strong emotional commitments or interests on either side of the question will probably concede that the arguments in this work are generally well reasoned and reasonable—even if they do not share the author's conclusions.

Professor Abboushi has contributed the most enlightenment to the matter by his lucid explanation of basic Arab culture, the Arab value system, customs, mores, and folkways as inputs into the issues. By doing this, and by going into the history of the Arab peoples and by dealing with deeply rooted, long-standing Arab hopes, dreams, ambitions, and desires, he has shown us what is behind the legalistic posturing. The root is to be found in the Arab culture, the Arab concept of things, and the Arab perception of things. Arab civilization is different from Western civilization, in which the English-speaking peoples live. Thus it is suggested, and quite correctly, that the Western world does not really understand the Arab position and that the Arabs are hampered by the fact that they lack articulate spokesmen who can translate their view into concepts and terms that Western man can comprehend. The Zionists, on the other hand, are Westernized men, and many of them have this capacity. Thus, according to Professor Abboushi, the Zionists have had the better of the argument in Western eyes because they were better at it, not because they were necessarily more nearly right. He hopes to be among those Arab protagonists who can remedy this disparity. That is the whole thrust of this work, and as a scholarly work with a "message" it is done well.

No matter what one's commitments, views, or feelings are on the Middle East question, one will find this a valuable book for its exposition of the culture of the Arabs as a people. It also is valuable as a calm exposition of current Arab feelings about (or against) various modern Western nation-states. Westerners will not always like what they read, but what

Professor Abboushi says is not offensively stated and certainly is not set forth in the style of the vastly overblown, flamboyant rhetoric of some Arab spokesmen. Here is a gentleman telling us why he does not like what we are doing and trying to persuade us that we might just be wrong.

Professor Abboushi deserves a hearing. He will not change any of the firmly committed on the issue one way or the other, but he does ask some hard questions that we probably would not like to answer and that maybe we should.

This book is a real contribution to the literature on the problem. All interested parties will have to face hard facts and realities. Professor Abboushi poses at least some of them.

DAVID N. ALLOWAY
Professor of Sociology
Montclair State College

Preface

This book is primarily a study in Arab-Western relations from the time of Mohammed to the present. In discussing the Arab view of these relations, I found the following sources especially useful: *The Arab World,* published by the Arab Information Center in New York; *The Palestine Digest,* published by the Arab Information Center of the League of Arab States in Washington, D.C.; and *The Middle East Newsletter,* published by Americans for Justice in the Middle East, an organization based in Beirut, Lebanon. I have also benefited from the work of Dr. Fayez Sayegh and the work of Dr. H. B. Sharabi on the various aspects of the Palestine problem. These two Americans of Arab extraction have written extensively on the Arab-Israeli conflict and on the background of the Palestine controversy. Also of benefit to me was the excellent work of Dr. Fred J. Khouri, *The Arab-Israeli Dilemma* (Syracuse University Press, 1968).

I am also indebted to many individuals for taking an interest in my work. My colleagues Professors Stephen E. Bennett, Kenneth R. Libbey, Abe Miller, and Henry J. Anna provided many opportunities for discussing some of the ideas embodied in this work. At the University of Cincinnati, Professor Norman C. Thomas, head of the political science department, and Professor Robert H. Wessel, vice-provost for graduate studies, encouraged me and gave me moral support. Mr. Robert Muir edited the manuscript. My research assistants and graduate

15

students Bassam Khoury, Diane Borgerding, and Brad Reese saved me many trips to the library. Mrs. Roxanne Smith was patient and efficient in typing two drafts of the manuscript.

Of course, I alone am responsible for any errors of judgment or fact that may be found in the book.

Finally, I should not forget to thank my wife, Leah, and my children, Shareef and Jenine, for lightening the burden of preparing the manuscript.

~ ~

I completed the manuscript for this book in the summer of 1973 and left the United States almost immediately for a period of study abroad. Thus, I was actually in the Middle East at the time of the Arab-Israeli fighting and its aftermath in the fall of 1973. I have refrained, however, from writing a new chapter to cover these events because it was important not to delay publication. I am convinced that what I wrote before the latest hostilities erupted is both important and relevant. My historical account of Arab-Western relations underlines Arab frustrations that impinge so directly on Western concerns today. And my position that the course of the Western powers can be both dangerous and self-defeating has been illustrated again in recent events. Now, with the prospect of a cold winter and in the midst of an "energy crisis," people will be asking new questions about the Middle East and will be listening for answers not only from Israelis but also from the "Angry Arabs."

W. F. A.

December, 1973

Introduction

In recent years, events concerning the Arabs have been very much in the news. Rarely a day passes without a headline report on some Arab country, leader, or activity. The intensity of this Western interest in Arab affairs, of course, results mainly from the Arab-Israeli conflict, which threatens world peace and which could involve the United States in a war having deeper effects on mankind than all previous wars.

If we are to deal with the deadly danger of war in the Arab world, a knowledge of the Arabs is needed—a balanced knowledge, if it is to be useful. Although English-language literature about the Arabs is not scarce, it is naturally based upon assumptions that are largely Western and the values employed by the writers for evaluation and judgment are derived from Western civilization. There is, therefore, a strong need for a new kind of literature, one that shows greater understanding of Arab values.

This book is an attempt to achieve such a balance and understanding. It is designed to show how the Arabs interpret historical controversies involving them, the Western world, and Israel. While it emphasizes the Arab view of these controversies, it does not ignore other views, and it offers opinions that are not popular in the Arab world. Also, since the Arab-Israeli conflict constitutes the major controversy, and the most recent one, almost half the book is devoted to an explanation of its history and its implications. This is wholly consistent

17

with the main purpose of the book, which is to explain why the Arabs seem bitter and frustrated in their regional and international relations.

Chapter 1 is designed to give the reader very basic information about life before the great Islamic conquests of the seventh century. The first few pages acquaint the reader with pre-Islamic Arab organization and customs. However, most of the chapter is about the Islamic religion, the force that motivated the Arab to build a vast empire and a great civilization.

The material in the first chapter is intended to straighten out the misconceptions among Western people about Arab customs and Islam. To do this I have selected on the one hand customs criticized in the West, and on the other, positive customs or traits that are not appreciated adequately by Western people. Also, the discussion of the Islamic religion attempts to give the reader a picture of this religion in juxtaposition with Christianity and Judaism.

Chapter 2 deals with the Arab-Islamic Empire in order to give the reader an appreciation of the Arabs as the builders of a great civilization. An account of Arab conquests is included, with a brief description of the political organization of their empires. But the main emphasis is on an analysis of Arab contributions to world civilization and, particularly, to Western civilization—followed by a discussion of how the Western world, specifically Europe, reacted to the Arab contribution. It is the thesis of this chapter that Europe benefited from the Arabs at the same time it discredited them; and that for a number of reasons the images Europe formulated of the Arabs and their Islamic religion were negative.

Chapter 3 discusses the downfall of the Arabs as rulers of a world empire. They were gradually replaced by the Ottoman Turks, under whose empire Arab culture stagnated. Special attention is given to Egypt, where events such as the construction of the Suez Canal, the politics involving it, and British occupation constitute important background for later Egyp-

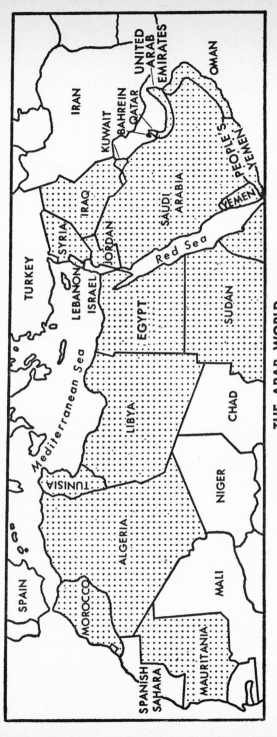

THE ARAB WORLD

tian problems. Egypt is seen as suffering under foreign rule
and domestic corruption, which helps explain why, later,
Nasser's Arab nationalism reacted strongly to these two problems.

Modern Arab socialism and the current issues of imperialism
both derive from the historical background discussed in this
chapter.

A tragic partition of Arab lands is related in Chapter 4.
After the downfall of the Ottoman Empire in 1916, the European powers took over the Fertile Crescent and divided it
into a number of small states. Iraq, Syria, Lebanon, Palestine,
and Transjordan emerged, dominated by France and Britain.
The partition of Syria (into Syria, Lebanon, Transjordan, and
Palestine) was the product of highly controversial international and regional activities. Secret agreements, promises,
counterpromises, and intrigue characterized these activities,
involving Britain, France, the Zionists, and the Arabs.

The ways by which Syria was divided were of doubtful
ethics and morality and the purposes of the divisions were of
doubtful wisdom. The experience was important to the Arabs,
who believed that the Western world had betrayed them. It
contributed both to bad Arab-Western relations and to the
development of an Arab nationalism that was characterized by
anti-Western feelings.

But it was the Palestine problem, the subject of Chapter 5,
that radically affected Arab-Western relations. The Zionist
movement, the mass immigration of Jews to Palestine, and the
British role in the controversy greatly angered the Arab nationalists, in whose eyes the establishment of the State of
Israel after World War II was to be seen as the climax of
Western imperialistic designs against them. This chapter gives
the history of the Palestine problem and documents Arab and
Zionist arguments on the subject. Although the Arab point of
view is elaborated, the Zionist point of view is not ignored,
and the reader is consciously made aware of it.

Chapters 6 and 7 consider the problems of war and peace

in the Middle East. Although no practical solution to the Arab-Israeli conflict is offered, the difficulties of peace and the implications of war are analyzed in order to provide the reader with an insight into the future of the controversy.

Finally, the closing chapter discusses Arab-American relations, which is a particularly pertinent subject since the United States is a superpower and is the leading Western country. Also, it will be close to the interests of American readers, for whom the book is primarily written. Perhaps the most important part of the chapter is the analysis dealing with Zionist pressure on the American Government and American interests in the Arab world. The conclusion that is drawn from this analysis is that the United States is torn between her domestic and social interests and her foreign economic and strategic interests. As a result, she has been unable to act as a peacemaker in the Middle East.

Outside intervention in the Arab-Israeli conflict might be useful to the superpowers but would prove detrimental to both the Arabs and the Israelis. At the same time, continuation of the conflict is bad for the Arabs in the short run and bad for the Israelis in the long run. Moreover, if the superpowers continue to identify with the main parties in the conflict, the possibility of World War III exists. Under no circumstances should they intervene without prior agreement among them on a solution. World War III threatens greater disaster for mankind than do continued Arab-Israeli wars, if limited to the local parties. In other words, regardless of the outcome of Arab-Israeli wars, mankind will be better off if these wars do not directly involve the superpowers.

Chapter 1

Arab Life
Before the Empire

Before the birth of Mohammed in A.D. 570 the Arabs were not among the most famous people of the world. They were mostly nomadic, and their land, the Arabian peninsula, was largely arid and inhospitable.

The Arabian peninsula is about one third the size of the United States, and all of it, with the exception of the extreme southern portion and a few patches here and there, is barren. Irrigation systems had been tried even before the time of Mohammed, but neither these nor their modern counterparts were enough to alter the harsh and cruel environment.

THE EARLY ARABS

The Tribe. The harshness of the countryside dictated a nomadic and warlike way of life. Arab tribes moved from one place to another to look for green lands, scarcity forcing them to compete fiercely among themselves. They became excellent warriors, developing a survival pattern in which rivalry characterized relations between the tribes and loyalty characterized the relationship of the individual to his own tribe. Even so, the concept of alliance was known to the Arabs. It was often necessary for tribes to join in coalition to offset the preponderance of the larger tribes or the preponderance of other coalitions. However, these alliances and coalitions shifted with changes in the power structure and the conditions of survival.

23

Of course, this pattern was one of political fragmentation. And although the tribal form of organization has declined and the contemporary Arab world has modern and semimodern communities, the pre-Islamic political fragmentation persists. This is the one element in Arab tradition which still contributes to rifts between governments and between Arab leaders.

Early Contact with the Outside. The nomadic life of the early Arabs did not prevent them from making contact with the higher civilizations that surrounded their peninsula. A small influential elite whose main occupation was trade traveled beyond Arabia. Thus, the early Arabs were never really isolated, and their awareness of life outside the peninsula increased after Mohammed.

However, because the pre-Islamic Arabs thought the Red Sea was dangerous, their contact with the outside was limited to overland commerce, with Egypt and the Fertile Crescent. During the time of the Roman Empire this trade declined. But there was enough of it to sustain the economics of the few settled communities in the western and southern parts of Arabia.

There were cultural exchanges and racial ties between the people of Arabia and the more advanced people of the Fertile Crescent, the area north of the peninsula. Like the Arabs, these people were of Semitic origin.[1]

Historians agree that the Arabs were distinguished for their eagerness to learn from the more advanced people and for their ability to put such knowledge to use. This accounted for the richness of the civilization they developed later. That civilization synthesized the contributions of earlier civilizations. It borrowed elements from the Byzantines, the Persians, the Indians, and the Chinese, added to them its own, and transmitted the product to others.

Some Early Customs and Traits. Certain early Arab customs have come under criticism in the Western world and they have been used to support anti-Arab feelings. One of these customs, practiced by a few pre-Islamic Arab tribes, was infanticide, the killing of a newborn child. Today infanticide is generally considered murder, but it was not always considered so. Greece and Rome, two of the most important ancient civilizations, permitted it. In most Greek city-states, the decision to kill the child was usually made by the father, but in a few such communities the mother made the decision. In Sparta, the decision was made by a public official. In all these communities, it was the coming of the great monotheistic religions that ended the practice. Judaism, Christianity, and Islam all prohibited it.

Another Arab custom was the blood feud. Like infanticide, the custom was not peculiar to the Arabs. Europe has had its share of blood feuds, and its history is filled with killing for revenge. Family feuds continue in Corsica, the Balkans, and Sicily, and in the mountain regions of the southeastern part of the United States. The feuds in the nineteenth century between the Hatfield and the McCoy families of Kentucky have become part of American folklore.

Arab rivalries and feuds produced some positive practices and customs. For instance, the pre-Islamic Arabs knew arbitration as an important method of settling disputes. This institution was a relatively well developed technique in Arabia, and the Arabs had a strong tradition of honoring agreements. In addition, tribal wars caused the Arabs to admire the brave and to exalt courage. A great deal of pre-Islamic Arab poetry testifies to this. There was also a strong emphasis on loyalty to one's family, clan, and tribe, which made a life full of rivalries more secure. The emphasis on friendship was strengthened by the custom of honoring one's ancestry. Arabs would trace their ancestries to find friendship between their families in the past. Thus the bonds of friendship took on the added sanction of tradition.

Although economic scarcity made war part of the Arab's way of life, peace was a desired goal. Every year there was a recognized time when all fighting ceased and Arabs visited

Mecca to worship (Mecca was a commercial center near the Red Sea). In Mecca, the Kaaba had religious significance for most tribes regardless of the differences in their deities. Mecca, the meeting place for the Arab tribes, was a symbol of religious tolerance as well as a symbol of peace.

The most admirable quality of the peninsula Arab was hospitality. The harshness of desert life necessitated the development of this characteristic. Without public facilities to accommodate the traveler, it became the duty of every Arab to open his home to visitors and to see to it that they were comfortable: Hospitality has remained an important aspect of Arab life, even though only a minority of Arabs still live in deserts. However, because they are time-consuming, the customs associated with Arab hospitality are considered somewhat tiresome in the modern communities of the Middle East. Nevertheless, the tradition of hospitality is still useful and necessary in the less-developed communities; and one must admit that it is a delightful tradition in a world that is largely materialistic.

THE ARAB PROPHET OF ISLAM

Early Life. The greatest single influence on the world of the Arabs was the coming of Islam; and the founder and chief prophet of the Islamic religion is Mohammed.

Born in Mecca in A.D. 570, Mohammed belonged to the Qureish family, the most powerful and the best-known family in the city. He spent most of his growing years in the care of an uncle, his father having died before he was born, and his mother while he was still a child. (He spent a short time in the care of his grandfather, but the grandfather, too, died while Mohammed was still young.)

Until Mohammed was forty, there was nothing very unusual about his character or behavior. He was an ordinary citizen with a reputation for honesty, gentleness, and devotion; and he showed no inclination toward revolutionary change. There were no signs that he would become the prophet of a great religion.

As a young man, Mohammed showed an interest in business. He and his uncle made a trip to Syria with a trade caravan. Later, he made more of these trips as the representative of Khadija, a rich widow in her early thirties. The widow admired Mohammed for his honesty and straightforwardness. Soon the business partnership became a marriage partnership. When the two were married, Mohammed was twenty-five and Khadija was forty. However, in spite of the difference in their ages, this proved to be a happy marriage.

While Mohammed attended to her business with diligence, she attended to his family with devotion. The couple had several children, but only the female children survived infancy. One of them, Fatima, married Mohammed's cousin Ali, who would later become the fourth caliph (successor).

Khadija trusted Mohammed and gave him complete authority to manage her business. Her wealth, however, did not corrupt him, and with her approval he gave some of it to the poor. He also freed her slaves at a time when slavery was acceptable and the Islamic religion had not yet come to him.

But honesty and compassion are hardly indications of a vocation to preach a new religion, or of a destiny to lead a movement that would become one of the most powerful in the history of the world. Indeed, Mohammed's new interest in religion at the age of forty seemed quite sudden (a fact which gave greater credence to the idea that he was chosen by God as his prophet).

Nor did the fact that Mohammed liked to spend part of his free time in meditation indicate anything special to his family and neighbors. True, he made a habit of retreating to a cave on a hill outside Mecca, but since he was a reserved person, no one knew what he did during his retreat, and never during this time did he show any dislike for, or opposition to, the paganism of the people of Mecca.

But it was during one of these visits to the cave, in 610, that Mohammed first communicated with God. According to his account, a mysterious voice ordered him to "read"; and when Mohammed answered that he could not read (he was illiterate), the voice said:

Read: In the name of Thy Lord Who Createth,
Createth man from a clot.
Read: And it is Thy Lord the Most Bountiful
Who teacheth by the pen,
Teacheth man that which he knew not.

This was the first revelation to come to him. He went home excited and disturbed, and unable to relate his experience to anyone but his trusted wife. Khadija advised him to speak to a relative, an old man "who knew the Scriptures of the Jews and the Christians." The old man agreed that God had revealed himself to Mohammed.

Mohammed's Ascendancy to Power. When Mohammed began to preach the new religion, few people believed him. Among the early converts were his wife, Khadija; Zaid, a slave that Mohammed had freed; Ali, the prophet's eleven-year-old cousin; and Abu Bakr, a wealthy friend who would later become the first caliph.

Most people in Mecca thought Mohammed had gone a little mad; they did not believe his claim that God communicated with him. But the number of converts increased, and as they did so, the opposition to the prophet and the new religion also increased. One good reason for Meccan concern was the new religion's threat to paganism—which brought pilgrims and trade to the city. Many attempts were made to assassinate the prophet. The new converts were also in danger and the Meccans treated them harshly. In 622, persecution compelled Mohammed to leave Mecca and go to Yathrib (later renamed Medina). The event marked the first year in the Muslim calendar. In history, it is known as the Hijra ("migration").

In Medina, Mohammed concluded an agreement with the influential Jewish tribes.² Under its terms, the Jews were to enjoy freedom of religion and the right to live under their own laws and customs. Soon, however, trouble developed between Jews and Muslims, mainly because the Jews felt uncomfortable with a rival monotheistic religion and the Muslims behaved as though they were the city's traditional authority. The Jews began to conspire with the Meccans against the prophet and his followers. After several unsuccessful efforts toward reconciliation and after reminding the Jews of their treaty obligation to defend the city against Meccan attacks, Mohammed declared war against them. Eventually, the Jews were forced to leave Medina and settle elsewhere in Arabia.

In Mecca, Mohammed was a preacher. In Medina, he was the head of a city-state. The feud between the two city-states, pagan Mecca and Muslim Medina, developed into open war. In the battle of Badr (A.D. 624), the Muslims won an astounding victory against the superior arms of the Meccans. This gave Mohammed greater prestige, but it also increased the determination of the people of Mecca to destroy Muslim power. Almost immediately after Badr, the Meccans began to prepare for the second round. In the next battle, Uhud (A.D. 625), the Muslims were defeated and there followed a decline in Muslim prestige, especially among the tribes.

In Medina, the Muslims felt threatened by Jewish conspiracy, and their position became more precarious. The Jews collaborated with the Meccans, and the alliance was supported by many tribes outside Medina. The Muslims dealt with the Jewish collaborators first, and the result was the expulsion from the city (in A.D. 626) of one of the Jewish tribes.

The anti-Muslim alliance, the "confederation," formed a large army, about twenty thousand strong. In anticipation of an attack on Medina, the Muslims dug a trench around the city. When the battle took place in A.D. 627, the Muslims were ready. During the siege, the Muslims were again threatened by the Jewish tribes. Fortunately for them, bad weather made the siege impossible for the invaders, who decided to abandon their project. Mohammed immediately took measures against the Jewish tribes that had collaborated with the Meccans, and after a month of fighting the Jews were forced to leave the city.

The battle of the Trench marked the beginning of Muslim ascendancy to power in the entire Arabian peninsula. Now the prestige of the Muslims was so high that many Arab tribes outside the warring cities became Mohammed's allies.

After the battle of the Trench, Mohammed wished to visit Mecca, his birthplace, which he had not seen for six years. The Kaaba was his main interest because it was associated with Abraham, the Arabs' "ancestral father" and one of the important prophets recognized by Islam; and thus the place had a special significance to the Muslims. The people of Mecca, aware of Muslim superiority, accepted the conclusion (in A.D. 628) of a treaty, the treaty of Hudaybiyah, which permitted Mohammed and the Muslims to visit Mecca after a year. In addition, the treaty stipulated that the war between Mecca and Medina would cease for a period of ten years. Although many Muslims believed the treaty was not in their best interests, Mohammed believed that the secession of hostilities would permit him to preach the word of God and gain new converts without resort to violence.

But the Meccans violated the treaty the year after it was concluded, by attacking one of the tribes allied with Mohammed. Muslim force gathered for a showdown, but the Meccans decided not to fight because of obvious Muslim superiority. Mohammed then entered the city unopposed, destroyed the idols the pagan Meccans worshiped, and declared that henceforth only the worship of one God would be allowed in the Kaaba.

After fighting one more battle, Hunain (A.D. 631), against recalcitrant tribes, this time with the Meccans on their side, the Muslims were the most powerful force in Arabia. Soon more of their enemies became their allies. New converts were won to Islam, and in a short time a large portion of Arabia was a Muslim country with Mohammed as its head.

In the tenth Muslim year, A.D. 631, Mohammed went on a pilgrimage to Mecca. (He had returned to Medina to live.) It was his last pilgrimage, and it is said that he knew his life was coming to an end. He spoke to a large crowd of people and urged them to obey the Koran and the things he taught them, to respect their women and give them their rights, to treat justly their prisoners of war, to respect individual rights, and finally to consider all Muslims brothers. This was his "farewell address," and he died a year later, in A.D. 632. He was buried in Medina, which became, after Mecca, the second holy city of Islam.

THE ISLAMIC RELIGION

Islam means submission, and a Muslim is one who submits to God. Under the Islamic religion, Mohammed is only a prophet. He has no divine qualities or supernatural powers. He performed no miracles, but he had two distinctions. God selected him to teach his message, and he was to be the last prophet.[3] Of course, he became the model of the believer, and Muslims emulated his conduct.

The Koran. Islam's sacred book is the Koran ("recitation" or "discourse"). Muslims believe the Koran was revealed to Mohammed by God over a period of about twenty-two years, from 610 to 632. It was not written down at the time, but committed to memory by the early followers. Consequently, there was concern about possible omissions and errors. The first caliph, Abu Bakr, had attempted to compile in writing the various chapters, but it was not until 650 that a single authoritative edition was published. This edition was ordered by the third caliph, Othman, who also ordered the destruction of all other sources of the Koran. Othman's edition survived, and it is the one in current use. Today, scholars generally agree that the Koran is a well-preserved document with very little doubt about its authenticity.

The Koran is revered by Muslims. Before a Muslim can even touch the holy book, he is required to be "pure" or to go through a "purification" ritual of cleaning certain parts of the body (sexual intercourse requires a full bath for "purification"). Muslims are encouraged to read the Koran in their spare time, and individuals who cannot read are usually able to recite from the Koran. Some commit the whole book to memory, beginning the task at a very early age.

Of course, the language of the Koran is Arabic. Many Muslim scholars believe that the Koran is the most important reason why the Arabic classical language has survived. They also believe that the Koran is an Arabic classic, the best writing in that language. Because of this, the book is read by Arab Christians, many of whom have learned to appreciate its literary value. It has been an indispensable source for literary scholars, whatever their religious beliefs. Especially in the latter part of the nineteenth century, the Lebanese Christian writers knew the Koran very well, and they were among the most outstanding contributors to the Arabic language and literature.

Early in the development of Islam, translations of the holy book were not authorized. Today such translations exist, but Arabic scholars believe that the book loses much of its vitality and literary beauty in translation; and anyone who can compare a translation to the classical Arabic would agree. In fact, many non-Arab scholars and writers had difficulty understanding and appreciating Islam because they lacked a strong command of the Arabic language. Those Western scholars who learned the Arabic language generally did better in their writing about Islam.

The Five Pillars of Islam. Islam imposes five religious duties on its followers. Known as the "pillars of Islam," they are: the profession of the faith, prayers, almsgiving, fasting, and pilgrimage.

Profession of the faith consists of the pronouncement of the formula "There is no God but God, and Mohammed is the messenger of God." A Muslim must make this pronouncement with conviction and a serious attitude. However, contemporary Muslims are in the habit of repeating the formula many times every day: it has become a convenient expression to reaffirm Islamic conviction and to remind Muslims of the significance of religion to their whole social existence.

Prayers are performed five times a day: at dawn, at noon, in midafternoon, after sunset, and at the end of the day. They are preceded by the purification rituals and consist of recitation from the Koran and certain prescribed bodily movements.

Almsgiving is of two kinds: the *zakah* (compulsory contribution) and the *sadakah* (voluntary contribution). The *zakah* may be considered a form of state tax which, above a certain minimum, ranges from one fortieth to one tenth of the value of ownership (property, money, cattle, agricultural produce, etc.). Only Saudi Arabia, and, to a certain extent, Pakistan, still collects this kind of tax. The other Muslim countries have tax systems similar to those in Western countries.

The *sadakah*, the voluntary almsgiving, is given by individuals directly to the poor and to charity organizations. Muslims give *sadakah* in the hope that it goes to their credit with God. In Muslim countries where the state no longer collects the compulsory tax, people still give *sadakah* for their own salvation.

Fasting takes place during the month of Ramadan, the month the first revelation occurred.[4] During the entire month, Muslims are required to fast from dawn to sunset each day—abstaining from food, liquids (alcoholic beverages are prohibited at all times), and certain kinds of pleasures such as smoking and sexual intercourse. Fasting is not required of the sick, the old, and travelers.

During Ramadan the pattern of life changes in the Muslim

world. During the day, working hours are shorter, people look tired, and places of food and pleasure are usually closed. At night there is vitality: restaurants, shops, and places of entertainment are open until early in the morning. In short, the night becomes day and the day becomes night.

Many Muslims believe this custom has rendered fasting meaningless and is, therefore, contrary to the spirit of Islam, particularly since the purpose of fasting is to give Muslims some appreciation of the dilemma of the poor. Others believe the custom has some advantages for health. But whatever the significance of the fasting, it must be remembered that Ramadan is the month of intense worshiping. It does remind Muslims of the sanctity of religious life and the generosity of God.

Modern life, especially city life, has made fasting extremely cumbersome. This, plus the fact that Ramadan sometimes comes with hot weather, has led to frequent violations of the rule. In some Muslim countries the law still requires places of food and pleasure to close during the day, and prohibits eating and drinking in public. In others, however, the individual is left to perform his religious duty without the interference of the government.

The last duty of the Muslim is pilgrimage. Every Muslim is required to visit the holy places in Mecca, Saudi Arabia, at least once in his lifetime. While on pilgrimage Muslims will usually go also to Medina to visit the grave of the prophet Mohammed. And some pilgrims will also stop in Jerusalem, the third holiest city of Islam. In the past the trip to Mecca was long, expensive, and tiring. Even train travel was an ordeal if distances were great, and some of the less fortunate had to journey on the backs of animals. Today, however, airplanes carry pilgrims regularly during the season from many parts of the Islamic world to Mecca. Of course, those who cannot afford the air fare still travel by the old methods. However, those who cannot afford it or are physically unable to endure the journey are exempted from the duty of pilgrimage.

The meeting in Mecca of Muslims from all over the world

every year symbolizes Islamic unity and signifies the religion's international character. It reawakens religious feelings in the pilgrims themselves and in those who wait at home for their return. Upon his return, the pilgrim is received with ceremony and is accorded special respect thereafter. He is considered to have become "clean" of sin and to be indeed a new man.

The Sources of Islam. Islam is a way of life, not just a religion. It is concerned with people's temporal affairs as well as their spiritual life. The sources of Islamic law are the Koran, the traditions, analogy, and consensus.

The *Koran* is absolute and has priority over the other three sources. Muslims believe there can be no conflict between the Koran and the traditions, which include Mohammed's statements, actions, and rulings. They argue that no one knows God's laws better than his prophet.

Although the Koran is "perfect" in that it cannot be wrong, it does not cover all human situations. While alive, the prophet dealt with some of these uncovered situations, and his solutions were the first of *the traditions.* Individuals who knew Mohammed recorded his statements and rulings either in writing or by memory.

Since these reports were not initially compiled in one single source, questions about their authenticity have arisen. To verify authenticity, the motives and circumstances of the reporters or recorders are investigated, and the reports themselves are examined for evidence of spuriousness. Authenticity is sometimes considered established if a fact recurs in more than one report or if the objectivity of the compiler or reporter has already been verified. Thus, precaution is required before any report on traditions is accepted.

In spite of these problems, the traditions constitute an important source of Islamic law. In addition, they are useful in explaining Islamic social thought in its historical context.

Analogy, the third source of Islamic law, is used when there

are no definite prescriptions in the Koran or the traditions to
apply to a certain case. The problem is then resolved by taking
the prescriptions or traditions applied in an analogous case
already decided and applying them to the undecided case,
providing the two are factually similar. Accordingly, Islamic
analogy approximates the Anglo-American judicial doctrine of
stare decisis (precedent). Like that doctrine, analogy con-
nects current and past legal practices to establish cohesive
legal traditions. Consequently, both the Arab and the Anglo-
American doctrines are conservative in nature and are often
inadequate to deal effectively with modern problems.

Legal problems not resolved by the Koran, the traditions,
and analogy are resolved by a consensus of Muslim scholars.
Consensus became important as the Islamic community expanded and as situations not existing in past practice developed. In this connection we should remember that the
Islamic state began as a city-state in Medina, became a "national" state in Arabia, and later developed into an empire,
one of the largest in history. Consensus was used to bridge
the gap created by the new developments. Muslims believe
that the method is an important aspect of Islamic democracy,
since it involves agreement. However, this democracy is limited to the knowledgeable people in the field of Islamic law
and doctrine. It does not include the public.

Points of Strength of Islam. From a theological point of view,
Islam is very simple and easy to understand. No great intellectual effort is needed to assimilate its basic doctrines. This is
one reason why it appeals to the illiterate or those with little
education. Consequently, although force was used to carry
the Islamic banner within and beyond Arabia, it was mainly
the simplicity of the religion which brought about its success.
Certainly the spread of Islam in the East Indies and Africa
did not result from the use of force. In Africa, Islam has been
more successful than Christianity because it is less demanding
of a people whose life is still simple.

Even so, the simplicity of Islam has not denied satisfaction to the intellectual and the educated. Islamic law, for instance, is quite challenging, and it is particularly complex in the doctrines regarding community relations and the state. But these aspects of the Islamic religion need concern only the professionals, not the ordinary Muslim.

The rewards that Islam promises to good Muslims are great and so are the punishments promised violators of its commandments. Muslims believe in a second life where there is hell for God's enemies and heaven for his followers. Hell in Islam is very much like hell in Christianity, but Islam's heaven (paradise) is very elaborate, and the Koran describes it vividly and in great detail. Perhaps this explains the intense devotion of early Muslims. Some believe that the early Muslims fought well because they were motivated by their clear vision of paradise. They were not afraid to die.

Points of Weakness. According to the standards of the twentieth century, Islam's major difficulty is that it is a legal and political order as well as a religious one. It is not merely a spiritual doctrine but a code of life as well, containing rules for personal and social conduct and establishing a political community with a governmental system. Consequently, the basic elements of Islam's legal and political order are largely God-made and God-given, and while man can give them his own interpretation, he cannot change them fundamentally.

Since interpretation provides only limited flexibility, many otherwise desirable changes in economic, political, and social relations would necessarily be inconsistent with Islam. Thus the pressures of modern times, especially twentieth-century needs, have forced many contemporary Islamic communities to ignore Islam as a legal-political system. However, the religion still maintains its spiritual force and appeal.

Another difficulty of Islam is that it is incompatible with nationalism. Although Christianity, also a universal religion, once had the same problem (before the development of the nation-state in Europe), it no longer insists on political loyalty as does Islam. Modern nations are no longer identified with particular religions, and consequently political and religious loyalties have become separate. Islam's fusion of both loyalties became a source of confusion only as a result of modern developments.

Islam, Judaism, and Christianity. Islam, Judaism, and Christianity are the three great monotheistic religions. The similarities among them are numerous, and Islam would not seem peculiar to Western people if they knew more about it. Actually, Muslims have understood Christianity and Judaism better than Christians and Jews have understood Islam, perhaps because from the beginning Islam recognized Jews and Christians as "the people of the Book," meaning the people who have a Bible. Accordingly, it treated them as believers in the one-God idea and not as pagans who, under Islamic law, were not recognized and whose religious freedom was not granted.

When in the early seventh century Islam became a political order, a state, it recognized the civil and religious rights of Jews and Christians, and whatever controversy developed was primarily political. For instance, when Mohammed fought the Jews of Medina in the 620's, the controversy was purely political. He never attacked Judaism, and he accepted the principle of religious freedom. However, he did demand of the Jews loyalty to the state, and when the Jews of Medina conspired with the Meccans against him, he fought them.

By the standards of the time, Christians and Jews were treated better under Islam than under any other political system. Only when their status under Islam is judged by the standards of twentieth-century Western constitutions does it seem inadequate. One must remember, however, that the obligations of full citizenship under Western systems are greater than those that were required of the Christian and Jewish minorities by the Islamic state. Moreover, Western practices with regard to certain minorities seem to impose upon citizens obligations greater than the rights they confer. Under Islam the rights of minorities were commensurate with the obligations, although in both cases minority rights have been far from ideal.

The Muslim treatment of minorities appears yet more favorable when weighed against the many centuries separating Mohammed and the modern West. The modern West, being the most recent, should be the most advanced in terms of humane developments; but some minorities in the Western world have not experienced any significant change in their status since Islam was founded. On the other hand, the treatment of the various minorities under the Islamic state was definitely a great improvement on anything that preceded Islam and was superior to the treatment of minorities in many civilizations that followed. The Islamic state offered nothing comparable, for example, to the Spanish Inquisition and to the persecution of the Jews in Germany.

Christ is greatly revered by Muslims. Islam considers him a major prophet. It accepts the theory that his mother was a virgin at the time of Christ's birth and gives her a respected place among people "close" to God. Islam also accepts the Christian belief that Christ performed miracles.

However, Islam does not accept the belief that Christ was crucified. Instead, it teaches that God had replaced Christ by someone who looked like him, and that while Christ's replacement was crucified, Christ himself was taken to heaven. Furthermore, Islam, which believes in the oneness of God, rejects the idea that Christ is Son of God. It teaches that the miracles which Christ performed were by the authority and power of God, not by Christ's own authority.

Some historians believe that the rejection of Christ's divinity was common among the heretic Christian groups of Arabia and that Mohammed might have been influenced by them. Of course, to the Muslims, the Islamic religion is the revelation of God; it was not borrowed.

In Islam, God is known by the Arabic word *Allah*. The

Hebrew counterpart is *Eloah* or *Elohim,* and the word form is also found in the Christian Syriac scriptures. The similarity goes beyond language, for according to Islam, Mohammed was sent not to any one race or ethnic group but to all mankind. The God recognized by the Muslims, then, is the God of mankind; and consequently, Islam recognizes no ethnic or racial minorities within the Muslim community. All Muslims have the same rights and the same obligations, and a non-Arab Muslim can aspire to become the head of the Muslim state. In fact, had it not been for this tolerance the Turks would have had greater difficulty wresting Islamic power from their Arab predecessors. Negro Muslims have held high positions in the Islamic state. The commander of the first expedition sent by Mohammed to Syria was a former Negro slave, although in his army there were more socially prominent men.

Islamic Divisions. Islam puts the responsibility of fulfilling religious obligations squarely upon the individual. It provides for no ordained priesthood to assist him in his task. Unofficially, self-ordained "ministers" do exist, but they are not part of a hierarchy as they are in the Catholic Church, for instance. Given such individual freedom, disagreement among Muslims on points of religion and politics inevitably developed. A number of sects arose, and they were to play an important role in politics. Even so, Islam has fewer sects than Christianity, and the religious wars involving Muslim divisions were not as intense as those fought among Christian denominations.

The majority of Muslims are Sunnite. They consider themselves the "orthodox" of Islam, and they accept the traditions as second only to the Koran. Their most reliable collections of traditions are those compiled by al-Bukhari (d. 870) and Muslim (d. 875).

The Sunnites also accept consensus as part of the official doctrine of Islam. They cite Mohammed's statement, "My community will never agree in an error," to provide the basis for consensus.

The second largest Islamic sect is the Shi'ite, which during the controversy over who should succeed Mohammed to the leadership of the Islamic community believed that the caliph should be a direct relative of Mohammed. They supported Ali, Mohammed's cousin and son-in-law, for the position and deplored the selection of Abu Bakr as the first caliph. They did not become a serious and visible movement, however, until the selection of the third caliph.

In time the Shi'ites divided into three groups. The Imamis, or the "twelvers," believe that the twelfth caliph or imam[5] disappeared in 873 and would reappear later as the Messiah, or the Mahdi. Today the Imamis constitute the majority of the Shi'ites and are concentrated in Iran (Persia) and southern Iraq. In Iran, Imami Shi'ite is the state religion. The second group of Shi'ites are the Ismailis, who believe the twelfth imam still lives. The "western" Ismailis believe he leads a normal life but is not known to the ordinary people. The "eastern" Ismailis believe he exists in the person of the Aga Khan, whom they revere more than Mohammed. The Ismailis live mostly in Pakistan and East Africa.

The third Shi'ite group are the Zaidis. These Shi'ites attribute no divine qualities to the current imam, and they do not believe that the twelfth imam disappeared. They elect the current imam from the Sayyid family in Yemen which, they believe, descends from Mohammed.

Other Islamic sects appeared from time to time. Some of them became so independent that some people consider them separate religions. The Druze sects, for instance, developed distinct characteristics as a faith and as a subculture. The Druze people live mostly in Lebanon, Syria, and Israel.

Part of the Druze religion is unknown because it is secret. The Druzes believe that God has, at times, been incarnated in a living person. They say that the last such incarnation was al-Hakim, the sixth caliph of the Fatimid dynasty of Egypt, who declared himself an incarnation of God in 1016. It is probable that the sect was named after an early follower of al-Hakim, Mohammed ibn Ismail al-Darazi. The Druze religious doctrine was given form and substance by Hamza, a Persian by origin.

It is said that the Druze sect has elements from Christianity and Judaism and that the Druze people can worship as Muslims when among Muslims and as Christians when among Christians. The Druze accept Jesus Christ as the incarnation of God. They also believe in the transmigration of the soul as a process by which final purification is achieved.

Chapter 2

The Arab-Islamic Empire

The death of Mohammed in 632 was a shock to Muslims, who had not anticipated the event. They had become used to the Islamic prophet's political and spiritual leadership and were not prepared to manage their affairs without him, although at no time had Mohammed given any indication that he was different from other men or that his death was not to be expected.

THE EARLY CALIPHS

The confusion that followed Mohammed's death precipitated what might be called a constitutional crisis, and one of the first magnitude. Who would govern Muslim society? How should he be selected? What was the nature of his position?

Neither the Koran nor the traditions gave clues to these questions. The disturbances among Muslims increased. At one point, the crisis became so great that a close associate of Mohammed, Omar, felt compelled to tell a group of worshipers that the prophet was immortal.

Abu Bakr. The crisis was finally resolved under the leadership of Abu Bakr, Mohammed's closest friend and later his father-in-law. One of the first converts to Islam, Abu Bakr had demonstrated his devotion to the prophet by accompanying him on the dangerous "flight" (Hijra) to Medina. Mohammed relied on him in time of crisis. It was Abu Bakr who finally dared to announce that the prophet was indeed dead, declaring that there was nothing unnatural about the event. He reminded Muslims that Mohammed was a man and must die like all men, and his reminder had a calming effect. The effect was reinforced by quick and resolute action from a group of the prophet's associates. They selected Abu Bakr to be the first caliph (successor) and asked Muslims to accept his leadership. The congregation acquiesced; and although no formal procedures were established for future successions, the constitutional question was at least temporarily resolved.

Although Abu Bakr's tenure in office was very short (two years), he was successful in asserting the authority of his position and in upholding its dignity. Those who deserted Islam because of the prophet's death returned; those who doubted the legitimacy of the new regime were given confidence; and Muslims who opposed the regime were either persuaded to declare their loyalty or were forced to do so. In short, Abu Bakr reunited the Muslim community and reaffirmed the authority of the state and the religion. Almost the whole of Arabia was under the caliph's authority. In addition, Abu Bakr was able to make incursions into territories outside Arabia, but the major conquests took place under his successor, Omar, who became the second caliph in 634.

Omar ibn al-Khattab. Omar was Abu Bakr's closest friend. Before his conversion, Muslims considered him a rough character. Afterward, however, his personality changed noticeably. He became known as kind, gentle, and fair, and many Muslims referred to him as "the just."

Indeed, Omar was to become a legend as well as a historic figure. Muslim historians record that he walked the streets late at night to make sure everything was well with his people. His modesty and incorruptibility were also legendary. The founder of a vast empire, with great wealth at his disposal, he is said to have had only one outfit to wear, causing his wife to complain that she could no longer patch it. Omar always insisted that the government's treasury belonged to the people, not to himself. He could spend on himself only what was needed to survive. In short, Muslims came to consider Omar the embodiment of the virtues of Islam, and the legend who launched their glorious political and cultural expansion.

Omar's Islamic conquests required a great deal of effort. To the north of the Arabian peninsula were the great Persian and Byzantine empires. However, the Byzantine state, whose capital was Constantinople in Asia Minor, was showing signs of weakness resulting from wars begun under Justinian and continued into the reign of Heraclius. Because of its frequent wars with the Byzantine state, the Persian Empire was also weak at the time the Muslims made their attacks. Consequently, in 636, at the famous battle of Yarmuk, the Muslims defeated the Byzantines. Then Persia fell, being completely overrun by 642. By 649, the Arabs were also in possession of Syria (including Palestine), Armenia, and Egypt.

What motivated the Arabs to do all this in such a short time? Many Western scholars reason that the Arabian peninsula could no longer support its growing population, and, consequently, the Arabs had to expand by conquest. However, this only partially explains the situation. After all, the Muslim Arabs created an empire greater than Rome's, extending far beyond any necessity imposed by the peninsula's population problem.

It was Islam, primarily, which inspired the Arabs to conquer. The religion united the Arabs and gave them a purpose in life. It generated the energy and provided the organization needed to mobilize Arab fighting skills and traditions. Furthermore, Islam enjoined Muslims to spread the word of God, either by advocacy or by the sword. Also (a point often ignored by Westerners) the religion had changed Arab values beyond their simple tribal traditions. A desert culture was inadequate for the new Islamic life. Islam, then, not only provided a new system of values, it encouraged conquest by requiring it for the realization of these values.

Othman ibn Affan (caliph, 644–656). After the conquests of Byzantium and Persia, the expansion begun under Omar was slowed by internal political conflicts, and in 644 Omar was murdered by a Christian (Persian) prisoner of war.

The problem of succession reappeared. (It has never been permanently resolved.) However, on his deathbed, Omar appointed a selection committee to choose a new caliph. The committee decided on Othman ibn Affan. Mohammed's son-in-law, Ali, had been a candidate for the office, and his supporters were not happy with the choice of Othman. They were to conspire against the state and contribute to a civil war.

The new caliph himself contributed to the coming civil disorder. Othman was a wealthy convert to Islam. He came from an influential family, the Omayyads, which had played an important political role in pre-Islamic Mecca. As caliph, he allowed himself to be influenced by his relatives, and his twelve years in office were characterized by nepotism. Many competent officials who had been appointed by his predecessor were replaced by friends and relatives, and dissatisfaction with his leadership grew into hostility. Unlike Abu Bakr and Omar, Othman failed to control dissenting elements in the state or to inspire Islamic society. In 656, his rule was also ended by an assassination, but of a different kind than the one which ended Omar's life. Othman was killed by Muslims —by a dissenting group from Egypt—and his death reflected serious divisions in Islamic society.

First, there was the old rivalry between Mecca and Medina, now transferred into internal conspiracy and intrigue. Secondly, the Islamic state was troubled by the tribal elements in the population, especially the nomads, who resisted centralized authority and contributed to political instability and uncertainty. Finally, there was a struggle for power which involved the supporters of Ali, who had been unhappy with

Othman's election to the caliphate. They were blamed for the assassination of Othman, but there was no evidence to incriminate them.

Ali ibn Abi Talib (caliph, 656–661). With the death of Othman, Ali got the office denied him by his predecessor's election. Again, however, the selection was made without following any established formal procedures, thus continuing a situation that was to divide loyalties and disrupt the unity of Islam.

As mentioned earlier, Ali was Mohammed's cousin and son-in-law. Becoming a Muslim at about age eleven, he was the youngest of the first converts. Because of his close relationship to Mohammed, he had always been a candidate for the high office. Ali's sympathizers multiplied after Othman's appointment, and they contributed to the weakness of the caliphate during Othman's tenure in office.

Ali also had his enemies. Among them was Mohammed's wife Aisha, and some of the early converts who did not approve of his election to the caliphate. Aisha's dislike for Ali was a personal matter which developed into open opposition. She went to Basra, in Iraq, where Ali's support was insignificant, but the caliph followed her with an army. In December, 656, they fought in the battle of the Camel, named so because Aisha was riding a camel while urging her soldiers to fight more vigorously. Ali won, but because many of the prophet's associates were killed in the battle his prestige was not enhanced. It was the first time Muslims fought Muslims.

After the battle, the capital of the empire moved from Medina, in Arabia, to Kufa, in Iraq, where Ali had a large following and where he felt more secure. The change indicated that Arabia was no more the center of power and that the Arab empire had been transformed into a "multinational" state. A new era had begun.

THE OMAYYAD EMPIRE

The strongest opposition to Ali's rule came from Othman's family, the Omayyads. As expected, Othman's relatives were not happy with the choice of Ali as the new caliph. They demanded the punishment of Othman's murderers, but Ali seemed reluctant to respond. Rather, the new caliph proceeded to replace Othman's friends and relatives in the governmental bureaucracy. Fearing the erosion of their power and influence, the Omayyads went into open opposition and revolt.

Muawiyah ibn Abu Sufyan. Their leader was Muawiyah. This talented statesman had converted to Islam in the same year Mohammed conquered Mecca. He became the prophet's secretary; and later, the second caliph, Omar, appointed him governor of Syria. Thus, unlike many other Omayyad officials, Muawiyah was not appointed by his cousin Othman. Nevertheless, he too was distressed that Ali did not take measures against the assassins of his cousin.

In contrast with Ali's larger domain, Muawiyah's province was orderly and prosperous. The Syrians were more advanced than the people of Arabia. Their ingenuity and adaptability helped carry Arab-Islamic civilization to heights rarely equaled in history.

Muawiyah did not take part in the Aisha-Ali feud. He waited, and while Ali's prestige went down, his remained undiminished. However, about a year after the battle of the Camel, the two men confronted each other in battle. Muawiyah would have lost had it not been for the tricky diplomacy he used. While the battle was going on, he suggested arbitration, and because many sincere people on both sides wanted to avoid further bloodshed, Ali had no choice but to accept. The judgment of the arbitrators was against Ali, who quickly charged that the arbitration procedure was abused. From among Ali's supporters a group of Muslims, called the Kharijites, felt that the situation had deteriorated to the point where neither Ali nor Muawiyah was likely to improve conditions and restore the Islamic state to its puritanical form. Consequently, they decided to desert Ali and oppose him as well as his rival, Muawiyah.

In fact, the Kharijites became an extremist group. They plotted to kill both Ali and Muawiyah. They succeeded in doing away with Ali, but Muawiyah survived after a slight injury. The death of Ali ended the era of the first caliphs, who were distinguished by having been Mohammed's close companions.

In 660, before Ali's assassination, Muawiyah had himself inaugurated as caliph in Jerusalem, ruling until 680. Syria and Egypt followed him, but Iraq and Arabia did not. However, the death of Ali enabled Muawiyah to extend his control over the whole of the empire.

Unlike Ali, Muawiyah was a strong leader. He can be considered the first "modern" Arab caliph because he understood the art of politics and ruled resolutely. He was an autocrat, but persuasion was his favorite political method. And the system he developed was an autocracy with the old forms of self-government retained. During his tenure, religion had to give way to politics; it was no longer the *raison d'être* of the empire. Under him the empire was united. Non-Muslims were relatively free and internal dissension was subdued by focusing attention on external enemies and on the need to expand the territory of the empire.

Characteristics of the Omayyad Empire. Two elements characterized the Omayyad state. First, it was dominated by the Arab aristocracy. Some historians refer to it as the "Arab Kingdom" to emphasize its Arab rather than Islamic character. The Omayyads showed no religious prejudice, and they utilized the skills and knowledge of the subject peoples who were more advanced than they. Remembering Byzantine and Persian high taxes and severe religious restrictions, Copts,

Jews, and Syrian Christians welcomed Arab rule and cooperated with the Omayyads.

Cooperation between subjects and rulers was greater under
the Omayyads than under other contemporary political regimes—for example, the Germanic kingdoms of Europe. In a
sense, the Omayyad society was the melting pot of the East.
Racial, religious, and ethnic groups mixed together to form a
highly productive system. And although the Arab aristocracy
was politically dominant, culturally the system was fluid.

The second element characterizing the Omayyad state was
dynastic rule. The lack of an orderly procedure for selecting
caliphs had encouraged rivalries and dissension in the previous Islamic regime. While the elective principle was recognized theoretically, the office was in fact hereditary. Although
occasional fierce competition occurred within the ruling family, the hereditary practice was a stabilizing factor. Fourteen
Omayyad caliphs ruled before the empire's downfall in 750.

The threat to Omayyad sovereignty came from the Shi'ites
who challenged Omayyad rule in the eastern section of the
empire. This movement had been revived when Ali's second
son, Husain, made his claim to the caliphate in 680. Husain
was brutally murdered by Omayyad armies at Karbala in
Iraq; but the incident gave the Shi'ites a martyr, and Husain
became the symbol of their spiritual unity. Ultimately, the
Shi'ites would participate in the final destruction of the Omayyad state.

Arab writers disparaged the contribution of the Omayyads
to Arab history. Most of those who wrote on Omayyad history lived during Abbasid rule, and Abbasid enmity toward
the Omayyads was reflected in their writing. Recent research
indicates that the Omayyad age was "formative and creative
and the most glorious in the annals of the Arab race." [1]

Omayyad Conquests. The most significant achievements of
Omayyad rule were the conquests, which enlarged their territory and enhanced their prestige. In the east they conquered

Khiva, Bukhara, Samarkand, Afghanistan, and the valley of the Indus. In the west they advanced along the Mediterranean coast, taking Carthage in 697 and winning the whole of North Africa up to the Atlantic Ocean by 708.

This last military campaign was not an easy task. The Berbers of North Africa resisted stubbornly, mainly because of their strong tradition of local autonomy. Once defeated, however, many of them converted to Islam. They too discovered that Muslim rule was better than Byzantine rule. In time, the Berbers became staunch supporters of the Omayyads. In fact, it was Berber support which enabled the Omayyad state to conquer Spain. Under Tariq, Arab forces, composed mostly of Berbers, crossed the sea to Spain in 711. In Spain, the Visigothic regime was suffering from internal divisions, and succumbed to the first major attack.

Gibraltar (Jabal Tariq) takes its name from Tariq, who became a legendary Arab hero. After landing in Spain, he destroyed his ships, telling his soldiers they could no longer return to Africa. There was no alternative to victory. His speech to his soldiers has become part of Arab literature: contemporary Arab students read it with pride and some of them recite it from memory.

Under Arab rule, Spain was to have a splendid history. Under its Omayyad rulers it became a center of cultural activity, and the vehicle through which Arab civilization influenced the civilizations of Europe.

The Muslim armies did not intend to stop with the conquest of Spain. They pushed northward into the Frankish kingdom. However, in 732 Charles Martel put an end to their plans by defeating them at Poitiers. Shortage of manpower was the main reason for Muslim defeat.

The Downfall of the Omayyads. The Omayyads built one of the greatest empires in history, greater even than that of Rome. And they accomplished this feat in less than a hundred years. Their territory was bounded by Byzantium in the north-east, the Frankish empire in the northwest, India in the east, and by the Indian and Arabian seas in the south. Their successful conquests, however, could not save them from several problems, which contributed to bring about their downfall in 750.

One major problem they shared with other empires was the difficulty of managing vast territories. There are territorial limits to political control and administrative efficiency, and these limits are largely fixed by communication and technology. Like the Roman Empire, the Omayyad Empire exceeded those territorial limits, and consequently, could not retain control.

But the most serious problem was the rivalry between the Omayyads on the one hand and the Shi'ites, Kharijites, and the Abbasids on the other. (The last-named group were the descendants of the prophet's uncle Abbas.) In 716 the Abbasids took over the organization of an extremist Shi'ite sect and gradually their claim to the caliphate was supported by the Persians, who resented Arab supremacy in the empire. In a sense, the feud was a manifestation of the rivalry between Syria and Iraq that had followed the conflict between Aisha and Ali. The rivalry ended with the victory of the eastern center, when in 750 Abu al-Abbas won a decisive victory over the Omayyads. The Omayyad family was wiped out, and the capital moved from Syria to Iraq. The Abbasid family became the new ruling dynasty, exercising control over all the Omayyad territories except Spain. In Spain, the administration was taken over by the one survivor of the destruction of the Omayyads, Abd al-Rahman. He arrived in Spain in 756, after having eluded the new rulers for several years.

THE ABBASID EMPIRE

The Abbasids ruled from Baghdad, a city built by their second caliph on the west bank of the Tigris. They relied on force to maintain their rule, but they were willing to tolerate the non-Arab Muslims and to grant them political rights. Thus a major difference between Abbasid and Omayyad rules was the emphasis of the new regime on the Islamic rather than the Arab character of the state. The non-Islamic minorities had benefited under the Omayyads, but under the Abbasids the benefit went to the non-Arab Muslims. However, the general level of tolerance was high in both regimes.

The Persians had a great deal of influence on the Abbasids. Consequently, the Abbasid system resembled the defunct Persian Empire in its inclination toward despotism. Also, Persian influence was conspicuous in the Abbasid style of living. The caliphs lived in fantastic luxury. Like the Persians, the Abbasids appreciated wine, women, and song. The legendary Harun al-Rashid (caliph, 786–809) was an example. However, Persian influences had to adapt to Islamic requirements. For the Abbasids, Islam was the common bond among their subjects, and they used it to stay in power.

The Abbasid caliphs encouraged economic activity. The textile industry begun under the Omayyads flourished. Silk manufacturing, learned from the Byzantines, was introduced and developed. Cotton, imported from India, was cultivated in Persia. Carpets, manufactured by the Armenians, were made almost everywhere in the empire. Many of these and other products were sold in domestic as well as foreign markets.

The Abbasid Empire manufactured a great variety of goods, from pottery and metalwork to soap and perfume. From the Chinese, the Abbasids learned how to make paper, and Harun introduced it in Iraq. Later, paper was manufactured almost everywhere in the empire. Arab traders traveled throughout the Far East. They appeared in China as early as the eighth century. Interest in trade forced the Arabs to learn how to master the sea. They built ships, drew accurate maps, and developed their knowledge of geography and astronomy.

Economic activity and prosperity influenced social life in

the imperial society. The Arabs "ceased to be a closed hereditary caste and became a people, ready to accept, by a sort of naturalization, any Muslim speaking Arabic as one of themselves." [2] The Arabic language became the vehicle by which minorities were assimilated into the culture of the empire. However, had it not been for the high absorptive capacity of the economic system, this assimilation would have been difficult. Of course, Abbasid tolerance was also a factor.

The Abbasid period of Islamic history is best known for its intellectual achievements. According to a highly respected student of Arab history, this period "witnessed the most momentous intellectual awakening in the history of Islam and one of the most significant in the whole history of thought and culture." [3] Abbasid intellectual activity was greatly influenced by non-Arabs: Syrian, Persian, Hellenic Greek, and Indian. The Abbasid state encouraged the translation of foreign works. It is said that the caliph al-Mamun paid an expert in gold the weight of the books he translated. The same caliph established in 830 an institution of learning called the "House of Wisdom," which included a library, an academy, and a translation service. Consequently, the Arabs were able to borrow from their great predecessors in history, and to develop knowledge by adding their own contributions. The result was a rich civilization, Arabic in the sense that the contributors wrote in Arabic, although often their ethnic background was not Arab.

The Downfall of the Abbasids. This glorious history of the Abbasids lasted for about half a millennium, from 750 until the Mongol invasion and the destruction of Baghdad in 1258. But, like all empires, the Abbasid Empire did not die suddenly; its decline began about 945.

What were the reasons for the Abbasid fall? Abbasid tolerance, while undoubtedly an element of strength, was also an element of weakness. The various nationality groups competed for greater influence over the government. Ultimately, some of them succeeded in dominating the caliph and breaking up the empire.

The deterioration of Abbasid military organization was another reason and it too was speeded by nationality differences. The army was organized along nationality lines; every important nationality group was represented, and the Arabs were not dominant. It was truly an Islamic army. However, gradually the military got mixed up in politics, and the nationality groups in the army began to compete for political influence. The Turks were the most successful. Beginning with the caliphate of al-Mu'tasim (833–842), they were the caliph's bodyguards. Their influence was great, and their activity grew to menace the capital's population. To avoid a people's uprising, al-Mu'tasim decided to move his capital to Samarra. (In 892, the capital returned to Baghdad.) Another caliph, al-Mutawakkil (847–861), attempted to curb their influence, but they murdered him in retaliation.

Since the Abbasids needed military force to maintain power, the disorganization of their armies was a serious blow. The size of the empire also contributed. Although Abbasid caliphs ruled as absolute monarchs, the imperial system was highly decentralized, especially in the tenth century and after. Many provincial governors consolidated power and became independent. Some of these were army officers of non-Arab descent. Thus, the more defection in the provinces, the weaker the army—and, therefore, Abbasid rule—became.

In the tenth century, Egypt went under Fatimid control. The Fatimids were Muslims from northwest Africa, who ruled Egypt for approximately two hundred years. During their rule Egypt was rejuvenated. The Fatimids founded the city of Cairo, and in 978 they founded al-Azhar, today the oldest Muslim university. Their empire stretched from Morocco in the west to southern Syria as far as Jerusalem.

The eastern part of the Abbasid Empire also changed. In 945, the Buwaihids, a Shi'ite Persian dynasty, conquered Iraq and occupied Baghdad. For about a century they ruled as sultans (kings) but they kept the Abbasid caliphs as the nominal heads of state to provide legitimacy to their political regime. In 1055, the Buwaihids were overthrown by the Sunnite Seljuk Turks, whose original home had been central Asia. Known for their fighting skill, the Turks had become the main security force of the Abbasid caliphs. As mentioned earlier, the caliphs relied on them for personal protection and in order to stay in power. Time proved that the Turks were no different from other nationality groups. They too wanted power. However, after their capture of Baghdad, they limited themselves to secular authority and left the Abbasid caliphs as the spiritual and ceremonial leaders of the Islamic community.

Gradually, the Seljuk rulers brought more and more of the Abbasid Empire under their control, including Syria, Palestine, and most of Anatolia in Asia Minor. Anatolia had once belonged to the Byzantines, and it later became known as Turkey.

Ultimately, the Seljuk regime also gave way to the forces of decentralization. Like its predecessor, it broke up into smaller states each headed by an army officer or a civilian governor. It was during this time, in 1096, that the crusaders invaded the Near East.

THE CRUSADES

The Crusades were a series of wars which Christian Europe launched against the Near Eastern Muslims between the eleventh and the fourteenth century. Their declared objective was to gain control of the Holy Land. The actual causes, however, were varied and complex. Of course, the religious factor was important, but it was more relevant to the first Crusade than to the others.

An outburst of religious and spiritual fervor at the end of the eleventh century made the idea of rescuing the Holy Land from Muslim rule very appealing to Europeans. But the idea of a church-sponsored war had no precedent in Christian history. Christian doctrines had not originally recognized war as morally right. In the fifth century, however, Augustine had introduced the concept of the just war, by which certain wars were recognized to be morally consistent with Christianity. In the eleventh century, Thomas Aquinas elaborated on the concept and made it more acceptable to the church. Finally in 1095, the concept was officially endorsed by Pope Urban II, and the idea of a Crusade to the Holy Land was initiated by him.[4]

Another factor contributing to the Crusades was the desire of the European princes to obtain new fiefs. This desire was consistent with the feudal culture of Europe. Since the Islamic Near East was then more advanced than Christian Europe, the idea of acquiring new fiefs in the more prosperous Near East was attractive to the European princes. In fact, the material incentive seems to have been stronger than the religious motivation. Mindful of this important fact, Urban II did not forget to point out to the European princes that the Levant was a "land of milk and honey." [5] However, the economic factor was not limited to the acquisition of prosperous fiefs, but included the prospect of promoting trade with the Oriental world.

The Seljuk threat to the Christian Byzantines of western Asia Minor was a factor. In 1071, the Seljuks defeated the Byzantines at the battle of Manzikert, and they captured Romanus IV, the Byzantine emperor. A large part of Asia Minor fell under Seljuk control. It was evident that unless Europe came to the rescue, the Byzantine state would disappear and the Muslims would then be in a position to threaten eastern Europe and perhaps western Europe also.

In sponsoring the Crusades, the Roman pope might also have hoped to reunite the two sections of the Christian church in addition to saving the Byzantines. The reunion would obviously enhance his prestige and power. Unfortunately, later events would show the futility of his project: Christian Europe and Christian Byzantium were to confront each other in the battlefield.

The Wars. The first Crusade was successful mainly because of Muslim disunity. Also, the Fatimids, who were in control of Jerusalem, had very little attachment to the city and they did not think it had important strategic values.

Thus, in 1099, the crusaders established the Kingdom of Jerusalem and until 1187 most of Palestine was under their control. In addition, they established three states in the northern part of the Fertile Crescent: Tripoli, Antioch, and Edessa.

Other Crusades followed the first. In these Crusades, religion was less important than economics as a motivation for organizing the campaigns and starting the wars. After the first Crusade, Europe's hope to save the Byzantine state and reunite the Christian church disappeared. Quarrels between the Byzantines and the crusaders developed and in 1204 the crusaders sacked Constantinople, the Byzantine capital.

The Byzantines had not been genuinely interested in the crusading movement, but they had hoped the movement would check Muslim power to the point where they could recover the territories captured by the Seljuks. With the sack of Constantinople by the crusaders, the Byzantines ceased to cooperate with the Europeans, and concluded treaties with the Turks, offering their Muslim enemy neutrality in the conflict. Relations between Europeans and Byzantines were at their worst during the second and third Crusades.

After the first Crusade, the Muslims showed new strength. In 1144, under the leadership of a general named Zangi, they regained control of Edessa. Then in 1171 Zangi's son, Nureddin (Nur al-Din) destroyed Fatimid power in Egypt and united that country with Syria. But it was not until Saladin (Salah al-Din), succeeded Nureddin that Christian power in the Holy Land was considerably weakened. Saladin recaptured Jerusalem in 1189, and in the remaining part of the Holy Land only a few coastal towns remained under European control.

The loss of Jerusalem to the Muslims shocked Christian Europe, and a third Crusade was hastily organized. The effort was largely unsuccessful. Frederick Barbarossa of Germany drowned in a stream in Asia Minor. Because of his quarrels with King Richard of England, Philip Augustus of France had to return to his kingdom after the capture of Acre. Only Richard the Lion-Hearted stayed on to continue the fight against the Muslims.

The two adversaries, Richard and Saladin, have been immortalized by legend. No doubt they represented the best qualities of their age. Honorable, friendly, and courageous, they distinguished between time of war and time of peace, and they were the best of men in both times.

The Arabs of today consider Saladin one of their great heroes. (He was in reality a Kurd, but in his time ethnic groups of the Near East were Arabized.) To contemporary Arabs, Saladin represents the kind of leadership they need. His success in uniting the Muslims against the European intruders is quite appealing to a people almost hopelessly disunited and threatened by outsiders.

Saladin created the Ayyubite dynasty and ruled an empire that included Egypt, North Africa, Yemen, Syria, and Palestine. Before his death in 1193, he virtually ended the crusaders' hope to dominate the Near East, although the crusaders kept trying.

The Aftermath. Contrary to their hope for unification, the crusaders really weakened the Byzantine state and it made it vulnerable to Turkish attack. And although in 1261 the Byzantines were successful in driving the Latins out of Constantinople, the event did not amount to significant recovery. Byzantine territory remained limited, including only a small part of Asia Minor and the Balkan region.

The hope of reuniting the Latin church and the Byzantine church had disappeared long before the end of the Crusades. In fact, it became apparent that the Byzantines preferred the

Muslim enemy over their Christian brothers. Furthermore, the pope, who had hoped to gain from uniting the two churches, lost prestige. From a religious point of view, the Crusades accomplished almost nothing.

Nor did the crusaders obtain the full benefit of contact with the more advanced Arab civilization. Europe learned more from the Muslims through Spain and Sicily than through the Crusades. However, there were a few benefits. The Italians established a trade with the Levant that survived the wars. In addition, the Crusades kept the Muslims out of eastern Europe for about two centuries. European military science advanced. Also, the Crusades renewed Christian interest in missionary work. And although missionary work was ineffective with Muslims, the spirit survived. Later, Christianity and Islam were to compete for the conversion of pagan peoples.

In the aftermath of the Crusades, important events took place in the Muslim world. The Ayyubite princes divided Saladin's empire, and in Egypt the sultan fell under the influence of his household slaves. Known as the Mamelukes, these slaves quickly established their own regime and expanded into neighboring countries. By 1271, they controlled most of the Near East, and in 1291 they took Acre, the crusaders' last stronghold. But their greatest achievement was to rescue Egypt and Syria from Mongol destruction. (The caliph had been driven out of Baghdad after its destruction in 1258 by the Mongol prince, Hulagu.) The Mameluke empires were Islamic, not Arab. Arab rule had come to an end with the fall of Baghdad in 1258. To legitimize their regime, however, the Mamelukes invited the Abbasid caliph to live in Egypt. But they allowed him only spiritual authority while they retained political control. Mameluke rule continued until 1517, when it was replaced by another non-Arab regime, that of the Ottoman Turks. But whatever its political fate, the Arab civilization that developed between the seventh and eleventh centuries contributed immensely to human civilization. Europe was the main beneficiary of Arab contributions, and it is important to understand Arab influence on the West and the reaction of the West to such influence.

ARAB INFLUENCE ON THE WEST

After the decline of Arab power, the torch and center of civilization shifted to Europe.[6] The new change was preceded by a learning process in which the "backward" Europeans assimilated the knowledge of the "advanced" Arabs.

Arab-European Interaction. While the Arabs were building their monumental civilization, Europe was asleep in the dark ages. The Europeans were not even aware of their Greek heritage and had it not been for the Arabs, they would not have rediscovered this important pillar of their civilization. By translating Greek works, the Arabs preserved Greek contributions. The Arab translations were retranslated into Latin by Europeans, and this was how Europe learned about such Greek philosophers as Aristotle and Plato. Of course, Arab commentary on Greek writing also influenced Europe's views of the Greeks.

Europe received Arab civilization and its influences through three channels. The first was Spain, where the Arabs created a "brilliant" culture. For about five hundred years, Arab (Moorish) Spain had been the center of intense cultural and scientific activity. Cordova, Toledo, Seville, and Granada had some of the best universities in the world, where Christians learned advanced scientific knowledge from Muslim scholars.

Sicily was the second channel through which the Arab contribution was transmitted to Europe. It was of lesser significance than Spain, but was important during Norman and Hohenstaufen rule there. Frederick II, emperor of Germany and Sicily, was an "Arabized" European in the same way that many rulers of the contemporary Arab world are "westernized." A Renaissance leader, he probably was the most pro-

gressive European monarch of his time, and he considered
the Arabs the most civilized people on earth. Frederick dressed
in Arab style, patronized Arab scholars and Arab art, and
emulated the Arabs in many other ways.

The third channel was established by the crusaders. We
mentioned earlier that the crusaders did not learn much from
the Arabs. Consequently, their function as transmitters of
Arab civilization was necessarily very limited. Nevertheless,
the little they learned from the Arabs was helpful in the process of European awakening.

The Arabs got little in return from the Europeans: "While
European civilization of the Middle Ages derived some of its
most worthy features from the Arabs, the latter gained practically nothing from their contacts with contemporary Europeans." [7] The crusaders were considered barbarians.

But while we evaluate Arab influence on Europe, we should
remember a few things about the makeup of Arab civilization.
As mentioned earlier, it was partly a product of foreign influences mainly Greek and Persian, and, to a lesser degree, Indian and Chinese. The word "Arab" described not the nationality of the civilization but the language by which it was
expressed. Arab tolerance was a factor in this diversity. The
Jew who could not find fulfillment in Europe, for instance,
"could still find in Arab communities a home, a livelihood, and
all of the tools for scholarly pursuits." [8]

Also, the Arabs learned from their predecessors much faster
than the Europeans learned from them. It took the Europeans
many centuries before they could begin moving. Furthermore,
if we take into consideration the fact that the original environment of the Arabs (the Arabian peninsula) was much more
difficult and limiting than Europe, we would appreciate more
the learning abilities of the Arabs.

The Substance of the Arab Contribution. The Arab contribution was not limited to a few areas of scientific activity. In
philosophy, the contributions of a number of men were im-

portant: particularly al-Kindi (d. ca. 873); Ibn Rushd (1126–1198), known as Averroës; al-Farabi (d. 950); Ibn Sina (980–1037), known to the West as Avicenna; Ghazali (1058–1111); and Ibn Arabi (d. 1240). All these scholars influenced Western philosophy and writing.

The philosophies of these men were connected with their Islamic religion. They were never completely secular and were very different from the philosophies of Western thinkers. Nevertheless, the outstanding Christian philosopher, Thomas Aquinas (1225?–1274), could not escape Muslim influence, especially the influence of Averroës. Professor Alfred Guillaume finds great resemblances between the writing of the two men, especially in the *Summa*.[9] In addition, the basic theories of Thomas Aquinas were also influenced by the Muslim thinker al-Farabi. Indeed, Christian philosophy owed a great deal to Muslim writers. Dante's conception of heaven and hell was based mainly on Islamic theories. He was influenced by Ibn Arabi.

Western writers who admitted indebtedness to the Arabs included Roger Bacon (d. 1294), Albertus Magnus (d. 1280), and John Duns Scotus (d. 1308). However, later scholars were not as frank. Credit should go to modern scholars such as A. J. Arberry for revealing the truth about Western indebtedness to the Arabs.

In mathematics, Arab contributions were still more significant. The Arabs were pioneers of algebraic theories, and al-Khwarizmi (780–ca. 850) is the acknowledged founder of this modern science. He wrote the oldest work on algebra, and its Latin translation was used as a text until the sixteenth century. (The word "algebra" is derived from Arabic.)

The Arabs developed the decimal system, whose impact upon science is obvious, and introduced the zero, the Arabic *sifr* ("cipher") which is indispensable to the decimal system. They might have taken their numerals from India, but they improved them and made them more useful. Arabic numerals replaced the Roman numerals in Europe.

In chemistry, the Arabs were the first to emphasize the importance of laboratory experiments. Jabir ibn Hayyan, known to Westerners as Geber and recognized as the father of Arab alchemy, was a pioneer in this field. In addition to his discovery of a number of chemical compounds, he introduced improved methods of calcination, reduction, evaporation, crystallization, melting, and sublimation.

Medicine was a fourth area of Arab pioneering. Rejecting the Greek theory that disease was born in human beings, the Arabs established the fact that diseases could be contagious. This was mainly the contribution of al-Razi (865–925), who also wrote a clinical account of smallpox. In the West, al-Razi is known as Rhazes.

In discovering the contagious character of disease, Arab scientists became interested in the discovery of cures. Consequently, the field of pharmacy became the object of their pioneering work. Ibn al-Baytar (d. 1248) described fourteen hundred drugs of medicinal value. He traveled from Spain to Syria to collect drugs and plants and wrote an important book on botany. Al-Hazen (al-Haytham), living at the end of the tenth century, made new discoveries in optics and his work influenced Western writers such as Roger Bacon, Leonardo da Vinci and Johannes Kepler.

The Arabs had high regard for medicine. Doctors and druggists were highly paid individuals, and they had to pass an examination before they were allowed to practice. There were Arab hospitals in the ninth century, and they were usually attached to medical schools. Europe had no hospitals until the thirteenth century.

Arab doctors knew how to operate on the cataract, and there were other aspects of medical science in which they excelled. As late as the sixteenth century, Europe relied on Arab medical science, and European languages borrowed a number of Arabic medicinal terms, such as "syrup" (*sherab*) and "julep" (*gulab*).

In geography, the Arabs produced accurate maps. Al-Idrisi

(1100–1166), for instance, drew seventy accurate maps of the then-known world. He believed that the earth was spherical at a time when prevailing theory described it as flat. In addition, Western knowledge of the African continent was based on Arab sources until the eighteenth century.

Arab interest in geography was stimulated by the religious duty of pilgrimage. Many Muslims had to travel long distances and therefore they needed to know about climate and other conditions of the countries they passed through; and they needed a technique for establishing locations and directions. Out of these needs grew an interest in astronomy, astrology, and trigonometry. Of course, their religious interest in heaven and earth was also a motive.

Many of the Western astronomical terms came from the Arabic language. The terms "zenith," "azimuth," and "nadir" are examples. Also, certain stars were named by the Arabs. Algedi, Altair, Deneb, and Pherkad are examples. Arab astronomical works were translated into Latin and transmitted to Europe through Spain. The so-called Alfonsine tables of the thirteenth century "were no more than a reflection of Arab astronomy." The West acquired its first lessons in spherical and plane trigonometry from the Arabs, who made their conclusions from the study of the stars.[10]

To a lesser extent, Arab literature also had an impact on the West. Of course, we are familiar with the classic known as the *Thousand and One Nights* or simply the *Arabian Nights*. This work was translated into Western languages in the eighteenth century and "introduced a distinctive element into European fiction writing." [11] It included tales from Persian, Greek, Indian, Hebrew, and Egyptian sources. Ironically, the *Nights* became more popular in the West than in the East.[12]

The Western mind usually finds it difficult to understand and appreciate Arab literature, whether poetry or prose. Classical Arabic is difficult and its grammar is complicated. It is a beautiful language, however, and those who have sufficient command of it find it very expressive. At one time or another,

Arabic was a language of poetry as well as one of science. Today it is no longer the scientific language it was, because the Arabs have not kept up with science.

In spite of the difficulties, the Arabic language contributed some vocabulary to English in addition to the scientific and medical terms already mentioned. Examples are the words "tariff," "muslin," "admiral," "sofa," "average," "alcove," "alcohol," "mattress," "cipher," "lilac," "arsenal," "sugar," and "cotton." In addition, Arab influence is evident in European literary works such as Chaucer's *Squire's Tale,* Boccaccio's *Decameron,* the French *Chanson de Roland,* the German *Rolandslied,* Beckford's *Vathek,* Samuel Johnson's *Rasselas,* and Goethe's *Westöstlicher Divan.*

The Arabs taught the Europeans to use and make paper, an art they had learned from the Chinese. This was a revolutionary event, since paper facilitated the writing of books and the appearance of modern libraries and bookstores. The Arabs had great libraries and collections of books, and large numbers of bookshops, long before Europe learned how to organize these educational facilities. European universities relied on Arabic sources for information and sought Arab scholars to assist in their educational programs. In short, Europe was what the Arab world is today, a "developing" area in need of help. And it sought help from the Arabs.

Muslim scholars were usually versed in more than one field of knowledge. Omar Khayyam, the author of the *Rubaiyat,* which is known in the West, was a good astronomer and mathematician as well as a poet. He calculated the length of the solar year with precision and solved complicated algebraic problems. Avicenna made contributions in medicine and also wrote valuable commentaries on Aristotle. Ibn al-Khatib wrote sixty works in such varied fields as poetry, history, geography, medicine, and philosophy.

Arab contributions to science and art made possible the development of European civilization. In the next section we will discuss the reaction of the West to the Arab civilizer. We will show that the reaction was negative, and that the West showed little gratitude to their teachers, certainly much less than the gratitude shown by the Arabs to their benefactors—mainly the Greeks, the Byzantines, and the Persians.

THE REACTION OF THE WEST TO THE ARABS

The Arab Image. The Western world first formed an image of the Arabs during the Middle Ages. It was a bad image, and since then it has changed but slightly.

The Arab was pictured as a rough and crude desert man who loved to fight. His moral standards were low. He was unfair to women, approved of slavery and violence, and loved women and song, though not wine (his religion prohibited drinking). His Islamic religion was a forgery, some of it plagiarized, and the plagiarism failed to give the religion any measure of respectability.

To the West, Islam was invented by a peculiar sort of person. Mohammed was thought of as a magician, who married a rich widow as a means to achieving power and wealth, who tolerated sexual license and authorized promiscuity, and who occasionally had fits which he explained as the moments of revelation. This thinking about the prophet was encouraged by many European writers, among them was the renowned Guibert of Nogent, one of the earliest biographers of the prophet.

Of course, this image of the Arab, Islam, and Mohammed is no longer acceptable to Western writers. It is too naïve and silly to be credible, especially in the days of advanced research. Unfortunately, the image appealed to Western imagination; and in spite of modern scholarship some aspects of it continue to be popular in the Western world.

After the middle of the twelfth century Western writers on Islam were less subjective than their predecessors. But they did not substantially improve the Arab image. In fact, Western scholars did not seriously begin to correct the image until after World War I. Even then the work of scholarship failed to influence public conceptions. Journalistic reports unfriendly to the Arabs had a greater impact on Western public opinion than did scholarship.

Reasons for the Bad Image. Why did the West distort the picture of the Arabs and Islam? Was the distortion intentional? Was there any real basis for it?

The bad image was partly the product of medieval European reaction to the rising power of the Arabs. Europe felt threatened by Arab ascendancy to world power. And the threat was real. After all, the Arabs were successful. Within a period of four hundred years, they had experienced an intellectual and cultural growth unparalleled in the history of Western Europe.

The success of a "superior" culture often evokes feelings of inferiority and bitterness in other cultures, especially when the others are in the process of development. Also, competing cultures usually do not see each other in accurate perspective, at least not while the competition is going on. This is exemplified in the twentieth-century competition between the Communist and "free" worlds.

The problem of perspective is partly the product of differences in the value systems of the competing cultures. But it is also influenced by propaganda, which in turn is the product of a desire to excel in the competition. Each competing culture propagandizes to discredit the other culture and to point out its own "superior" qualities. This last objective is usually considered necessary to establish a people's unity and to create a desire for cultural self-preservation. All these elements were present in Arab-European relations.

In addition to the sensibilities involved in power competition, there was the competition between Christianity and Islam. Although the origin of the two religions was the Middle East, Christianity had become associated with Europe.

Consequently, geography complicated the political and religious competitions: it made them territorial.

At the beginning, Christian Europe considered Islam an inferior religion and the Arabs to be savages. Europeans were convinced that savage physical power was the substance of Arab threat and Arab success. Later, when the Arabs showed intense cultural activity, Europe became still more insecure. She had to learn from the Arabs, but it was necessary to deny them credit. Indeed, Europe managed to denounce the Arabs and Islam while absorbing Arab learning.

Unlike individuals, nations find it difficult to express gratitude. However, unlike the Europeans, the Arabs did not denounce their predecessors. They simply incorporated their civilizations into their own. In this instance, one might say the Arabs were at least more gentlemanly.

More often, however, the outcome of cultural competitions is not gratitude. In the twentieth century, the Arabs denounced the West at the same time they learned from it. Russia and China acted similarly, adopting a Marxist, Western ideology and denouncing the source. However, in the case of the Arabs, the Western powers ruled them and this was an important factor in the Arab attitude.

Finally, image-making was not confined to the Western cultures. Every culture creates images of other cultures and peoples; and as mentioned earlier, the Arabs saw the European crusaders as barbarians. However, the need for better understanding of the Arabs has existed in the Western world since medieval times. Since the Western and Arab worlds are important to each other, the lack of understanding is very dangerous. If the need is not filled, the alternative is enmity, which usually results in negative consequences.

Islam in European Literature. The Europeans' view of the Arabs was largely conditioned by their view of Islam, and the Arab image in European writing was enormously colored by this view.[13]

Before 1100, Western writers knew nothing about Islam. Their conception of Islam was the product of imagination and fictitious reports. R. W. Southern compares their ignorance to that "of a man in prison who hears rumors of outside events and attempts to give a shape to what he hears, with the help of his preconceived ideas." [14] The Spanish writers caused the greatest damage to the Arab image. From a Christian point of view, Spain was a victim of Islam; it was a European country whose Christian culture had been successfully challenged by the Muslims. Consequently, the Spanish writers were extremely bitter about Spain's "unfortunate" experience. Their bitterness and fanaticism were further aggravated by the defection of Christian youth to Muslim cultural and intellectual activity. While Spain was under Muslim rule, its Christian writers and intellectuals were left with only a small number of followers.

During the first half of the twelfth century in western Europe, literature on Islam and the prophet Mohammed continued to be influenced by "the fireside stories of returning warriors [crusaders] and clerks far behind the line of battle." [15] However, the situation began to change in the second half of the twelfth century. Although the Western view of Islam remained negative, the Western world became better informed about the religion. The first Latin translation of the Koran appeared in 1143, the first serious step in improving Europe's sources of information. The task was undertaken by Robert of Ketton, and Peter the Venerable (the Abbot of Cluny) financed the project.

Between 1150 and 1175, translations of al-Kindi, al-Farabi, and Avicenna also began to appear. Through these translations Europe recovered its Greek heritage. In the thirteenth century, Arab-Islamic influence on Europe was very strong. It was not uncommon to see the names of Augustine and Avicenna appear side by side in the writings of Western scholars.

Unfortunately, fourteenth-century Europe returned to fiction and fantasy about Islam. The European attitude toward Islam was cynical, but cynicism characterized the attitude toward all religions, not just Islam. Thus, the literature of this period considered Moses, Christ, and Mohammed imposters. Moreover, Europe continued to fear Islam, but primarily as a "moral and not physical danger." [16]

However, in the fifteenth century, there was a very real physical danger. In 1460, the Muslim Turkish armies were at the doors of Europe. Logically, there was a great need for European writers to analyze Islam critically, but they failed to do so. They "got to grips with each other but they failed to get to grips with Islam," and the old fictions continued.

The Turkish threat to Europe continued into the sixteenth century, and in 1542 Hungary was overrun. Anti-Islamic literature naturally increased with the increase of the threat, but with no increase in critical thinking or objectivity. About this time, Luther translated Ricoldo da Montecroce's *Confutatio Alchoran* into German, one of the strongest indictments of Islam written in the thirteenth century.

In the late sixteenth century, Europe became interested in the Western hemisphere. New frontiers were open to Christianity and Islam ceased to be a source of danger to Europe. Nevertheless, Europe's conception of Islam continued to be negative, and since the Middle Ages, Europe had made only a slight effort to change it.

Europe associated Islam with the Arabs and the European view of Islam affected the Arab image. Because it is really Islam and not Arabs that Europeans base their views on, the more fanatic Muslim Turks ultimately were able to escape the image problem. Much later, in the 1920's, they were to sever relations with their Islamic past, and when they did so Turkey came to be considered a "Western" country, and was admitted to the family of "modern" nations. Thus, the Turks were able to improve their image in the Western world, whereas the Arabs, who remained "loyal" to Islam, had no similar success.

The Religious Controversy. Christians of medieval Europe did not understand Islam, and the few who did judged it by the standards of Christianity. Christians believed, consciously or subconsciously, that religion could not be anything but perfect since it was the word of God and God was perfect. To these Christians, Islam was not truly a religion because it was not perfect: it did not prohibit slavery, it approved of war, it allowed marriage to more than one woman, it was punitive, and it had other "peculiarities."

Furthermore, Christians believed Christianity was more humane: it did not approve of violence or war, did not approve of slavery, and it emphasized great ideals.

Objectively, the difference between Islam and Christianity is in the emphasis and in certain theological arguments. Generally speaking, Christianity is something one "lives up to," while Islam is something one "lives by." While saying this, we must remember that there are many things in Christianity to live by and in Islam to live up to. Again, the difference is in the overall emphasis of the two religions.

The Christian religion, for instance, did not endorse any form of violence. On the other hand, while Islam had a great deal to say about peace and nonviolence, it permitted war under certain circumstances such as against the nonbelievers in the one God. (No war can be waged against Jews and Christians if they give allegiance to the Islamic state. In return for this political act, they are guaranteed religious freedom.) Muslims are asked to be fair and merciful to others, but if this does not work, then they can use force in self-defense. They may also use force to spread the faith to nonbelievers.

We have another example in the attitude toward slavery. Christianity prohibits it altogether. Islam does not, but it prescribes specific ways for setting the slave free and promises rewards to those who do so. What this means is obvious: God does not like slavery. However, to prohibit slavery altogether would be impractical since it was a well-established custom. Islam, therefore, prescribed procedures for its eventual disappearance. The change was to be gradual.

Islam took into consideration the customs, the conditions of life, and the institutions of the Arabs at the time the religion was "revealed" to Mohammed. Its strategy was to help people move from the *status quo* to the ideal. Islam was practical and evolutionary. An illustration of Islamic pragmatism is the provisions on women. Before Islam, women were much inferior to men. Islam greatly improved their status but did not go all the way to make them equal to men. The inequality was more the outcome of the difference in the social roles assigned to them by the religion than in the religion's outlook toward people.

It took Europe many centuries before the status of women reached the point where it was under Islam. Only in modern times did Europe surpass that point. Furthermore, in the contemporary Muslim world the inferior status of women has not been the direct product of religion. Although Islam is partly responsible for the failure of Muslim women to achieve greater freedom, economic factors are also relevant. For instance, the females receive half the share of the males under Islamic inheritance laws because economically the family was the responsibility of the male. A woman was her father's or husband's responsibility and so were the children.

Polygamy, which Islam tolerates, has no absolute religious support. The Koran allows the Muslim a maximum of four wives but requires the husband to give equal justice to the four. To the Christian, this may seem peculiar, if not ridiculous. It must be remembered, however, that polygamy was the custom in pre-Islamic Arabia, and also that initially Islam confronted a shortage of men as a result of war. Moreover, Islam discouraged a multiplicity of wives where the husband could not give them the required equal justice; in such cases the Koran enjoins him to marry only one. Here again we see that Islam is realistic: it takes into consideration the prevailing customs of the people, and it allows change to a different condition. Monogamous marriages can be the social rule if Muslims choose to have it so. Islam no more outlaws monogamy than it requires polygamy.

Islam is a code of life in addition to being a spiritual doctrine. It is not limited to beliefs and ideals, but prescribes rules of practical conduct. In its early development, it manifested a great deal of realism. It was a "brilliant" balance between goals and means. Like Christianity, it required effort and diligence. However, because of its idealism, early Christianity ran against a number of problems that Islam avoided. Christians needed an Augustine and a Thomas Aquinas to resolve the problem of how to deal with warfare. The two men had to develop a theory of the "just war" to adjust Christian principles to the realities of political life. Islam, on the contrary, accepted from the beginning the concept of the "holy war." It did not endorse all wars, and it looked forward to times of peace.

In its later developments, Islam lost much of its relevance. Many factors contributed to this situation. Some aspects of Islam could not be adjusted to modern life. In other words, there was a limit to Islamic realism which modern life surpassed. Other aspects of the religion were flexible enough to keep up with modern life but were neglected by Muslims, who failed to adjust them. As the gap between Islam and social life widened, secular laws and practices gradually replaced Islamic rules of conduct. Today, Islam is more a spiritual force than a code of life.

Chapter 3

Decline and Disaster in the Arab World

With the disintegration of the Abbasid Empire went the glory of the Arabs. The rulers who succeeded the Abbasids were Persian- or Turkish-speaking, and the Islamic world came under non-Arab leadership not only politically but also culturally. Arab influence remained conspicuous in both Persian and Turkish cultures, but these cultures developed independently nevertheless.

After their loss of power, the Arabs stagnated culturally. Few really outstanding scholars appeared, among the more notable being the Tunisian historian and sociologist Ibn Khaldun (1332–1406). His *Muqaddimah* ("Prolegomena") has been translated into English and is considered an important contribution to sociology.[1]

The Ottoman Empire

As we have seen in the previous chapter, the Mongol invasion of the Near East had its greatest impact on Iraq. The effect of the destruction of Baghdad, the seat of Abbasid power, was enormous; and Iraq was not to recover again for centuries. However, the invasion left the Mamelukes of Egypt and Syria largely unharmed. And in Asia Minor the Ottoman Turks managed to recover from Mongol attack. It was the Ottomans who soon became the new power in the Near East.

75

The Ottomans were aided by the decline of Byzantine power in Asia Minor. Although the Byzantines revived somewhat in 1261, their control was limited to Constantinople, and a small area on either side of the straits. The Byzantines were no match for the rising Ottoman power.

Ottoman Conquests. The Ottomans had originally been commissioned by their predecessors, the Seljuk Turks, to safeguard the northwestern borders of their empire against the Byzantines. As a people they were "militaristic," a cultural trait that may have resulted from the continuous wars with the Byzantines. In any case, the Ottomans were known for their discipline, and were excellent soldiers. They developed organizational abilities which later enabled them to set up the complex bureaucracy necessary for the administration of their vast empire.

In 1299 the Ottomans established their own dynasty under Osman I, who gave them their name. Early in the fourteenth century, they had already conquered most of Asia Minor, and about the middle of the century they established settlements on the European side of the straits. At this time, Europe was disunited and preoccupied with internal feuds. The strongest initial opposition came from the Serbs, but they were defeated in 1389 at the battle of Kosovo. With the Serbs defeated, Hungary was exposed, raising the possibility that the Turks might overrun the whole of Europe. To stop them, the pope organized another Crusade—of Germans, Hungarians, and Frenchmen. But even this effort failed. In 1396, the crusaders were defeated at the battle of Nicopolis.

Europe was at the mercy of the Ottomans, and had it not been for Mongol attacks on the eastern front, they might have advanced deeper into Europe. For nearly forty years, the Turks were incapacitated, and their central authority was dissipated by Mongol pressure. During that time local princes ruled, and they quarreled among themselves. However, neither the Mongols nor the rivalries among the princes significantly weakened the militaristic characteristics of the Ottomans; and they recuperated sufficiently in the 1440's to resume their European activities.

After several wars with the Hungarians, Europe lay open to the invaders; and in 1529 they were knocking at the doors of Vienna. Fortunately for Europe, Vienna proved to be the turning point. Turkish attempts to take the city came to nothing, and western Europe escaped Ottoman control.

While battling with the Hungarians, the Turks had sufficient strength to crush their old enemy, the Byzantines. In an attempt to save his throne and his little kingdom, Constantine XI consented to the uniting of the Greek and Latin churches under the pope, something that had been attempted several times earlier but unsuccessfully. However, the union came too late: the popes had already lost their influence in Europe and they could not effectively defend the Byzantine kingdom. In 1453 the Turks captured Constantinople and the emperor was killed. This was the end of the Byzantine state, which had existed for fifteen hundred years.

By 1517 the Turks had defeated the Mamelukes in Egypt and Syria and annexed their territory. Shortly afterward, they conquered Tunisia and Algeria, and by 1639 almost the whole Arab world was under Turkish control. This dominion did not end until World War I.

THE ARABS UNDER OTTOMAN RULE

The "Treacherous" Turks. Many contemporary Arabs, especially the nationalists, believe that the Turks had betrayed their Arab rulers and were responsible for ending a glorious Arab history. Historically, this belief refers to the time when Abbasid caliphs recruited the Turks as bodyguards and relied on them to safeguard the state and its territory. In time, the Turks dominated the caliph and ruled his empire, and to contemporary Arabs this Turkish takeover was no more than a subversion of the system of the Abbasid Arabs.

There is no doubt that the Turks exploited Abbasid racial

tolerance to their own advantage. Whereas the Abbasids emphasized the Islamic character of their state rather than its racial composition, the Turks considered their common ethnic background a more important focus for loyalty. Consequently, Turkish "usurpation" of power was ethnically motivated. In a sense, it was an act of betrayal, but only insofar as the Arab rulers were concerned.

In a sense, however, the Turkish takeover was no more than a military coup d'état similar to the coups d'état of the modern world. That it was gradual does not change this fact. In the contemporary world, there are instances where men engineering coups d'état stay in the background and do not come out in the open until later. What makes the Turkish coup different is its ethnic character: political power became a Turkish monopoly.

The fact that the Turks were able to subvert the Abbasid system indicates that the system was weak. Even without the Turks, Abbasid disintegration was inevitable. Still, it is understandable that contemporary Arab nationalists read history and interpret it in the light of their own interests. Nationalists elsewhere do the same. In any event, although there are different premises from which history may be interpreted, and the Arab premise is only one, it is not, therefore, necessarily incorrect.

However, this belief in Turkish betrayal is not the only source of the present Arab view of the Turks—there is a religious and cultural question as well. After World War I, the Turks renounced their Islamic cultural tradition and began to affiliate with Western culture. In the 1920's, the Kemalist republican regime introduced and implemented extensive programs for modernization. The old Islamic social and political structure, with its own laws, customs, and symbols, was abolished. Of course, the Turks continued to be Muslims but their public institutions and laws were fundamentally Western. The last link with the Islamic tradition was severed in 1928 when the Arabic script was replaced by the Roman.

The Arabs were hurt that their coreligionists were no longer identified with the Islamic tradition, and Turkey's defection from the Islamic camp reinforced their belief that Turks were treacherous. Ironically, the progressive Arabs respect Kemal Atatürk, and they consider him a great revolutionary. When Gamal Abdel Nasser became their hero in the late 1950's and early 1960's some of them likened him to Atatürk; and some likened him to Saladin, of the period of the Crusades.

The rift between Arabs and Turks widened still more after World War II, when Turkey became pro-Western in its international relations. Turkey's recognition of the State of Israel came as a shock to the Arabs; and the situation was not helped when the Arabs began to complain about Western "imperialism" and Israeli "aggression." Arab revolutionary regimes of the postwar period have found no identity with Turkey. In fact, they have contributed to the widening of the cleavage between the two peoples.

But it must be remembered that the Turks have their own case against the Arabs. They think the Arabs betrayed them when in 1916 the Arabs took up arms against the Ottoman state and cooperated with the British during World War I. The war, of course, ended the Ottoman Empire. Thus it might be argued that the Ottoman Empire had its beginnings in Turkish "betrayal" of the Arabs and ended with Arab "betrayal" of the Turks.

Obviously, Turkish-Arab relations are beset by a crisis of confidence, a crisis that has developed historically. Whether relations between the two peoples will improve in the future is uncertain. However, as the Arabs become culturally more Westernized and Turkey becomes politically more Middle Eastern, the gap separating the two peoples might narrow.

Arab Rebellions Against the Ottoman Turks. The Arabs "slept" through the Turkish-Ottoman period of history. During most of the time, they felt more Islamic than Arab and they gave their loyalty to their Turkish rulers, who were alien in lan-

guage and ethnic background. Their situation was characterized by "general spiritual and cultural decadence, a complete
dissipation of the sense of nationality, and a real social degra-
dation." [2]

Consequently, although there were Arab rebellions against
Ottoman rule in the seventeenth, eighteenth, and nineteenth
centuries, they were not nationalistic in character. They largely
arose from economic or social factors or from the ambitions
of particular rulers. Nevertheless, they are important to a clear
vision of Arab history.

In the first half of the seventeenth century, Fakhr al-Din, a
Syrian Druze leader, attempted to free himself from Turkish
control. He failed, and was executed in Constantinople. Another leader, Bashir al-Shihabi, revolted at the beginning of
the nineteenth century but was equally unsuccessful. More
important was Mohammed Ali's challenge to the authority of
the sultan during the third decade of the nineteenth century.

Mohammed Ali (1769–1849) served in the Ottoman army
and distinguished himself during the campaign against Napoleon. In 1805, the sultan appointed Ali governor of Egypt,
and soon he was so powerful that he became virtually independent of Ottoman central control.

Ali tried to industrialize Egypt with the assistance of Western technology. He introduced several economic and social
reforms with the intention of making Egypt militarily strong.
He also involved himself in several military campaigns to boost
his prestige and give himself a reputation as a strong and dynamic leader. The first campaigns were on the side of the
Ottoman sultan. Ali helped the sultan quell the Wahhabi rebellion in the Arabian peninsula, and in the 1820's he sided
with the sultan against the Greeks who were trying to gain
independence from Ottoman rule. However, Britain, France,
and Russia brought about his defeat at the battle of Navarino
in 1827.

When Ali realized that fighting on the side of the sultan did
not add enough to his prestige and influence, he invaded Syria
in 1833, and occupied it for ten years. His success in the

Syrian adventure induced him, in 1834, to extend his military operations to Asia Minor. But again, the European powers forestalled him. They threatened to intervene to save the weak sultan, whom they preferred to the ambitious and independent Ali. In the end, the sultan and Ali concluded a treaty in which the sultan agreed to make the Egyptian governorship hereditary. Until 1952, Egypt was governed by Ali's family, King Farouk being the last representative of the family to rule.

Mohammed Ali's career was motivated by his personal ambitions. Although his origin was Macedonian, he appealed to the Arab people of Syria. But his movement did not involve a conception of Arab nationality. Like the other rebellions, his was a personal one.

Only one revolt was truly Arab, the Wahhabi revolt of the Arabian peninsula, which Ali helped crush. The origins of the revolt go back to a religious reform movement started in central Arabia by Mohammed ibn Abd al-Wahhab (1703?–1792) in the middle of the eighteenth century. The movement aimed at "purifying" Islam from secular elements and restoring it to its original form. By 1800 it had developed political interests and controlled a few places in Arabia. After its expansion outside the Arabian peninsula was stopped, with Ali's help, the movement became linked with the Saud family. This family controlled more than two thirds of the Arabian peninsula, early in the twentieth century, in what is known today as Saudi Arabia. In a sense, the Wahhabi movement succeeded in the Arabian peninsula. Politically, it gained autonomy, although it remained within the Ottoman Empire.

TROUBLE IN EGYPT

The most dramatic political events of the nineteenth-century Arab world took place in Egypt. They were significant because they complicated Egypt's political future and culminated in Britain's occupation of the country.

Many of Egypt's present problems are caused by past events

and historical developments, and to understand contemporary Egyptian politics we must study Egyptian history. Historically, Egypt suffered from two evils: internal corruption and foreign intrigue. The first evil, internal corruption, was a social illness that afflicted Egyptian governments on and off during both the nineteenth and the twentieth century. The second evil, foreign intrigue, continued until the military coup of 1952. Both left marks on the psychological makeup of the Egyptians.

The Capitulations. Foreign control in Egypt began in 525 B.C. and was almost continuous until 1922. Egyptian students need read no more than a brief account of Egypt's history to understand the impact of foreign rule upon their country. It is natural, therefore, that they would be against anything foreign and insist on sovereignty and independence as important criteria of national security. Such reactions are hardly abnormal for a people with a long history of foreign domination.

As long as Egypt was under foreign rule Egyptians were second-class citizens: foreigners had advantages Egyptians did not have. These advantages were mostly the product of what was called the capitulation system, which continued to give special privileges to foreigners and inferior status to Egyptians even after independence (1922).

The capitulations had been introduced to promote trade. The first such treaty was concluded in 1535, between the Ottoman state and France; and it came at a time when French trade with the Middle East was growing. Similar treaties between the Ottoman sultan and other European countries followed. This body of agreements became the basis of the capitulation "system." The system existed for centuries and did not really come to an end until the late 1940's.

The capitulation treaties gave European nationals living in the Ottoman Empire such special privileges as exemption from the jurisdiction of Ottoman courts. Foreign nationals remained subject to the laws of their mother countries even though they were living on Ottoman territory. In addition, they were exempt from the payment of certain types of taxes. Being part of the Ottoman Empire (until 1914), Egypt too was, for the most part, obligated by the capitulations.

From the sixteenth to the eighteenth century, these capitulations were not controversial and were accepted as a normal part of the legal system. In fact, they were consistent with the Islamic millet system, which allowed non-Muslims (Christians and Jews) to live under their own community law and custom.

However, in the nineteenth century, new features were introduced into the system; and those and other factors made the capitulations a political and economic issue. Foreign privileges were extended to new areas of law and taxation; and state sovereignty was further limited. The new features were the product of two developments. State authority had weakened as a result of internal problems at the same time that foreign diplomatic pressures had increased and became more effective. Also, European nationals had become interested in owning land in Egypt, where previously their interests had been limited to business and commerce.

Foreign governments began to intervene in civil and criminal justice. Disputes were often settled with very little regard to evidence, and foreign litigants were favored. In criminal cases, foreigners were tried before their own consular courts, many of whom were "sufficiently unscrupulous as to connive at certain criminal acts performed by their own nationals." [3]

The system was used to promote the economic interests of the European nationals. Egypt's industry and commerce were controlled by foreigners, who had the support of their powerful governments as well as a favorable tax structure. Since Egyptians did not have the privileges provided by the capitulations, they labored under serious economic handicaps. Another effect of the capitulations system was that it denied tax revenues to the Egyptian government from important sources of income. Consequently, public projects and economic reforms were almost impossible without borrowing.

The most striking example of the damage done to Egypt's

economy by the capitulations was the lack of foreign interest in developing the cotton industry. Egypt's primary agricultural product was spun into yarn outside the country, and until 1930 only one third of Egyptian cotton was processed in Egypt. "The capitulation treaties discouraged the protection of infant industry, and the Levantine mercantile community, where financial power lay, was oriented to the service of the European manufacturers." [4]

The cotton-processing problem was later one of the main concerns of the Nasser regime. As a result of the regime's conscientious policies, over three fourths of Egypt's medium staple cotton is today spun by Egyptian mills. Between 1952, when Nasser took power, and 1967, textile production increased almost four times.[5] Of course, the disappearance of the capitulation in the late 1940's paved the way for the Nasser regime to introduce the new policies and carry them out.

The capitulations created chaos in some legal transactions. This problem became more complicated in the latter part of the nineteenth century, as the volume of trade between Europe and Egypt increased. In time it became necessary to reconstruct the legal relations of Egypt and the foreign nationals. An unsuccessful attempt was made in 1869, when an international conference consisting of Britain, Germany, France, Russia, Austria-Hungary, the United States, and Italy met to discuss the matter. In 1873, however, a second conference was held in Constantinople and this met with better success. The conference resolved to establish a system of mixed courts to adjudicate civil cases in which Egyptians and foreigners or foreigners of different nationalities were involved. The old consular courts continued adjudicating criminal cases in which foreigners were involved (even if an Egyptian was a party to the case) and those civil cases involving foreigners of the same nationality.

The mixed court system did not change the status of foreign nationals. It merely regularized the system of civil justice and eliminated some of the confusion that had existed previously.

Two aspects of the new system denied the Egyptian govern-

ment greater control over the foreign nationals. First, the majority of the judges serving on the mixed courts were foreign,
and the courts applied French law rather than Ottoman or
Egyptian law. Secondly, Egypt's ruling family and government
were not exempt from the jurisdiction of the mixed courts. In
other words, whenever foreigners were involved in a particular case, the mixed courts had jurisdiction even though the
other party was the Egyptian government. This was contrary
to the prevailing legal principle that a state could not be sued
against its will. In effect, the European governments denied
the Egyptian state what they considered a universal right of
all states. The resulting humiliation for Egypt was later an
important issue with Egyptian nationalists, who denounced
the mixed court system and after independence argued that
it was a violation of Egyptian sovereignty.

Moreover, Egyptian nationalists viewed the capitulations as
instruments of foreign exploitation and symbols of foreign superiority and Egyptian inferiority. This view was reinforced
by the fact that the capitulations had been extended to include all foreigners and not only the nationals of the capitu-
latory powers. Anyone who could secure the necessary certification from a foreign consulate would have privileged status
in Egypt. Expediency prompted sued Christians and Jews born
in Egypt to apply for certification. When Nasser came to
power, he found the situation intolerable. A high proportion
of Jews born in Egypt had not bothered to obtain Egyptian
citizenship. To a much lesser degree, this was also true of the
non-European, non-Egyptian Christians.

**The Suez Canal: A Lesson in Internal Corruption and For-
eign Intrigue.** The Ottoman sultan, long before the death of
Mohammed Ali in 1849, had decreed that the office of governor of Egypt would be hereditary.[6] Consequently, Ali's family ruled Egypt until 1952. Events after 1849, however, succeeded in destroying the semi-independent status of the office
built up by Ali.

The building of the Suez Canal was the most decisive of

these events. It was a major cause of the expanding European intervention in Egyptian affairs that culminated, in 1882, in British occupation of the country. This period in Egypt's history, therefore, requires consideration of the international politics surrounding the construction of the canal as well as the impact of the canal itself on the political status of Egypt.

The immense political and commercial value of a waterway between the Mediterranean Sea and the Red Sea had long been recognized. Indeed, an indirect route had existed as far back as 2000 B.C., when a canal connected the Red Sea and the Nile River. Maintenance of the canal had been too much for the ancient governments, however, and reconstruction was considered too costly.

But the appeal of the idea persisted, and it gathered momentum with the Anglo-French trade rivalry of the nineteenth century. British trade around the Cape of Good Hope to the Far East was hurting the French seaports on the Mediterranean;[7] and so it was the French who revived the idea of the canal, and who were its most strenuous advocates. It was a Frenchman who ultimately directed the construction of the hundred-mile waterway between Port Said and Port Taufiq, near Suez—perhaps one of the greatest engineering enterprises ever devised by man.

Frenchmen made many attempts to secure concessions for the construction of the canal from Turkish and Egyptian authorities; but none was successful during the first half of the nineteenth century. Mohammed Ali believed, and events proved him right, that the canal project could not benefit Egypt politically and that Egypt would become susceptible to foreign political influence as well as outright domination by the European powers. Ali's successor, Abbas I (governor, 1848–1854), also resisted similar attempts. Additional obstacles were raised by the British, who were naturally fearful that a French canal in Egypt would result in political advantages for France and a decrease of British influence in the area. The British used their influence over the Ottoman sultan to prevent the realization of the project.

In addition to British pressure and the resistance of Egyptian governors, there was also another important obstacle: the widespread belief that the Red Sea and the Mediterranean were not at the same level and therefore could not be joined without flooding Egypt. The construction of the canal was thus considered an impossibility by most people.

But the succession of Said to the governorship of Egypt (1854–1863), and the findings of an international committee showing the physical practicability of the canal project disposed of the two main obstacles. The succession of Said brought favorable political conditions in Egypt, because of the personal friendship between the new Egyptian ruler and Ferdinand de Lesseps.

De Lesseps had devoted most of his life to realizing the idea of the canal, and it was his friendship with Said—developed during Said's early years when de Lesseps was serving as a French diplomat—that finally achieved the concession in 1854. The concession, however, was not valid without ratification by the sultan, Said's overlord; and, ironically, France was not yet ready to use her influence with Britain or the sultan on behalf of de Lesseps. France and Britain were allies in the Crimean War against Russia (1854–1856), and France did not wish to antagonize Britain. Mainly for this reason, the project was to be postponed for nearly another decade.

The year 1864, however, was a fortunate one for de Lesseps. Britain had a Liberal government, which showed little interest in the whole Suez affair; and it was possible for the Ottoman sultan to ratify the concession which Said had granted to de Lesseps. The Suez Canal project became legally possible and construction could begin.

The financial arrangements had already been worked out by de Lesseps.[8] (Indeed, shares had already been sold six years before the concession was ratified.) The Egyptian government was entitled to 15 percent of the net profit; the promoters were to receive 10 percent; and the shareholders the remaining 75 percent. When the shares of the Suez Canal Company, which was chartered in France, were put up for sale in 1858, the French bought the majority of them and the Egyptian government became the second largest owner. But within a short time Egypt's shares began to diminish. In 1874, Ismail (governor, 1863–1879),[9] Said's successor, sold part of his shares to the British, and, shortly after his deposition by the Turkish sultan in 1879, the Anglo-French controllers of the Egyptian treasury sold the remaining part, leaving Egypt with no shares whatsoever. Thus Egypt lost some 44 percent of the Suez Canal Company's shareholding. Great Britain became the largest single owner of the company's shares.

When the construction of the canal was completed in 1869, the total cost of the operation was 16,000,000 Egyptian pounds.[10] Of this the Egyptian government paid about 11,500,-000 pounds in return for 15 percent of the Company's net profits. These figures clearly indicate that Egypt had paid by far the largest portion of the bill for the construction of the canal, although she was entitled to only a small part of the profit. The promoters and the shareholders, who paid little more than a quarter of the cost, were entitled to the remaining 85 percent of the profit.

The political aftermath of the construction of the canal was still more detrimental to the future of Egypt than the unfair financial arrangements. Beginning in 1876, Egypt began to lose her semi-independent status. In 1882, Egypt was occupied by the British, although it was not until 1914 that the legal status of the country was changed. In the meantime, Egypt continued to be part of the Ottoman Empire, with the British in actual control of her domestic and international affairs.

The British in Egypt. As mentioned earlier, Ismail, who succeeded Said as governor of Egypt, borrowed too much money to finance his ambitious projects, including money for building the Suez Canal. His predecessor had also incurred heavy debts in the name of Egypt. The creditors were European businessmen interested in business ventures in Africa. They charged exorbitant interest on their loans,[11] and when their Egyptian debtors were unable to pay on time, they attempted to use their governments' political influence to bring about Egyptian compliance. The Egyptian financial situation grew progressively worse until, finally, in the mid-1870's, Ismail had to accept Anglo-French supervision of the Egyptian treasury, which the French and English considered necessary for ensuring the payment of the Egyptian debt to the European creditors. Thus the financial problem of Egypt was the most important cause of her fall under European control.

After Ismail was deposed by the two European powers in 1879 (with the sultan's approval) and replaced by his son Tewfik (governor, 1879–1892), there was further deterioration in the political situation of the country. Nationalist sentiments ran high, while army officers conspired against the foreign intruders. The Arabi rebellion, which took place in 1881, succeeded in putting nationalist officers in positions of power. Its leader, Colonel Ahmed Arabi, became minister of war in a government that looked with favor upon the cause of the nationalists.

Naturally, the rebellion threatened Anglo-French dominance in Egypt, thereby giving England and France a pretext for direct military intervention. There were possibilities for reconciliation between the aims of the rebellion and the financial interests of France and Britain, but France had already decided in favor of intervention by force. At the beginning, the British were not receptive to the French idea, but, ironically, when intervention did finally take place in the summer of 1882 the British went in alone. A change of government in Paris prevented French participation.

British occupation of Egypt thus began in 1882. At the time, Britain believed that it would be temporary, until a program of financial reform could bring Egypt out of her debt. Consequently, she left the existing governmental institutions almost unchanged. The Egyptian khedive (the title had been held by Egyptian governors since 1867) continued to issue his customary decrees and preside over an Egyptian ministry; but real power and the actual formulation of policy was British.

Again because Britain did not intend a long occupation, the

economic reforms she undertook were also temporary. The British were not motivated to attempt rehabilitation of the entire economy through long-range planning, but preferred limited reforms that could produce sufficient surplus in state revenues to pay the Egyptian debt and balance the budget. These policies emphasized agriculture at the expense of industry. Industrial development, Britain feared, would hurt her own export industries. Also, Egyptian agricultural products were compatible with the British economy, which needed food products to feed its population and cotton for its textile industry. The agricultural improvements did increase the revenues of the state, but because of population increases they failed to raise the standard of living of the Egyptian fellahin (peasants).

When it became clear by the end of the 1880's that state finances were improved to the point where it was possible to pay the larger portion of the Egyptian debt, the question arose of the moral justification for British presence in Egypt. This question troubled not only Egyptians but also the British.

Political developments in the Sudan at the time provided the British with a temporary argument for continued occupation. They could say that they must remain in Egypt to quell a Sudanese revolution that had broken out in 1881, which they considered a serious threat to the security of the Suez Canal and therefore to British trade interests in the East. A second argument arose from pre-World War I political conditions. Britain pointed to the strategic importance of Egypt to her military operations in the Middle East.

Familiarity with the problem of the Sudan, and with the situation prior to World War I, is important for an understanding of this period in Egyptian history. Let us, therefore, consider these two subjects before going further.

British Involvement in the Sudan. British interest in the Sudan began with the Sudanese rebellion against Egyptian control in the 1880's, which threatened the Suez Canal and the British role in Egypt. Egyptian interest had begun with Mohammed Ali, who sent an expedition to establish authority in that country. Originally, Ali was mainly looking for new recruits for his armies. But he was also interested in dominating the Sudan trade, which included such important items as gold, ivory, and slaves. In 1842, the Ottoman sultan officially recognized the fact that the Sudan had become part of Ali's domain.

After Ali's death Egyptian interest diminished for a time; but beginning in 1865 Ismail became interested in controlling the sources of the Nile to guarantee the continuous flow of water to Egypt. To strengthen and perpetuate his control over the Sudan, Ismail attempted to involve Britain by announcing his intention to end the slave trade there, something about which Britain had shown concern. Also, in 1869, he appointed a British citizen to the governorship of Equatoria, a Sudanese province under Egyptian control. The British, however, remained neutral on the Sudan question, even after they occupied Egypt in 1882.

In 1881, however, a rebellion led by a Muslim Sudanese called the Mahdi (the guide) broke out against Egyptian rulers. The rebellion continued for several years, becoming more violent and intense after the death of the Mahdi in 1885 and the assumption of leadership by a more determined man known as the Khalifa (the successor). And when the Khalifa declared his intention to invade Egypt herself, the rebellion threatened Britain's interests in that country and in the Suez Canal.

A more important factor affecting British neutrality in the Sudan was the fierce struggle at this time among many European countries for control of Africa, mainly France and Italy. At one point also, there was danger of a military showdown between Britain and France over spheres of influence in the area. Finally, late in 1896, the British government decided to occupy the Sudan and suppress the rebellion. An expedition largely composed of Egyptians was sent to the Sudan under Sir Herbert Kitchener. After a series of battles with the rebels, culminating in the famous battle of Omdurman (September, 1898) Kitchener was able to destroy and disperse the rebel forces almost completely. The Khalifa was killed in a minor battle shortly after Omdurman and the Sudan was finally brought under foreign rule.

What type of governmental arrangement in the Sudan would be acceptable to the British? To leave Egypt with sole control of the Sudan would be illogical since the British were in control of Egypt itself. Also, the Egyptian administration which existed in the Sudan before the Mahdi rebellion was unpopular and had the reputation of being irresponsible and exploitive. The new arrangement Britain worked out was unusual in terms of colonial administrative theory. The Condominium, as this arrangement was called, established a joint rule by Britain and Egypt.

The Sudan Convention of 1899 was the legal instrument upon which the Condominium was based.[12] Ratified by both Egypt and Britain on January 19, 1899, the Convention basically required: (1) that the flags of the two countries be raised over public buildings in the Sudan; (2) that a governor-general, appointed by the khedive (Egypt's ruler) upon the recommendation of the British government, should possess all military and civil powers in the Sudan; (3) that no import duties could be levied on goods entering the Sudan from Egypt; (4) that Europeans must have no special privileges in the Sudan; and (5) that the slave trade be abolished once and for all.

In the years after the establishment of the Condominium in the Sudan, it became obvious that Egypt was less than a partner in the administration of the country. Very often the British ignored Egypt, and the Condominium was no more than unilateral British rule, an extension of British control over Egypt itself.

The Sudan was very important to the Egyptians. Egypt relied on Nile River water for her agriculture; and the source of the Nile is in the Sudan. Whoever controlled the Nile, Egyptians argued, also controlled Egypt. Many people thought this Egyptian argument was an exaggeration based upon imaginary fear. However, there were others who appear to have accepted the Egyptian view. For instance, when in 1924 Sir Lee Stack, the British governor-general of the Sudan, was assassinated in Cairo, the British high commissioner of Egypt declared that there would no longer be any limitations upon the Sudan's use of the Nile waters. Previously, such limitations existed by mutual agreement between the two countries to ensure sufficient water supply for both. This declaration was meant as a punitive measure against the Egyptian government, which the British commissioner thought was indirectly responsible for the incident. It would seem, therefore, that the British agreed with the Egyptian argument regarding the strategic position of the Sudan.

World War I and Its Aftermath. Political developments within the Sudan—considered important only in relation to the security of the Suez Canal—were only one reason why Britain did not leave Egypt sooner. A second was World War I.

When Turkey entered the war on the side of Germany, thereby becoming a British enemy, a crucial issue developed concerning the legal status of Egypt, which was still part of the Ottoman (Turkish) Empire. Although they occupied and controlled Egypt, the British recognized this legal status. But now, since Britain could no longer recognize Turkey's sovereignty in Egypt, she had only two alternatives: either grant Egypt independence or bring her into the British Empire.

The British considered independence impractical in view of the military necessities, which included defense of the canal and also a base from which Britain could launch an offensive against Turkey. The second alternative, therefore, was adopted by the British policymakers: Egypt was given the legal status of a British protectorate.

What is a protectorate? Usually one country becomes a protectorate of another upon the request of the first and the acceptance of the second. No such procedure took place with Egypt, however. The change was accomplished by a unilateral act of Great Britain.

After the war, Egyptians demanded independence. As it became clear that the British were not willing to grant the demand, at least not in the immediate future, the Egyptian people revolted. Support for the revolt was increased by Britain's refusal to allow an Egyptian delegation, under the leadership of Saad Zaghlul, to argue Egypt's case before the Paris Peace Conference.

Zaghlul became a national hero, and his delegation ultimately became the basis of a political party, organized in 1924. He was sent into exile several times as a result of his revolutionary activities. The role of revolutionary was a strange one for Zaghlul, who was essentially a moderate and had been a good civil servant in the British-controlled government of Egypt. But this shows how difficult it was for a moderate leader to accept as permanent British occupation of Egypt. As the nationalist movement grew in number and intensity and as British opposition to independence continued, the conflict became more polarized, more violent, and more difficult to solve.

However, the revolution ultimately succeeded and Egypt became legally independent in 1922, although she did not really shake off British interference. Great Britain wanted a treaty guaranteeing her interests in Egypt and the Sudan. Zaghlul could not understand how Egypt could be independent with such limitations upon her sovereignty, and he refused to make the treaty concessions the British demanded. But he accepted Egypt's new constitution (1923), participated in the elections which followed, and became Egypt's first prime minister.

From then on, Egypt was torn by rivalries among the king, the British, and Zaghlul's Wafd ("delegation") party. King Fuad, Farouk's father, was authoritarian and wanted power for himself. The British continued to press for a treaty guaranteeing their interests. They continued to interfere in the internal politics of Egypt; they controlled Egypt's foreign relations; and they remained in occupation of her territory. The Wafd also wanted power, and was supported by the people. The party won almost every free election held between 1922 and 1952.

For Egypt to be truly independent it was necessary for her to be free of British occupation and control. For her to be democratic it was necessary to limit the king's powers and allow the Wafd party to rule in accordance with the constitution. Because these elements were lacking, Egypt was neither independent nor democratic.

There was no political stability: elections were usually not free; the king was arbitrary; and after the death of Zaghlul in 1927 the Wafd gradually became the party of the privileged and the rich. As for the British, they too would not relinquish power without concrete guarantees. The triangular struggle for power obstructed economic development and reform, and it was the people of Egypt who suffered most.

True Independence at Last. Between 1922, the year of independence, and 1936, when an Anglo-Egyptian treaty finally was signed, Egypt remained in constant political turmoil.

In 1936, however, King Fuad died, and one factor in the struggle was eliminated. His successor, Farouk, was young and inexperienced in politics, and the Wafd had a chance to rule the country without competing with the palace. In addition, the circumstances were ripe for settling the old controversy with the British. Italy's invasion of Ethiopia in East Africa forced both Egypt and Britain to the realization that Mussolini's ambitions could threaten Egypt. Consequently, the two countries were able to conclude a treaty, which, broadly speaking, guaranteed British interests in the area, but also gave Egypt some benefits.

The modification of the capitulations and the promise to abolish them twelve years later meant that Egypt could now levy direct taxes. Until then the Egyptian government was afraid to do so because foreigners were exempt while Egyptians were not. The hope was that the direct taxes would give the Egyptian government additional revenues to begin economic and social improvements.

With the limitations on foreign privilege, Egyptian citizenship acquired some prestige. However, it was not sufficient to encourage foreign residents to become Egyptian nationals. The vast majority of them continued to hold foreign citizenships until the advent of the Nasser regime in 1952.

Unfortunately, the Anglo-Egyptian treaty did not end British interference in Egyptian affairs. Nor did it end British occupation of Egypt. For instance, during World War II a controversy developed over the proper treaty relationships of the two countries. It was clear that the 1936 treaty did not require Egypt to declare war on Britain's enemies. Egypt tried to provide minimum cooperation with the British and to avoid assistance not specifically required by the treaty. Britain wanted more cooperation, although she did not demand an Egyptian declaration of war. Britain's position became more difficult as the German army advanced toward Egypt. And in order to guarantee the support of the Egyptian people during the crisis, the British told King Farouk to appoint Mustafa Nahas as prime minister.[13] Nahas had been the leader of the popular Wafd party since the death of Zaghlul in 1927. The British thought Nahas would have better control of the country than the palace governments, which were unpopular.

Farouk refused to appoint Nahas; and on February 4, 1942, British troops surrounded the royal palace. The British ambassador bluntly told the king that he had two alternatives, to abdicate or make the appointment. Farouk made the appointment.

The Egyptians never forgot the incident and they remembered it as a day of national humiliation. Furthermore, they were convinced that Egypt could not become truly independent as long as she was bound to Britain by the 1936 treaty;

and they began to assert their opposition through occasional street demonstrations and even violence. Consequently, in the postwar period, successive Egyptian governments made efforts to negotiate a new treaty, one that would leave Egypt in control of her destiny. But every effort failed.

In 1951, in desperation, the Nahas government decided to abrogate the treaty unilaterally. Ironically, Nahas was the man the British had wanted as prime minister in 1942, and he was the man who negotiated the treaty in 1936. Nahas' position recalls another irony: Zaghlul, who had led the 1922 revolution that gave Egypt her independence, had also held high positions in British-controlled governments. Could it be that the British were so unreasonable as to turn friends to enemies, moderates to extremists, and evolutionaries to revolutionaries? Or is it just coincidence that both of these initially cooperative men later turned revolutionary?

In any case, the Wafd government became involved in a life-and-death struggle with the British, and the outcome was disastrous to Egypt. Immediately after the abrogation of the treaty, civilians fought British troops in the Suez Canal area. University and high school students interrupted their educations and went to fight. Many people were killed on both sides. Nahas began to realize that the crisis was getting out of hand, but he did not know what to do. King Farouk, who disliked Nahas and his party, hoped the perilous policy of the government would backfire and Nahas would soon be out of power. The British simply awaited events.

Meanwhile, civilian groups, including students, were coming to the belief that the government had betrayed the people. Nahas had abrogated the treaty; but, they believed, he did nothing more. The civilian fighters wanted the government to help them with arms and to allow the army to enter the local war in the Canal Zone. Finally, as their hopes were not realized and their demands were not met, they set Cairo on fire.

On Saturday, January 26, 1952, a mob burned a number of

buildings, including famous restaurants, elegant movie houses, hotels, and foreign establishments. On that day, the skies of Cairo were filled with smoke and the city was in the midst of confusion: neither the police nor the army attempted to restore order to the city. For reasons still unknown, these forces did not act until late in the day.

The next day, the city was awakened by the news that the king had dismissed Nahas and a new, anti-Wafd government had been formed. The Egyptian people did not know how to react to all this. On the one hand they did not like Farouk. His failure during the Arab-Israeli war of 1948, his manipulation of the electoral process, his unconstitutional acts, and finally, his failure to provide the country with constructive leadership, all these contributed to his bad reputation. On the other hand, they felt Nahas was not forceful enough, although he was considered the best of the available leaders in the country. When he abrogated the treaty, they had made him the hero of Egypt; but now he was a failure, and they did not like failures. The Egyptian people had no alternative but to resign themselves to the situation. They might hope for a change, almost any kind of change; but they did not know when they might expect relief, or how it might be accomplished.

The political parties were also impotent: they were either corrupt or disabled by circumstances: The Muslim Brotherhood, a political organization in existence since 1928, was too extreme and doctrinaire to rule responsibly. Other parties not identified with the palace were too small and too weak to be effective. The Wafd party had had its chance, and proved incapable. Moreover, many Egyptians thought the Wafd was corrupt and that it had fallen under the influence of the exploitative big landowners.

Only the army was in a position to do something about the situation. In the armed forces, a small number of young officers (average age, thirty-two) were already organized into a conspirational underground movement, calling themselves the Free Officers. Under the leadership of Gamal Abdel Nasser, these officers staged a successful coup and took power in Egypt. Farouk was forced to abdicate, and in 1953 the monarchy was abolished.

It is not our purpose at present to delve into the policies of the new regime except to assert the important fact that it was under this regime that Egypt became free of British influence. In 1954, the Egyptian military regime reached an agreement with Great Britain which brought about the end of British occupation. With the departure of British troops, Egypt was finally the master of her own destiny.

Chapter 4

The Western Powers
Dismember Syria and Iraq

Under Turkish rule, the Fertile Crescent consisted of eight administrative divisions, three in Iraq and five in Syria. The Syrian provinces corresponded to the present-day territories of Lebanon, Israel, Jordan, Syria, and the Turkish province of Alexandretta. Of the original five provinces, only Lebanon enjoyed a substantial degree of political autonomy under the Turks, and this was due to the heterogeneity of its population and to foreign influence.

In all these administrative units, the socioeconomic structure was feudal, as it remained until recently. In spite of occasional attempts at reform, the Ottoman administration was either inefficient or corrupt. The Turkish rulers were more interested in the collection of taxes than in economic development. Consequently, economic stagnation, as well as political and cultural inertia, characterized Syria and Iraq throughout the Turkish period of their histories. Economic sophistication has come to these territories only recently.

The present chapter discusses two main topics: First, how Arab independence was denied by the European powers—particularly Britain and France—after the Arabs had been led to expect independence in return for their support in World War I. Second, the chapter considers how these powers divided Syria up between themselves.

ARAB-BRITISH RELATIONS DURING WORLD WAR I

The 1916 Arab revolt against the Turks was largely caused by the Arab belief that the support given the British war effort by the rebellion would be repaid by British support for Arab independence.

Without this incentive there was little reason for the Arabs to side with the British against their coreligionists. Indeed, during most of Turkish rule, the people of Syria had been more conscious of their Islamic identity than they were of their Arab identity. Of course, they were aware of their history and culture as a people, but this awareness held very little in the way of political implications. Arabism did not affect them until the latter part of the nineteenth century.

Nevertheless, World War I confronted all Arabs, Syrian and non-Syrian, with the serious question of whether they should support their coreligionists, the Turks, or oppose them. Some Arabs felt the Turkish Islamic state should have their loyalty; others wanted reform as a condition of loyalty; but very few thought of separation.

This last idea was to become dominant during the war, however; and it received encouragement as well as material support from the British. Of course, Britain wanted to bring down the Ottoman Empire, one of its adversaries in the war; and part of British strategy was to arouse the Arab population. The British believed this would provide desperately needed additional manpower and would enable them to conquer Ottoman territory with the aid of Ottoman subjects.

The British problem was to persuade the Arabs to side with them—a very difficult task: Most Arabs were loyal to the Ottoman state because it was Islamic. Some, however, were dissatisfied with the Ottoman administration: influential Arab families and landowners were especially sensitive to Turkish subversion of Arab culture and language.

The best British hope lay in Syria. At the time, Syria was

the center of Arab nationalism. But the difficulty of the Syrian Arab nationalists was a lack of strong leadership. Many of the rank-and-file Arab nationalists were Syrians, but the leadership was not. This problem of *imported leadership* still characterizes Syria's Arab nationalism. Also, the revolt could not start in Syria because of the firm control Turks had of the area. In fact, the Turks arrested and even hanged nationalist leaders.

As it happened, just before the 1916 Arab revolt, the Syrians were seeking a leader—at about the same time that the British were looking for an Arab to lead the revolt against the Turkish state. Both the Syrians and the British decided, separately, on Sharif Husein, King of Hejaz, on the Arabian peninsula. The fact that he was a direct descendant of the prophet Mohammed was important. The British thought Husein could effectively rally the Arabs behind him by calling for a jihad (holy war) against the Turks.

It was easier for the Syrians to reach an understanding with Husein than it was for the British, who had to offer something in return. After all, the British were neither Middle Eastern nor Muslim, while their Turkish enemy was both.

British Promises to Husein. Arab cooperation, Syrian and non-Syrian, was exchanged for a British guarantee of Arab independence.[1] The guarantee was made to Husein by Sir Henry McMahon, the British high commissioner of Egypt, and it was the culmination of a correspondence between the two men.

Initially Husein had sought to gain British guarantees of Arab independence in an area limited "on the north by Messina and Adana, to the 37th parallel, including Biridjek, Urfa, Mardin, Jezireh, and Amadia to the Persian frontier, on the south by the Persian Gulf and the Indian Ocean, with the exception of Aden, and on the west by the Red Sea and the Mediterranean to Mersina." [2]

McMahon did not recognize independence within the limits prescribed by Husein. The British had to accommodate

France, which had ambitions in the Arab Fertile Crescent; and they were reluctant to commit themselves in areas which in their opinion were not "purely Arab." Nevertheless, the British committed themselves to Arab independence in a more limited territory. In 1931, Harry Howard interpreted these British commitments as follows:

> It seems clear that Great Britain was undertaking, conditional on an Arab revolt, to recognize Arab independence, south of the 37th parallel, except Bagdad and Basra, and exclusive of districts where French interests predominated. It also appears that Great Britain, without the knowledge of her allies, was attempting to construct an Arab state or confederation under positive British control. Finally, it is evident that Husain had more far reaching ambitions which he did not renounce in his agreement with the British—such as claims against the British in southern Mesopotamia [Iraq] and against the French in Syria which he proposed to settle at the end of a victorious war.[3]

Thus, although Husein wanted more than the British could promise him, the establishment of an independent Arab state was the substance of the British promise. In return, the Arabs took up arms against the Turks. The ensuing 1916 Arab revolt was of immense value to the British war effort as well as to the Arabs themselves. According to one writer, it accounted for "something like 65,000 troops, thus freeing a number of British divisions for other tasks. It also compelled the Turks to fight on hostile soil, even though the battlefields lay within their own legal territory. Unquestionably, the British campaign in the Near East owed much of its ultimate success to Arab aid." [4] The revolt also gave the Arabs hope for a better future, and it was the Arabs' first recent experience in pursuing a major "national" goal. Of course, the outcome of the revolt was the disintegration of the Turkish Empire.

Conflicting Promises. Britain, however, had also been making promises elsewhere. About the same time that she was negotiating with Husein, she was also conducting negotiations with another Arab leader, through her Indian office. This was Ibn Saud, King of Nejd, Husein's rival in the Arabian peninsula, to whom the British promised the same territories in central and eastern Arabia that they had promised to Husein.

Finally, there was France, Britain's ally in the war, who was kept uninformed about British ambitions in the Arab world and about Arab aspirations for the future. However, in 1916 France and Britain became parties to the Sykes-Picot Agreement, which divided the Fertile Crescent.[5]

The terms of the treaty relating to the Arab Fertile Crescent were as follows: (1) France was to govern directly an area that included Cilicia, the northern coastal line of Syria, the province of Adana and part of central Anatolia. (2) Britain was to govern directly southern Mesopotamia (Iraq), including Baghdad and Basra, in addition to Haifa and Acre on the Syrian coast. (3) A "zone of influence" under French "protection" was created, to include Syria, Lebanon, and the northern part of Iraq. (4) A British "zone of influence" was created, to include the territory between the Mediterranean and the Iranian frontiers. (5) Palestine was to be international.

With this agreement, the Arab hope to become independent vanished. The victorious European powers had divided the Fertile Crescent among themselves.

The Sykes-Picot Agreement was negotiated in secret, with Russia later becoming the third party. But in 1917 the revolution took place in Russia, and the new regime made public the secret agreement. Only then did the Arabs learn of it. They reacted with a mixture of disappointment, doubt, and fear.

It is obvious that Arab aspirations for independence, guaranteed by Britain in the Husein-McMahon correspondence, were largely ignored. Not even in the zones of influence did the agreement establish any Arab independence: according to the agreement, an Arab administration was to exist with British or French "protection." The Arabs already knew what the word "protection" meant to the British. Egypt had been a British protectorate, which made her in effect a British colony.

The mandate system, established later in the Fertile Crescent, was not much different from the usual colonial administrations of Britain and France in other parts of the world.

Interpretations of British Conduct. The Arabs were not alone in their hatred of the Sykes-Picot Agreement. Many Western historians and writers agreed with them. For instance, the British historian Arnold Toynbee had the following to say in 1927: "The private and secret treaty indicates . . . the way in which, anticipating the successful outcome of the war, the allied representatives carved up an empire and planned new states as if the countries and peoples of the world were jig-saw puzzles to be toyed with, shaken up and refitted as a statesman's pastime. Upon such individual decisions rested the future fate of extensive Ottoman territories." [6]

Many other Western scholars recognized the conflict between the Sykes-Picot Agreement and British promises to the Arabs. Among them is George Lenczowski, of the University of California: "McMahon's pledge to [Husein] preceded by six months the Sykes-Picot agreement. The latter was obviously incompatible with the former and, to put it bluntly, constituted a breach of the pledge to the Arabs." [7]

As to the impact of the secret agreement upon the contemporary Arab nationalist, Professor William Spencer wrote: "The most famous (or notorious) of the secret agreements was the Sykes-Picot (1916). These two names, when coupled, still cause Arab nationalists to foam at the mouth; and indeed, few more blatant examples of arbitrary action exist in the annals of international relations." [8]

In the late 1930's, George Antonius, a Christian Arab, wrote a book called *The Arab Awakening*. This book, the first to contain the Husein-McMahon correspondence, brilliantly revealed the events surrounding Arab-Western relations during and after World War I.

It is evident from the book itself that the research which the author conducted was original and meticulous. The highlight of Antonius' analysis was a description of how the Western powers, mainly Britain, divided Arab land. The author concluded that the Arabs had been betrayed by European secret diplomacy, British promises to Husein constituting the major basis for the charge.[9]

In recent years, a few scholars have contested the validity of the "Antonius thesis." One of these is George Kirk, who maintains that the Arab nationalist movement of the nineteenth and early twentieth centuries did not involve the Arab masses and was nothing more than the activities of "privileged Muslim families," not a genuine national movement embodying common Arab aspirations.[10] Kirk states that Husein, the leader of the 1916 Arab revolt, "was pursuing personal and family interests rather than those of the Arab nationalist societies in the cities of the Fertile Crescent."

No doubt the Arab movement of 1916 was not a *mass* movement. In the feudal societies of the Ottoman Empire, mass movements were not possible. However, Kirk seems to imply that a movement that does not conform to modern Western criteria cannot be national. Although the Arab movement was not a mass movement, it was nevertheless a national one, aimed at freeing the Arabs of Turkish control and at establishing Arab independence. Also, Kirk seems to forget that nationalist movements elsewhere, including Western and Zionist movements, did not begin as mass movements.

Of course, like statesmen and politicians elsewhere, Husein did have personal ambitions and family interests in mind when he agreed to lead the Revolt. Indeed, it would be naïve to assume that a politician, whether Arab or Western, has no personal ambitions in political projects he is associated with. However, this does not mean that politicians cannot be sincere about the aims of their movements and the interests of their people. Husein tried to combine his personal and family interests with the interests of the Arab people, and to pursue both without endangering either. Ironically, he succeeded in pursuing his family interests while failing to secure his own position. Two of his sons became rulers of two Arab countries, while he himself was left without a country to rule.

There is also disagreement between Kirk and Antonius on the nature of the Husein-McMahon correspondence. While Antonius believes the letters contained definite and legally binding promises, Kirk believes they "did not result in a formal agreement" and that they "ended on an inconclusive note that thinly veiled a deep-seated disagreement."

The correspondence did reveal McMahon's intention to make a formal pledge. McMahon wrote Husein on behalf of the British government, and in his letter of October 24, 1915, he declared, "I am authorized to give you the following pledges on behalf of the Government of Great Britain." Furthermore, the letters did not "end on an inconclusive note," although Britain may have been less serious about its pledges to the Arabs than the letters indicate. McMahon's last letter to Husein sounded cheerful and optimistic: "The Arab countries are now associated in that noble aim which can be attained by uniting our forces and acting in unison. We pray God that success [in the war] may bind us to each other in a lasting friendship which shall bring profit and contentment to us all."

ZIONISM: NEW THREATS TO ARAB SELF-DETERMINATION

In addition to the assumption of overlordship by Britain and France, Arab rule over Arab territories was also threatened by the Zionist drive for a national Jewish state, which the Zionists believed should be in Palestine, despite the fact that the territory had been Arab for 1,300 years and had a decisive Arab majority.

The Palestine Dilemma: Who Shall Pay for the Jewish National Home? The basic assumption of Zionism is that the establishment of a Jewish state is the best solution to the problem of Jewish persecution. Since the Zionist movement had decided that Palestine should be the place of the Jewish state, the task of populating the area by a large number of Jews became its primary responsibility. Until the establishment of Israel in 1948, the Zionist movement did everything possible to encourage Jewish immigration.

With the growth of political consciousness, the Arabs of Palestine opposed the admission to Palestine of a large number of Jews. On many occasions, such as in 1922, 1929, and 1936, they revolted in protest. Consequently, the British were caught in the dilemma of Arab-Jewish relations, and they spent a great deal of their effort not in the betterment of Palestinian life but in quelling revolutions and mediating differences.

The reaction of the Arabs was understandable: they saw the Jewish immigrants as aliens who sometime in the future could threaten their majority status in Palestine. Had the new immigrants been Polish or Russian or French or English, Arab reaction would have been the same. At least initially, the fact that the new immigrants were Jewish was not important to the Palestinian Arabs. What really mattered was that these were aliens coming into Palestine in large numbers. Arab resentment was further increased by the knowledge that the new immigrants wanted a separate state based on Jewish nationality.

Arabs argue that the solution to the problem of Jewish persecution cannot be brought about at their expense. They stress the fact that they did not create the Jewish problem. If anyone should provide the solution, they argue, it should be the Europeans.

Historians argee that the Arabs were a tolerant people. The well-known American historian Carlton J. H. Hayes recognizes Arab tolerance in his famous textbook *History of Europe*. There he points out that the Jews "were only too glad to exchange Byzantine masters for Mohammedan." [11] When the Arabs were the leaders of civilization they gave their religious minorities a status considered good by the standards of the time. There were times when Jews could find homes in the Arab world when they could not find them in Europe. And they were able to attain intellectual and cultural fulfillment:

> Jewish scholarship at the time of its greatest fertility cannot be assessed apart from its Arab setting. Even in later years, when the Jew had come to be as a pariah in most European countries, he could still find in Arab communities a home, a livelihood, and all the tools required for scholarly pursuits.[12]

Until recently, minorities in the Arab world had a better status than the Arabs themselves. Under the capitulations, for instance, and until the 1940's, a foreigner had more privileges in Egypt than an Egyptian. Many Jews who were born in Egypt enjoyed the special privileges.

From an Arab point of view the Jewish problem was solved at the expense of the Arabs. This the Arabs believe is unfair. They insist that if it were not for European prejudice and Zionist exploitation of the Jewish plight there would be no Arab-Israeli conflict today.

The Zionist Movement. In the background of Zionism is the religious notion that God promised Palestine to Abraham and his descendants. (Both Jews and Arabs claim to be descendants of Abraham.) However, not until Jacob, Abraham's grandson, did the association of the Hebrews (Israelites) with Palestine begin. Without the idea of the Promised Land, Zionism could not have sustained the long and difficult struggle for the establishment of the State of Israel. Even the non-Zionist Jew could not escape being influenced by this notion:

> Whether ethnologically true or false, the fact remains that for more than two millennia Jewish children have been inculcated with this belief in their origin and their historic right to their Palestine homeland. Zionism reaches back deep into the roots of Jewish history for its sustenance and derives much of its strength from an emotionalism unique in political movements (one of which it has become).[13]

Ever since the destruction of their state by the Romans in A.D. 70, the Jews religiously yearned to return to Palestine.[14] Late in the nineteenth century, the implications of this yearning became largely political because Palestine was Arab and the return of the Jews required overcoming Arab opposition. In a sense, therefore, the Zionist movement was responsible for providing the political means by which its religious goal could be achieved.

At the turn of the century, the Zionist movement's greatest difficulty was to persuade and induce many reluctant Jews to settle in Palestine. Some Jews thought their "return" was dependent upon an act of God, rather than on the efforts of men, which were considered almost sacrilegious. Others believed that the solution of the Jewish problem required the assimilation of the Jews into non-Jewish cultures. European liberalism of the eighteenth and nineteenth centuries made the assimilation theory very appealing. In addition, many Jews were apprehensive about some of the implications of Zionism: they feared the possibility that non-Jews might doubt the loyalties of Jews to their countries of birth and citizenship. This, they believed, was the most significant and most dangerous implication of Zionism.

Zionism derived at least some of its impetus from the alarm felt by many eighteenth- and nineteenth-century Jewish leaders over the apathy of Jews toward their religion and culture. Moses Mendelssohn (1729–1786), for instance, advocated the strengthening of religious values; and Zionists believed that if the Jewish religious-cultural identity were to be preserved, a territorial base was a necessity. True, Palestine was not the only territory that could fulfill the goal of Jewish survival. Sociologically speaking, any territory could accomplish this objective. However, from a religious point of view, Palestine was the ideal place because it answered the religious as well as the cultural needs of the Jews. Furthermore, eastern European Jews favored Palestine because many Jews from eastern Europe had already gone there.

The Zionist movement remained largely intellectual until the 1890's, when Theodor Herzl (1860–1904) became its leader. Herzl, who was born in Budapest and later lived in Vienna and then in Paris, was a journalist. In his early years an advocate of Jewish assimilation, he, like many of his Jewish contemporaries, became a convert to Zionism as a result of the Dreyfus affair,[15] which convinced him that "Jews could overcome anti-Semitism only by becoming sovereign over a given territory."[16] In 1896 he published a pamphlet entitled *The Jewish State*, which made him famous.[17] Essentially, Herzl was uncommitted about the location of a Jewish state, although he thought Argentina and Palestine were possible sites. In 1897, however, the First Zionist Congress met in Basel, under Herzl's leadership, and resolved on the creation of a Jewish home in Palestine. Subsequently, Herzl, as the first president of the organization, set out to secure a charter from the Turkish sultan, which would permit the Zionists to organize Jewish colonization in Palestine. The sultan rejected his request, in effect warning the Zionists that the road to Palestine would be a long and arduous one.

But the Zionist movement was by no means united in its goal to create an independent Jewish state in Palestine. Early in 1901, Ahad Ha'am (Asher Ginsberg), a Jewish social philosopher, argued a theory of "cultural Zionism," which emphasized Jewish culture over political involvement. Ginsberg believed that the settlement of Jews anywhere was more urgent than the question of possible "political self-government in Palestine," and that the former should not depend on the latter.[18]

A more serious matter divided the Zionists in 1905. The British offered the Jews the possibility of making Uganda, East Africa, their national home; and the question was to be decided in the 1905 meeting of the Zionist Congress. Although the majority favored rejecting the British offer, a minority known as the "Territorialists," led by Israel Zangwill (1864–1926),[19] withdrew from the conference on the grounds that the urgency of the Jewish problem required immediate refuge for the Jews.

Zionist leaders fought over many other issues, but none of the disputes prevented the movement from being effective and dynamic. Under Chaim Weizmann, who assumed leadership in the World Zionist movement after 1920, Zionism achieved an extremely impressive record of accomplishments in a very difficult task—one that some people thought was impossible. Weizmann believed in "synthetic Zionism," the theory that colonization was attainable by diplomatic action. His approach was responsible for the increase in Jewish immigration to Palestine in the early years of the British mandate. But it is also true that without the cooperation of the British before 1939, Zionism would have had greater difficulties in furthering its aims. This cooperation began early in 1917 when the British government issued the famous Balfour Declaration.

The Balfour Declaration. In addition to the promises they made to the Arabs in the Husein-McMahon correspondence, and to the French in the Sykes-Picot Agreement, the British in 1917 made another promise to the Zionists. The Balfour Declaration promised the Jews "a national home" in Palestine. In spirit, this conflicted with both the other British commitments: in the Husein-McMahon correspondence Palestine was to be made part of an independent Arab state, and in the Sykes-Picot Agreement it was to be internationalized.

The Balfour Declaration was the culmination of Zionist pressure on the government of Britain—a pressure that began early in 1915, when Chaim Weizmann, a respectable British scientist of Russian origin, first approached the British government on the subject of Palestine. The first effort produced no tangible results, despite the fact that Weizmann had found two members in the cabinet of Prime Minister Asquith who were sympathetic to Zionist ideas: Herbert Samuel and Lloyd George. Asquith, however, found the idea distasteful, as it would add to the already complicated responsibilities of Britain.

Furthermore, there was some opposition to Zionist plans outside the government. Most English Jews were not Zionists. Some, of course, felt the historical ties between Judaism and Palestine, but they differentiated between their religious beliefs and their political aims. Consequently, they were generally reluctant to support the idea of an official British commitment to the Zionists.

However, when Lloyd George became prime minister in December, 1916, the situation changed, and the Zionists made another attempt. They also had the support of the foreign secretary, A. J. Balfour. Consequently, the Zionists were able to secure the following commitment, in the form of a declaration, from the government in November, 1917:

> His Majesty's Government view with favor the establishment in Palestine of a national home for the Jewish people, and will use their best endeavours to facilitate the achievement of this object, it being clearly understood that nothing shall be done which may prejudice the civil and religious rights of existing non-Jewish communities in Palestine, or the rights and political status enjoyed by Jews in any other country.[20]

What prompted the British government to issue the Balfour Declaration? This is an important question, since most British Jews did not sympathize with Zionism.

No simple answer can be provided. Lloyd George was not motivated by humanitarian reasons and this fact was known to Asquith, the former prime minister, who wrote in his *Memories and Reflections,* "Lloyd George . . . does not care a damn for the Jews or their past or their future, but thinks it will be an outrage to let the Holy Places pass into the possession or under the protectorate of agnostic, atheistic France." Others thought Lloyd George was a realist: his pro-Zionist policy was not motivated by emotion or sentiment.[21]

Another argument was that the British wanted Palestine for strategic reasons. Palestine separated Egypt, a British protectorate, from the Persian Gulf where Britain had economic interests. If Palestine were to go under French control, British interests in the Near East and India might be threatened. A commitment to the Zionists would give the British stronger bargaining power vis-à-vis the French. The British could argue they could not give Palestine to the French because they had already promised the Jews a national home in Palestine.

Still another view states that Britain was motivated by her need for the financial support of international Jewry. Finally, Lloyd George himself admitted that the British hoped to use Jewish influence to bring the United States into the war.[22] American participation was necessary to bring the war to an early conclusion.

Whatever the reason for issuing the Declaration was, the document was a masterpiece of tricky diplomacy. Its wording permitted different interpretations, and therefore, flexibility. For instance, the term "a national home" was obviously vague. Did it mean a national state? To the Zionists, it did. Did it mean a place where Jews can live with relative freedom? To the Arabs, that was what it meant: "a national home" was not a national state.

The Arabs argued that the Zionists interpreted the term "a national home" to suit their political aims, and that they deliberately ignored the remainng part of the declaration, which stated that "nothing shall be done which may prejudice the civil and religious rights of the existing non-Jewish communities in Palestine." Later, the Arabs would argue that the establishment of Israel violated the civil and religious rights of the Palestinian Arabs since over a million of them were displaced.

Perhaps the British had intended the document to be vague so as to allow flexibility of policy:

> It [the Balfour Declaration] was susceptible of any interpretation which would best meet the interests of His Majesty's government at the time. If it were in British interests to evacuate Palestine, such action would not violate the strict letter of this "promise" to the Jews. Palestine was to be a "national home," not a national state for the Jews. If British

interests in the Near and Middle East and India dictated a
long tenure in Palestine the declaration would become a
sacred pledge of national honor to remain in that much
troubled country. It is no mere coincidence that in the year
1918, Palestine finally passed into British hands.[23]

Once British control was established, however, the Declaration became less flexible and more troublesome. Arab opposition to Jewish immigration forced the British to issue an
official statement denying that "a national home" meant a national state. According to this statement, "a national home"
was simply "a center in which the Jewish people as a whole
may take, on grounds of religion and race, an interest and
pride." [24]

THE POSTWAR SETTLEMENTS:
CUTTING THE TERRITORIAL PIE

Immediately after World War I, the Allied powers were
confronted with the task of settling the issues arising out of
the war. Specifically, they had to determine who got what
among the territories of the defeated Ottoman Empire. Although Britain and France had secretly agreed to settle some
of these issues while the war was still going on, not all of
their pledges were honored. France was willing to abide by
the Sykes-Picot Agreement but Britain was not. The British
thought conditions had changed, making the agreement obso-
lete. Even Mark Sykes, the British negotiator of the agreement, thought the agreement had become unrealistic. Moreover, the British argued that since Russia was no longer a
party (she withdrew after the Bolshevik Revolution), the
Sykes-Picot Agreement was not binding. In any case, when the
Peace Conference met in Paris in January, 1919, many of the
war issues were not yet settled.

The Arab Position. Having contributed their share to Allied
victory, the Arabs hoped that the big powers would consider

their aspirations for independence and freedom. This hope characterized their attitude in spite of the jolt they had received upon learning of the Sykes-Picot Agreement.

The Arabs were soon to be disappointed. The British, who were in control of Egypt, prevented an Egyptian delegation, headed by Saad Zaghlul, from presenting the Egyptian case to the peace conference. The disappointment was even greater when the conference decided to allow the Zionists, who represented no country or territory, to present their case.

Amir Faisal, a son of Husein, did attend the conference, the only Arab spokesman there. He tried to limit big power and Zionist ambitions in the Arab world; but because he did not speak English or French, he could not communicate effectively with the European statesmen. Europe was a strange place for him. He had never been there before, and he could comprehend neither the European culture nor the shameful diplomacy of the European statesmen. Occasionally, he would seek the help of the United States, the country he trusted most, against the ruthless European politicians. Unfortunately, President Wilson had his own problems and he could do very little to help; his own position was complicated by obstructionists in the Paris conference and in the American Congress. Thus, Faisal was always alone in trying to save the day for the Arabs.

During the conference, Faisal had to deal with the British demands for Iraq and Palestine, the French demands for Syria and Lebanon, and the Zionists' demands for a national home in Palestine. In the end, he was forced to give up his original position, which envisaged Arab independence, in order to save as much as possible of Arab land from colonial control.

Of the three opponents at the bargaining table he preferred the British to the French and the Zionists. Upon the advice of the now-legendary T. E. Lawrence ("Lawrence of Arabia"), Faisal did negotiate an agreement with Chaim Weizmann in which he accepted the Balfour Declaration.[25] However, Faisal "made his consent conditional upon the fulfillment by Great Britain of her pledges respecting Arab independence. The stipulation was inscribed by him on the Text of the Agreement which he signed." [26] At that time, Faisal had no idea the Zionists would later interpret the Balfour Declaration to mean a promise to create a Jewish state in Palestine. Arab sources claim that Weizmann had assured Faisal that the Jewish people had no intention of establishing a state in Palestine, and that they desired economic cooperation with the Arabs.[27]

At the conference, Faisal insisted that the Arab people should be consulted before decisions affecting them were made. This was also the desire of President Wilson, who was on record as supporting the principle of self-determination. Consequently, the American President proposed the establishment of an Allied commission to ascertain the wishes of the Arab people. France refused to participate in the proposed commission and Britain showed very little enthusiasm for it. Later, the British withdrew from the commission, leaving the United States as the only country to participate. The American members were Dr. Henry C. King, president of Oberlin College, and Charles Crane, a businessman. In May, 1919, the two men visited the Middle East to discharge their responsibilities as a fact-finding committee.

The King-Crane Report. King and Crane held hearings in Syria and Palestine for a period of six weeks (May–July, 1919). While in Aleppo, in northern Syria, they had an opportunity to interview a delegation representing Iraq.

In these hearings and interviews, the following points became clear to the American investigators:[28] (1) there was "an almost unanimous desire for independence"; (2) the people of Syria wanted an independent Syria that would include Lebanon and Palestine along with the Syrian hinterland; (3) in case independence was impossible, the Syrians preferred the United States as the mandatory power, or Great Britain as a second choice; (4) there was strong opposition to France

"except for a number of pro-French petitions from Lebanon";
(5) both Christians and Muslims were opposed to Zionism.

The Iraqi delegation wanted independence for Mesopotamia and Syria. It also voiced strong opposition to Jewish immigration and to the establishment of a mandate system in the Arab Middle East. However, it indicated willingness to accept technical and economic assistance from the United States.

Arab preference for the United States indicated that America's image in the Arab Middle East was good. The Arabs thought the United States was basically honest and fair. Later, of course, the image changed drastically.

The King-Crane Commission made the following recommendations: (1) Syria was to become an American mandate (if this was impossible, then Britain should become the mandatory power); (2) Syria should not be divided, and should include Palestine; (3) Iraq should not be divided, and should become a British mandate; (4) Faisal should become Syria's king; (5) the holy places in Palestine should be internationalized; and (6) Zionist aspirations should not go unrestrained, and the Peace Conference should work out a "limited program" for the Zionists.

These recommendations reflected an awareness of the danger that might come from a plan which divided Syria and left Zionist aspirations unchecked. Had the Peace Conference seriously considered the King-Crane recommendations, the later turmoil in the Middle East might have been avoided. Unfortunately, the Peace Conference ignored them completely. (In fact, the recommendations remained secret until 1922.) Nor did the recommendations have any impact upon American policy. President Wilson's health and America's return to isolationism were the main reasons.

Arab Reaction to Big-Power Politics. As the big powers discussed their interests in, and plans for, the Arab Middle East, the Arabs remained deeply concerned about the future of their lands. They were aware of European intrigues, and they were doubtful of their ability to withstand the forces of foreign domination. In 1919, French troops were in the northern coastal area of Syria and British troops were in the south (Palestine). In Iraq, British occupation was already a fact of life. Only the Syrian hinterland was under Arab control.

In April, 1919, Faisal returned from Europe and informed the Syrians that their case was hopeless. He knew that independence could be obtained only by force, and he knew the Syrians did not have the physical strength to challenge the European powers. Consequently, he advocated a middle course: to save as much as possible without resorting to force.

The Syrians were disappointed with Faisal's policy, which they believed was not aggressive enough. Their new spokesman became the Syrian congress. Although this body was not elected directly, it was, nevertheless, fairly representative, a fact recognized by the King-Crane Commission.[29] In June, 1919, the congress resolved: (1) for the full and unqualified independence of Syria and Iraq; (2) to set up a monarchical democratic Syrian regime; and (3) to reject French and Zionist claims in Palestine.

In September, 1919, Faisal revisited Europe for more negotiations with the big powers. He found the British and the French more in agreement than before; and he concluded that the British had decided that an agreement with France was more urgent and useful than an agreement with the Arabs. In desperation, Faisal decided to abide by any solution that received the consent of the United States. He hoped the United States would be able to mitigate European greed and Arab grief. But, as mentioned earlier, the United States was unable to take a greater interest in Arab-European affairs.

In January, 1920, Faisal returned again to Syria and found nationalist feelings running high. About two months later, the Syrian congress declared him king of Syria (including Palestine and Lebanon), although the Syrian nationalists continued to complain that Faisal was not aggressive enough. He was, after all, still considered to be the hero of the 1916 revolt.

Faisal and the nationalists continued to be opposed on the question of how to establish independence. He and his supporters, "the diplomatists," believed in negotiations and the gradual attainment of goals. The "revolutionists" believed negotiations had already failed and the only course left was force. Unfortunately, neither group had enough ammunition for either successful diplomacy or a successful war.

Even before there was any official agreement, the two European powers, especially France, began to show toughness in dealing with the Arab nationalists. After the San Remo Agreement (April, 1920), this policy involved the use of force. In July, 1920, the French addressed an ultimatum to Faisal demanding Arab recognition of a French "right" to control Syria. Faisal accepted the demand but the Syrian congress refused. Rather, the congress repeated its previous declaration embodying Arab aspirations and added its rejection of all treaties to which it had not consented.

Faisal's refusal to heed nationalist demands to declare war on France precipitated a crisis. The two sides clashed, and there were casualties on both sides. At the same time, the French, ignoring Faisal's acceptance of the ultimatum, decided to attack Damascus, Syria's capital. Arab volunteers and regulars met the French force at Maisalun outside Damascus, with Azma, Faisal's minister of war, defying orders and joining the battle. The Arab force was defeated, and Azma lost his life in the fighting. The Syrians commemorate Maisalun and the hero's death of Azma every year.

The French occupied Damascus, and Faisal was ordered to leave the city. The Syrian king left on July 25, 1920, and with his departure the Syrian hinterland passed on to French hands.

The San Remo Agreement. At San Remo in 1920, the European powers (including Britain and France) resolved the question of who got what in the Arab Middle East. France became the mandatory power in northern Syria (the hinterland and Lebanon) and Britain became the mandatory power in southern Syria (Palestine) and in Iraq.

The mandate system had been established by the Covenant of the League of Nations. The Arab territories assigned to France and Britain by the San Remo Agreement received classification A. This meant that they would eventually become independent. In 1922, however, the League's agreement with Great Britain also incorporated the Balfour Declaration into the Palestine Mandate.

Although article 22 of the League's Covenant stipulated that "the wishes of these former Ottoman communities must be a principal consideration in the selection of the Mandatory," [30] the San Remo Agreement selected the mandatories for Syria without any consideration at all of the wishes of the populace.[31] Neither Faisal nor the Syrian congress was invited to the San Remo Conference. On the other hand, the Zionists had many opportunities to talk to the delegates and influence their positions. They were aided by an avalanche of telegrams from Zionist organizations and sympathizers all over the world. In short, while the conference allowed Zionist pressure and influence, it ignored the Arabs.

More Territorial Divisions

It seemed that neither Britain nor France was satisfied with the already mutilated picture of the Arab Fertile Crescent. After dividing the area between themselves, they proceeded to divide their separate domains into smaller units. From an Arab point of view, the rationale behind the new divisions was to make it easier for the two European powers to rule the area. But there were other considerations, as we shall see. In any case, the new divisions were irrational from both the economic and the social point of view.

British Fragmentations. The creation of Transjordan as a separate political division in the Fertile Crescent was initially the product of the Cairo Conference (March, 1921) on Middle

Eastern affairs. The conference was headed by Winston Churchill, then the colonial secretary of Great Britain, and it included a number of British administrators in the Middle East.

This conference recommended that Iraq's throne be offered to Faisal, who had been ousted by the French from Syria. Since the Iraqis had already chosen Abdullah, Faisal's brother, as their monarch, it was necessary to persuade the two men to accept the arrangement worked out by the conference. T. E. Lawrence, who attended the Cairo Conference, would persuade Abdullah to give up his claim to the Iraqi throne in favor of his brother. In return, Abdullah would be promised the territory east of the Jordan River (Transjordan).

The British had practical political reasons for proposing the arrangement. After the French deposed Faisal, Abdullah had begun organizing a military campaign to restore his brother on the Syrian throne. This disturbed the British, who had recognized French control of the Syrian hinterland. Consequently, the creation of Transjordan was intended to help pacify Abdullah by providing kingdoms for both himself and Faisal. The deal was completed in a meeting between Abdullah and Churchill, held in Jerusalem immediately after the Cairo Conference.

Abdullah's territory lacked the necessary ingredients for statehood. Its population was too small, about 300,000. One fifth of the people were semiurban and the rest were either Bedouin or rural. The territorial boundaries were artificial, running through mostly desert land; and the territory itself was largely desert, with only 3 percent of the land being cultivable. Transjordan was not economically self-sufficient and there was little hope that the country could become self-sufficient in the future. Arab nationalists would later argue that the British created the country to ensure Arab dependence and to make more difficult future efforts to unify the Arab countries.

The creation of Transjordan had unpleasant side effects for

the Zionists. The Balfour Declaration had applied to the territories on both sides of the Jordan River; but in September, 1922, the British excluded Transjordan from the application of the Declaration.

British action was consistent with the policy of the League of Nations, which earlier that month had given the British greater latitude in Transjordan and in Palestine.

The British did not divide Iraq as they had divided southern Syria. But even there they had trouble because the Iraqis did not want to be dominated by a foreign power. Immediately after the conclusion of the San Remo Agreement, Iraq revolted in protest against the mandate. Some 65,000 troops were required to break the power of the Iraqi rebels, and it cost the British government approximately $100,000,000.[32]

In an atmosphere of tension, the Iraqi mandate continued until nominal independence in June, 1932. That this independence was more theoretical than real is evidenced by the 1930 Anglo-Iraqi treaty, which went into effect in October, 1932, and which bound Iraq to Britain in a twenty-five-year alliance and obliged Iraq to consult Britain on foreign affairs. Since Britain was a big power and Iraq was small and weak, consultation in foreign affairs meant British domination. The treaty also committed Iraq to assist Britain during war by furnishing facilities such as airports and railways. More important, British troops were to be stationed at Basra and west of the Euphrates. The treaty made obvious the fact that Iraq was no more independent after 1932 than she had been before.

French Fragmentations. In dealing with her Syrian territory, France was still more unscrupulous than Britain. In 1920, she established the state of Lebanon, allegedly to safeguard the interests of the Christian Syrians who were concentrated in the area. The assumption was that a Muslim majority was a threat to Christian interests. Consequently, the two communities were to be politically separate.

The idea of political separation along religious lines was not

a French invention. Islamic law encouraged political autonomy
for Christians and Jews. But the separation put into effect by
the French envisaged independence for Lebanon, and the two
Syrian communities were encouraged to develop separate
identities.

During Ottoman rule, Muslim law was not the only reason
for Christian autonomy: foreign intervention was also a factor.
The European powers showed interest in religious divisions,
and they identified themselves with the various religious
minorities of the Empire, posing as protectors of these minorities. France ostensibly was the guardian of the Maronites
(Catholics), Britain and Russia were the guardians of the
Druzes and the Orthodox Christians respectively. In the nineteenth century the Turkish state was vulnerable to European
influence, and political divisions along religious lines sharp-
ened as a result.

The predecessor of French Lebanon was the autonomous
Ottoman territory known as Mount Lebanon. Mount Lebanon
was created in 1861 because of serious local conflicts as well as
foreign intervention. Its predominant population was Christian. It was not conceived as having the potential of becoming
a sovereign state. In fact, its governors from 1861 to 1915
were not Lebanese.

The Lebanon which the French created was much larger
than Mount Lebanon of the Ottoman Empire and included a
large Muslim minority. In time the Muslim population increased faster than the Christian population, because of a
higher birthrate. Today many scholars believe that the two
Lebanese communities are either equal in number or are un-
balanced in favor of the Muslims. Thus, Lebanon's raison
d'être was lost because of developments that took place after
1920.

However, in order to conceal the changes in the composition of Lebanon's population, the Lebanese state ceased to take
a full census after 1932. The French left the country in 1946
after they had succeeded in giving Lebanon a Christian politi-

cal identity. After independence, the tradition continued, although occasional civil strife still threatened the delicate political balance between Christians and Muslims.[33]

In the Syrian hinterland, France pursued the same policy as in Lebanon. It attempted to divide the country along religious lines. Unlike Lebanon, however, Syria had very little political tradition to support the division attempted by the French.

Four states were created: Aleppo, Damascus, Jabal ("mount") Druze, and Latakia. In the Muslim state of Aleppo there was a large Christian minority. Damascus was largely Sunnite Muslim. In Jabal Druze, the people belonged to an old Islamic sect known by the same name as the area. The Druzes had in common certain customs in addition to religion. They were, and still are, a subculture. In Latakia, the Alawis were the dominant population. Like the Druzes, they were, and still are, a subculture. Religiously, they grew out of the Shi'ite sect of Islam.

Geography enabled the Druzes and the Alawis to exist as autonomous groups: mountains separate them from the rest of Syria. However, the two groups did not desire a different political identity from the other Syrian areas. The Druzes, for instance, led the 1925 Syrian revolution against the French. And they participated in the Arab national movement of the 1920's and after. With the exception of a small Armenian minority, the Christian Syrians were thoroughly Arabized. In subsequent years, they would participate in important national events. One of them, Faris al-Khouri, reached the second highest political position in Syria, that of prime minister. Another, Michel Aflaq, founded the Baath party, which for a time was the voice of Arab nationalism.

Thus, none of the Syrian religious groups wanted a state for itself. They opposed centralized authority but they were content to remain within an Arab political entity.[34] The creation of the four states was, therefore, a French exaggeration of Syrian religious differences. It might be argued that France

was actually pursuing a policy of "divide and rule" in order
to govern Syria more easily.

In any case, the French separatist policy in Syria failed. In
1925, France had to merge the states of Aleppo and Damascus
to form the state of Syria. Later, she brought Jabal Druze and
Latakia, the two remaining states, into the Syrian union. However, an adequate degree of integration was never achieved
by the French authorities, who continued to treat the religious
groups as if they were politically separate.

In addition to dividing Syria, the French caused the loss
of the sanjak ("province") of Alexandretta, the country's
northwestern territory. In 1920, Alexandretta was part of the
Syrian mandate, of course under French control. At the time,
Turkey did not recognize the province as part of Syria and
protested its status. The population of the territory included
Arabs, Turks, Kurds, and Armenians.[35]

In 1936 the dispute between Turkey and France (as the
mandatory power in Syria) over Alexandretta was brought to
the League of Nations. And in 1937 the League's council resolved that the province be given a special status. Internally
it was to have autonomy, but externally and economically it
was to be joined with Syria. The League's recommendations
angered the Syrians, who believed that France was abandon-
ing Syrian territory in order to appease Turkey. The special
status of Alexandretta was rejected by the Syrian parliament.

France was anxious to win the friendship of Turkey to
balance the German threat,[36] believing that Turkey was more
useful in the Mediterranean than were the Syrians, whom
France controlled anyway. Consequently, France was willing
to make concessions to the Turks. Thus in 1938 France agreed
to share the responsibility for Alexandretta's security with
Turkey, and Turkish troops were allowed to enter the territory.
About the same time, the two countries signed a treaty of
friendship.

In 1938 an election took place in Alexandretta. Turkish
troops were in the area along with French troops to maintain

order, but their activities were suspicious. With 39 percent of the population, the Turks were allotted 63 percent of the electors.[37] Consequently, 22 out of the 40 seats in the legislature went to Turks. In 1939 Turkey and France concluded an agreement of mutual assistance, and soon afterward French troops withdrew from the province. On the same day, the two countries signed another agreement in which France ceded Alexandretta to Turkey.[38] Historian Stephen Longrigg describes the tragic event as "a crude example of power politics," and "a regrettable yielding by France of another's rights." [39]

Conclusion

The people of Syria (the hinterland, Lebanon, and Transjordan) desired independence during and after World War I. This fact was supported by the resolutions of the General Syrian Congress and the report of the King-Crane Commission (which also attested to the representative character of the congress).

Arab hopes for independence were raised by President Wilson's declaration on the right of self-determination, which the Arabs justly considered to apply to them, and by an Anglo-French declaration of November 7, 1918, which promised the establishment of national governments and administrations deriving their authority from the initiative and free choice of the indigenous populations (of the Ottoman Empire).[40]

In the Husein-McMahon correspondence, Great Britain promised the Arabs independence. The extent of the promise in terms of territory is controversial. Some writers play down the promise and its implications; some deny altogether that it was a legally binding promise; and still others affirm it in legal and moral terms. Whatever the British promise meant, the Arabs were deliberately led to believe that it was legally and morally binding. The British effort to arouse the Arabs against the Turks quickened the Arab hope for independence.

Without such hope, the Arabs would have had no reason to fight their coreligionists.

The division of Arab territory into numerous small units was obviously not in the best interests of the Arabs. Certainly it was not consistent with any positive economic and social considerations. In addition, it was to complicate the future political picture of the Arab Middle East, and it was directly responsible for many of the area's later problems.

Finally, the European powers decided the future of the Arab Middle East without consulting the Arabs. This was inconsistent with the big powers' own declarations as well as the Covenant of the League of Nations. The inconsistency gave the Arab nationalists an anti-Western argument. Arab bitterness increased as Arab nationalism grew more intense.

But Arab experiences after World War I were not the only factors that caused Arab frustration with the Western world. More recent experiences were also relevant. In the following chapter, we will discuss these new experiences and show how Arab-Western relations deteriorated to the point where they are today.

Chapter 5

The Palestine Problem

In the twentieth century, Arab-Western relations were damaged primarily by two important experiences. The first was the failure, after World War I, of the European powers to grant the Arabs independence, and their partition of Arab territory—which was considered in Chapter 4. The second experience was Western support of Zionism, first by facilitating the mass immigration of Jews to Palestine and later by assisting in the establishment of the State of Israel. This second experience not only has numerous implications for the Arabs in the Middle East and North Africa, it has profound implications for world peace.

The Events

Jewish Immigration to Palestine. From the seventh century until the establishment of the State of Israel in 1948 the majority of the population of Palestine was Arab. There had always been Jews in Palestine, but after the destruction of the Temple at Jerusalem in A.D. 70 their numbers dwindled until they were well below 10 percent of the population. Jews and Arabs lived together in Palestine for centuries in relative peace, until the European Jews organized the Zionist movement to promote their Palestinian "return."

Zionist sources estimate that there were 12,000 Jews in

129

Palestine in 1839 and 35,000 in 1880.[1] By 1900 the number was 50,000, but this was less than one half of one percent of the world's Jewish population, estimated at 11,000,000. The Zionist policy of mass immigration was a long way from realization, largely because most Jewish emigrants preferred to go to countries other than Palestine. Between 1840 and 1900 only 3.6 percent went to Palestine, while about 88.8 percent preferred to go to the United States. Only in the 1930's, particularly during the depression, did the rate of Jewish immigration into Palestine exceed the rate into the United States.

The reason for Jewish lack of interest in Palestine was mainly economic. Palestine was underdeveloped, and it offered very little opportunity for advancement. Furthermore, in the early years of Jewish immigration, the Turkish (Ottoman) state usually opposed the admission of alien elements such as the Jews to the predominantly Islamic community of Palestine.

In 1919, at the time that the big powers were still discussing the fate of the Arab territories of the Ottoman Empire, and while the Zionists were still trying to obtain international guarantees for the Balfour Declaration, the Jewish population of Palestine did not exceed 58,000. In that same year, the Arab population (Muslim and Christian) was 642,000.[2] In other words, less than 10 percent of the population of Palestine was Jewish.

In the 1920's, Zionist efforts to induce Jewish immigration to Palestine continued to be only moderately productive.[3] Except for the years 1924–1926, immigrants numbered less than 10,000 a year. However, after 1933 the number of Jewish immigrants increased sharply. For instance, in 1935 alone, 66,500 Jews entered Palestine. Some of the reasons for the increase were the rise of Hitler in Germany and the economic depression in the United States.

In 1931 the Jewish population of Palestine was 172,000. By 1939 it had grown to 445,000, with the Arabs numbering 1,044,000. The increase in the Jewish population was mainly the result of immigration; the increase in the Arab population resulted largely from natural growth (i.e., the excess of births over deaths).

Arab reaction to this sharp increase in Jewish immigration, especially after the high point reached in 1935, was one of fear and resentment. The Arabs feared that the Jews would ultimately become a majority; and, more important, they resented the admission in mass, without their consent, of an alien element. In 1936 the Palestinian Arabs revolted, and their struggle continued until 1939. The revolt and the advent of World War II forced the British to reevaluate their Middle Eastern policy. The British concluded that if the Arabs were unfriendly, their security in the Middle East would be jeopardized during the war. Consequently, they decided to conciliate the Arabs.

Thus in 1939 the British government issued a White Paper embodying a new policy,[4] under which Palestine was to become independent within ten years. Meanwhile, no more than seventy-five thousand Jews would be allowed into Palestine during the next five years; and after that, Jewish immigration would be conditional upon Arab consent.

Today the Zionists make light of the significance of the 1939 White Paper, which was obviously damaging to their case. In their propaganda they stress the importance of the Balfour Declaration and the Mandate Agreement. Some Arabs, on the other hand, emphasize the importance of the White Paper and argue that it supersedes the Balfour Declaration since it is the more recent expression of British policy.

In spite of the White Paper, massive Jewish immigration continued during World War II, prompted by Hitler's brutal Jewish policy. Although the immigration violated the policy set down by the White Paper, the British were confronted with a serious moral issue. Nevertheless, the Arabs complained that Britain, and indeed the entire Western world, was being generous at Arab expense.[5] They asserted that the Western nations did not want to take the Jews into their countries.[6]

Still, although by 1946 there were 608,200 Jews in Palestine, there were also 1,221,900 Arabs (Christian and Muslim); this was a ratio of two to one in the year preceding the partition of Palestine by the United Nations. Arabs argue that Jews did not have the right to determine the future of Palestine because they were numerically a minority and because their land ownership was limited to a very small proportion of the country.[7]

Palestine Under the British Mandate

The British controlled Palestine for approximately thirty years under a League of Nations mandate, and their rule ended with a disaster. In this time, Zionism and Arab nationalism became strong opposing forces, and the British failed to force the establishment of common public institutions for Arabs and Jews that could mitigate the differences and instill in them the habit of cooperation. In part, then, the present conflict between the Arabs and Israel results from the failure of the British mandate in Palestine.

The Nature of British Rule. Although the League of Nations intended to give Palestine a special status, one that would emphasize self-government and ultimate independence,[8] the British governed the territory according to the usual patterns of colonial rule. At the head of the Palestine administration, the British high commissioner had almost unlimited executive and legislative powers. An all-British council of senior civil servants assisted him. Only a few Arabs and Jews were able to secure high positions in the government, and they were always supervised by British senior officers. The judiciary did enjoy a degree of independence and was the most reputable branch of the government; there were a number of Arab and Jewish judges. Still, it was headed by a British chief justice.[9] Within the governmental services the Muslim Arabs were underrepresented, while the Christian Arabs and the Jews were overrepresented. It is true that the Muslim Arabs had a lower literacy rate than the other religious groups,[10] but this was not the only reason for the low Muslim representation. Another important one was the British policy of "divide and rule."

As mentioned earlier, the British failed to give emphasis to the principles of self-government and cooperation; they were handicapped by their conflicting policies toward Arabs and Jews. Had they not begun their mandate by confusing the Arabs and the Jews about their aims, cooperation between the two groups would have been possible. Admittedly, the task would have been difficult. The Arabs wanted greater control (self-government) than the British were willing to concede, and the Zionists consistently refused to enter into joint endeavors with the Arabs. From the beginning, the Zionists charted a separate political future.[11]

In spite of the confusion they created over their aims, the British did make some attempts to establish common institutions for the two Palestinian groups. Twice, in the 1920's and in the 1930's, they proposed plans to set up a quasi-legislative body to represent Christians, Jews, and Muslims; but their proposals were rejected by all parties concerned. The Arabs objected to the plans because the British high commissioner was given absolute veto power over the decisions of the proposed advisory council. The Zionist leadership opposed them because they did not wish "to enter a council dominated by an Arab majority." [12]

Jewish Political Development in Palestine. During the British mandate, the Jewish community was "a state within a state," [13] a status that was partly an extension of the Balfour Declaration policy and was given formal support by the Mandate Agreement between Great Britain and the League of Nations. For nearly a quarter of a century Jewish quasi-governmental institutions coexisted with the British administration, giving

Jews in Palestine training in self-government, and at the same
time diluting any incentive the Jews might have had for cooperation with the Arabs. The training in self-government
proved to be very useful after the establishment of Israel.
When they became a sovereign community the Jews had
very little difficulty in running their government.[14]

Under the mandate the Jews had two main public institutions, the Jewish Agency and the Community Government.
The first of these was recognized by the British government
from the beginning and took charge of Jewish relations with
the mandate government. Article 4 of the Mandate Agreement
authorized the Agency to "take part in the development of the
country" and to assist the mandate government "in such economic, social, and other matters as may affect the establishment of the Jewish national home." [15]

The Jewish Agency's aims, as formulated by itself, were to
work for the establishment of a Jewish state in Palestine
through mass Jewish immigration and the creation of "a Jewish majority in Palestine, and development projects." [16]

The executive department of the Agency resembled the organization of a sovereign state and performed similar functions. Consequently, the department was easily transformed
to a government when Israel came into being in 1948. Its
chairman, David Ben-Gurion, became the first prime minister
of Israel, and Chaim Weizmann, the president of the Agency,
became Israel's first president. During the British mandate, the
Agency was a sponsor of the Haganah, supposedly a secret
"defense force" for the protection of Jews from Arab attacks.
The Haganah later became part of Israel's regular army.

The second institution, the Community Government, controlled the internal affairs of the Jewish community. Until
1927 the organization was not recognized by the British; afterward, however, the Community Government was not only
recognized, it was granted the power to tax Jews in Palestine.
Thus, the Community Government acquired responsibilities
and powers not required by the League of Nations. In a

sense, they were privileges which the Arab population of Palestine could not have with British consent. Arabs complained that this situation was most unfair and that British policy was clearly biased in favor of the Jews.

The British mandate had the effect of widening the gap between Jews and Arabs. Opportunities to bring up new generations of Arabs and Jews with common ideals were lost. The result, as we now know, was disastrous.

THE EMERGENCE OF ISRAEL

During World War II the Zionists pressed for the repeal of the White Paper policy. The British were reluctant to acquiesce to Zionist demand, but the war prevented a confrontation between the two groups. However, immediately after the war, Jews in Palestine took up arms and battled the British. A Labor government in London decided to refer the question of Palestine to the United Nations.[17] Britain had come to the conclusion that she alone could not solve the problem, and that since she was governing Palestine on behalf of the League of Nations, whose successor was the United Nations, the latter international body had the responsibility to find a solution to the Palestine problem. Later the Arabs would charge that Britain began her involvement in Palestine with confusion and ended it with more confusion. For them, the British were simply washing their hands of the whole affair.

The Partition Plan. On April 28, 1947, the General Assembly of the United Nations met in a special session to discuss the question of what to do with Palestine. The delegates from different Arab governments attempted to get the Assembly to recognize Palestine as an independent and sovereign state, but members would not agree to put their proposal on the agenda. Furthermore, in spite of opposition from the Arab governments, the Zionists were allowed to present their case before the Assembly's political committee. On May 15 the Assembly resolved to establish a special eleven-member committee to make recommendations on the Palestine question.[18]

The resulting UN Special Committee on Palestine (UNSCOP) visited Palestine, some Arab countries, and Jewish refugee camps in Europe. Zionist representatives cooperated with the committee, but the representatives of the Palestinian Arabs did not. The latter group declared that the committee had more pro-Zionist than pro-Arab members.[19] In September, UNSCOP reported to the General Assembly.[20] The committee's report included two plans. The majority plan favored the partition of Palestine into two states, one Jewish and one Arab. The Arab state was to have the smaller and less prosperous area of Palestine (about 43 percent). It would have had an Arab population of about 725,000 and a Jewish population of about 10,000. The Jewish state was to have 56 percent of Palestine's territory, the more prosperous area, and a population almost equally divided between Arabs and Jews (497,000 Arabs and 498,000 Jews).

No transfer of population was envisaged by the plan. The two states were to be joined in an economic union which would take charge of matters like conservation, irrigation, currency, customs, and interstate communication. Jerusalem, which amounts to one percent of the total area of Palestine, was to have an international status under the UN Trusteeship Council.

Seven of the eleven members of UNSCOP voted for the partition plan. Australia abstained because she wanted the committee to propose alternative plans without supporting any one of them. Possibly also she was influenced by Britain's neutral stand on the Palestinian issues. India, Iran, and Yugoslavia submitted their own plan (usually referred to as the minority report). They proposed the establishment in Palestine of a federal state to join an Arab province and a Jewish province. Jerusalem was to become the capital of the federal state.

The Zionists showed interest only in the partition plan, although they would have liked more territory than was allotted under the majority plan. Even before the General Assembly approved the majority report, the Zionists had announced their determination to oppose any plan that did not establish a sovereign Jewish state.[21]

The Arabs, on the other hand, opposed partition. They attacked it on several grounds. First, they considered the territorial distribution unfair. The plan gave the Jewish state jurisdiction over 56 percent of Palestine, in spite of the fact that Jews were only one third of the population, that many of them were not native Palestinians, and that they actually owned less than 7 percent of the land. It gave the Arab state jurisdiction over less than 45 percent of the land even though the Arabs constituted a two-thirds majority of the population of Palestine.

Second, Arabs were doubtful about the economic union which the plan envisaged, since it required cooperation between Jews and Arabs. The Arabs contended that during the British mandate the Zionists would not cooperate with the Arabs. After all, if the Jews were willing to cooperate in economic matters, why was partition necessary? Why not have a single state for Jews and Arabs, a state in which economic cooperation would be more complete and would be strengthened by political and social integration?

Third, the Arabs denied the legal or the moral right of the UN to partition Palestine. They asked if the United States, or any other country, would permit the international organization to divide its territory and establish a sovereign state within its borders. Why, then, should the Palestinian Arabs, the majority in Palestine, submit to such a UN plan? Partition, the Arabs argued, would violate their right to self-determination, a principle recognized by the United States and many other countries.

The Adoption of the Partition Plan. The majority and minority plans were discussed by the General Assembly for two months. From the outset the first plan had a better chance of adoption simply because the majority of UNSCOP was behind it.

Both Arabs and Jews tried to influence the member states. The Arabs had the advantage of being represented by the delegations of six Arab countries. The Zionists, however, were allowed to present their case although they did not represent any recognized state and could not have membership in the UN. Moreover, the disadvantage of nonmembership was more than offset by the support they received from the two superpowers, the United States and the Soviet Union.

The Zionists were more successful in influencing members than were the Arabs. Unlike the Arabs, they had no problem communicating with the Western countries which, at the time, had a great deal of influence in the UN. Many Zionists were Europeans and Americans; therefore, there was no cultural gap to prevent effective communication. Furthermore, there were Jewish populations in many of the member states. As indicated by various sources, American Jews were extremely helpful in lining up the support of the United States. Their pressure upon the U.S. Government was too strong to be ignored.[22]

There were officials in the U.S. Government who tried unsuccessfully to resist Zionist pressure and who tried to persuade Mr. Truman not to submit to such influence. Among them was Secretary of the Navy James Forrestal, who believed that the Palestinian question should be kept out of partisan politics. He feared that pro-Zionism would hurt American interests in the Middle East.[23] In addition, both the State Department and the Joint Chiefs of Staff warned the President of the danger to American interests of a pro-Zionist American policy. Nevertheless, Zionist propaganda in the United States had long been active and a sympathetic American public had been assured.

Once a pro-Zionist policy had been established in the United States, American pressure on some Latin American countries was a major factor in securing the necessary vote for the partition plan.[24]

The Arabs, having a non-Western culture, found this cultural difference their main obstacle in communicating with the powerful Western countries. Some of their attitudes, their emotional behavior, and even their style of life, limited their effectiveness in communication. Furthermore, in 1947 the Arabs had very little experience in international affairs, which in Arab countries had for a long time been dominated by foreign powers.

While Zionist strategy assumed that right depended on might, the Arabs seemed to believe that right was might. Zionist talent for artful manipulation characterized Zionist policy.[25] In an attempt to save the situation, the Arabs, on November 11, 1947, suggested to the Security Council that the International Court of Justice be consulted on the legal issues involved in the Palestine problem. Specifically, they wanted to know the extent of the UN's competence in partitioning Palestine.[26] However, the draft resolution lost by one vote.

The adoption of a plan required a two-thirds majority of those voting in the General Assembly. On November 29, 1947, the partition idea won by such a majority. The famous "Resolution 181 (II)" passed by 33 affirmative votes.[27] Thirteen states voted against the resolution and ten abstained.[28]

According to the resolution, the Palestine Mandate was to be terminated and British troops were to leave Palestine by August 1, 1948. With minor modifications, the UNSCOP majority plan was adopted. What remained was implementation, either through the cooperation of the Arabs and the Jews or, if this was not possible, through Security Council action.

Reaction to the Partition Resolution. Four factors made possible the adoption of the partition plan: American influence, especially on the Latin American members; Soviet support, which eliminated big-power contention during the Assembly's discussion; Zionist artfulness and political manipulation; and the fact that in the 1940's the UN was Western-dominated. Had the question of Palestine been brought to the Assembly ten years later, or certainly twenty years later, the State of Israel would not have been "established" by a UN resolution.

This, of course, does not mean that Israel would not have come into existence. While Zionist political influence made possible the adoption of the partition resolution, it was mainly Zionist military prowess which made possible the creation of the Israeli state.

In fact, early developments outside Palestine after the adoption of the resolution indicated that the Zionist victory in the UN was being challenged. Britain declared she would not help implement the resolution. She made known her determination to evacuate Palestine by May 15, 1948, ten weeks before the scheduled date.

The Arabs declared they would oppose, by force if necessary, any effort to implement the partition resolution. They reminded other states that under the Charter of the UN, the Assembly had the power only to make recommendations and not to make binding decisions. Most authorities on the subject of international law seem to agree with the Arab argument.[29] In addition, President Truman distinguished between the principle of partition and its enforcement. He said that the General Assembly had accepted the principle but did not provide for its enforcement.[30]

Ironically, in 1960 the representative of Israel in the UN advanced an argument similar to the one that the Arabs had held thirteen years earlier.[31] (By 1960 the UN was showing some opposition to Israeli policy.) If anything, the Arabs seem to have had a better case, since they presented their argument before the so-called Uniting for Peace Resolution of 1950, which enlarged the General Assembly's powers and political role.[32]

Immediately after the General Assembly passed the partition resolution, Arabs and Jews confronted each other in the battlefield. This serious situation forced the United States to have second thoughts. (President Truman had naïvely assumed that the two Palestinian groups would peacefully cooperate in enforcing the UN resolution.) State Department officials were seriously worried about American interests in the Arab world and the possible intrusion of Russia into that part of the world.[33] In January, 1948, they decided that the Assembly's resolution was unworkable. In March they called the resolution "a mere recommendation," thus agreeing with the Arabs on the legal nature of the Assembly's resolutions. Finally, the United States came out in favor of a temporary trusteeship for Palestine.[34]

Some of the countries that voted for the partition also had second thoughts. Among them were France, Belgium, and Panama. Only the Soviet Union and the Ukraine continued to support partition without hesitation. In fact, the Soviets were one important reason why the trusteeship idea suggested by the United States did not have a chance of adoption.

The Security Council, which had the responsibility to implement the Assembly's resolution, failed to do so.[35] However, it did resolve to call the Assembly for a special session "to consider further the question of the future government of Palestine." On May 14, 1948, the Assembly resolved to appoint a mediator "to promote a peaceful adjustment of the future situation of Palestine" and to relieve the Palestine Commission, established under the partition Resolution 181 (II), of its responsibilities.[36]

The Zionist leadership's reaction to partition was one of pleasure. They indicated that, although the partition resolution would require a great deal of sacrifice on their part, they would accept it and unwaveringly "implement" it. They also declared that the United Nations had the competence and authority to partition Palestine. For the Zionists, therefore, there was no question about the legality of the Assembly's resolution. In addition, they argued that the UN did something morally right, since it "reestablished" Jewish "rights" in the Holy Land.

The Zionists argued that "the Arab states had no claim to an inch of the territory of Mandatory Palestine." They viewed

the interest of the Arab governments in the Palestine question to be tantamount to intrusion.[37] They also denounced
Britain for not cooperating in implementing the Assembly's
resolution.

Nevertheless, the Zionists did not hesitate to criticize the
content of the partition resolution. They argued that the UN
had drawn artificial boundaries and had envisaged an economic union which was not in the best interest of future
Jewish immigration.[38] In essence, the Zionists would have
liked to obtain more territory for the Jewish state.

The partition resolution had one important effect upon the
Zionist movement: it reduced Jewish opposition to Zionism.
Prior to the resolution there were Jews who for various reasons opposed the establishment of a Jewish state. The strongest
opposition came from those who feared that Jewish identification with Israel might raise questions about the loyalties of
Jews to the countries of their citizenship. Many Jews saw
themselves simply as Americans, Frenchmen, or Englishmen
who happened to belong to the Jewish faith. After the adoption of the partition resolution, a number of anti-Zionist Jews
more or less accepted the Jewish state as a foreign state established by the world community.

While the Security Council procrastinated in implementing
the Assembly's partition recommendation, and while some
states were having second thoughts about its workability and
wisdom, the Zionists showed determination "to carry it out."
On March 23, 1948, the National Council of the Jewish Agency
declared that the Jews would oppose by force any alternative
to partition, including the trusteeship proposal sponsored by
the United States. In April, as Arabs and Jews battled over
Palestinian territory in the early stages of the 1948 war, prepa-
rations for creating the organs of the Jewish state went on,
and it seemed that no force, whether from within or without,
could prevent the coming of Israel into being.

The State of Israel. The British Mandate was coming to an
end and the British had announced their intention to with-

draw by May 15, 1948. On May 14, the State of Israel was proclaimed by Zionist leaders. David Ben-Gurion was elected prime minister of the provisional government and Chaim Weizmann was elected the first president of the new state. Since the state was born under unclear legal circumstances, it became necessary for it to seek recognition of its sovereign status from other countries. First to recognize Israel was the United States of America, only eleven minutes after Israel's "declaration of independence." [39] Four days later the Soviet Union followed suit;[40] and by February 1, 1949, thirty-three countries had recognized the Jewish state, Britain among them.

The next step in Israel's efforts to obtain international recognition was to gain admission to the United Nations. On November 29, 1948, she applied for membership but failed to receive the necessary votes in the Security Council. The existence of war conditions in Palestine was the reason for the rejection of Israel's application. However, immediately after Israel and Egypt signed the Armistice Agreement on February 24, 1949, Israel renewed her application, and this time the Security Council voted to recommend admission. On May 11, the General Assembly passed a resolution to accept the Council's recommendation, and Israel became officially a member of the United Nations.[41]

The admission resolution assumed and anticipated that Israel "would unreservedly accept the obligations of the United Nations and undertake to honour them from the day when it becomes a member of the United Nations." It reminded Israel of the partition resolution of November 24, 1947, and of the resolution of December 11, 1948, which stated that "the refugees wishing to return to their homes and live at peace with their neighbors should be permitted to do so at the earliest practicable date." [42]

Arguments, Issues, and Attitudes

Very few problems are as complicated as the Palestine problem. The issues involved are moral, legal, cultural, historical, and religious. They are so complicated that it is not easy to explain them, let alone resolve them. Nevertheless, some issues need clarification, since they have become material for propaganda.

Ancestral Rights. The Zionist movement made several questionable assumptions about Jewish history and Jewish culture which contributed to their effectiveness in uniting Jews. One of these was that contemporary Jews were the heirs of the ancient Jews. And from this assumption Zionists drew several conclusions: that the present State of Israel is successor to the ancient Hebrew and Judean kingdoms; that Jews who emigrate to Palestine are "returning Jews"; that Palestine belonged to the Jewish people as a matter of historical right whether they lived there or not.

Arabs see many weaknesses in this argument. First, this argument ignores the fact that two thousand years have passed since Palestine was Jewish and the fact that Palestine had had an Arab population for thirteen hundred years before the establishment of Israel. In 1948, the Arabs of Palestine could claim the country on the basis of their own ancestral rights as well as on the basis of their birth rights, the latter being the more important.

Secondly, the argument ignores the fact that many changes have affected the Jews since their dispersion. To assume that the Moroccan Jew, the French Jew, and the Chinese Jew have a common culture and identity is a great exaggeration, if not completely false. Although Jews do retain common religious customs and share some cultural similarities, the claim of the Zionists that Jews everywhere constitute one national identity is more myth than reality. The changes that have affected the Jewish culture are best illustrated in Israel's own social existence, where Jewish social scientists recognize significant cultural differences among Israeli Jews. Nadav Safran wonders if in fact there is not more than one Israeli nation. He asserts that "cultural differences are consciously felt and expressed" by Israelis.[43] The conflict between the Ashkenazi (European)

Jew and the "Oriental" Jew is very real. After the election of November, 1969, Prime Minister Golda Meir organized a new cabinet which had only one Oriental Jew out of a total membership of twenty-four. This irritated Yeshe' Yahu, the former minister of postal service and a Yemenite Jew, who declared that "after forty years it became clear to me that the Ashkenazim have not let down the barriers." [44] The ultimate Israeli nation will be very different from the Diaspora Jews and there will be strong cultural differences between the Israeli Jews and the non-Israeli Jews.

Thirdly, conversions to Judaism, abandonments of the Jewish religion, and intermarriages raise serious difficulties for the theory of ancestral rights. Thus many Arabs jokingly ask if Sammy Davis, Jr., the famous American Negro singer who converted to Judaism, has the right to "return to Palestine." Some Arabs humorously remark that they "look more Jewish" than Abba Eban and Yigal Allon.

The argument of ancestral rights makes the Palestinian Arab a bitter man. He cannot understand why he cannot return to his home in Palestine, which he still remembers, while Jews from other countries can immigrate to an Israel they have never seen and become citizens.[45] He argues that the "myth" of ancestral rights cannot be more important than Arab birth rights and the Arab right to self-determination, a right denied to the Arabs when they were the majority in Palestine.

The Religious Argument. To all Jews, Palestine is the promised land. This concept is essentially a religious one. It was transformed by the Zionists and their supporters into a secular doctrine and a program of political action. It is doubtful if the Zionists would have been interested in Palestine had it not been for this religious notion and the fact that Palestine was at one time Jewish.

The idea of the promised land has meant different things to different Jews. Some believed that Palestine would become Jewish by an act of God and not by man's deliberate design. These Jews were ridiculed by the Zionists, who could not understand how God could fulfill his promise without man's cooperation. The Zionists, therefore, considered their efforts to be part of God's design, even though many of them denied the connection between religion and the political realities of Zionism or Israel (a contradictory denial, since the Jewish religion has been the basis of Jewish identity). Whatever the contradictions, however, the religious idea has acquired a secular meaning; and the religious idea is the psychological force behind Zionist dedication, motivation, and determination. Without it, the Zionists could hardly have thought of Palestine as the site for the Jewish state.[46]

The Arabs take issue with the political meaning that has been attached to Jewish religious beliefs. Although they do not deny the Jews the right to believe whatever they wish, including the notion of the promised land, they object to the transformation of these beliefs into a political program that conflicts with their own "legal and political rights." Religious beliefs, the Arabs argue, confer upon the Jews the right only to worship freely, not the right to establish a state.

Furthermore, the Arabs argue, Palestine has a religious meaning for them too. There are in Palestine many Muslim holy places that are as significant to the Arabs as the Jewish holy places are significant to the Jews. In addition, the Muslim Arabs revere both Christian and Jewish holy places because Islam recognizes the two religions. In other words, Jewish and Christian holy places have a religious meaning for the Muslims.

The Arabs cannot understand why the Christian Western world supports the Jews instead of the Christian Arabs. However, the more sophisticated Arabs know that religion has very little to do with Western support of Zionism; what is probably more relevant is that the Arabs are Eastern while the Zionists and the Israelis are Western.[47]

The *Fait Accompli* Argument. This Israeli argument states that regardless of the legal or even moral arguments, Israel exists, and this is a fact that no one can deny. Even the Arabs, who do not recognize Israel, cannot ignore it. In fact, they know more than anyone else that Israel exists, for it has become an important part of their daily concern.

Zionists often ask why the Arabs refuse to recognize the State of Israel. They inevitably come to the conclusion that the Arabs are "unrealistic," "stubborn," "misguided," and "extremists." The Arab hope to destroy the Israeli state is a "fantastic" dream. This hope cannot be fulfilled and all the Arabs can do is bring disaster upon themselves.

This *fait accompli* argument is Israel's strongest propaganda weapon against the Arabs. It has succeeded in influencing public opinion in many countries. It neutralized the opposition of those who agreed with Arab legal and moral arguments. In fact, it caused many pro-Arabs to attempt to limit Arab demands in favor of Israel's "right" to exist as a state. Today, very few people other than the Arabs want to see Israel disappear as a state, although many might not like what Israel is doing and might desire concession to the Arabs.

The *fait accompli* argument is not entirely a propaganda weapon. Israelis give it legal implications. They argue that many countries have recognized Israeli statehood, and that this recognition has become the legal foundation of the state. Certainly many scholars agree with the Israeli argument, but there are many others who do not. Most scholars, however, consider recognition more a question of politics than a question of law.[48] "English and American courts generally designate questions of recognition as 'political questions.'"[49] Hans Kelsen, the well-known authority on international law, states that "before recognition, the unrecognized community does not legally exist *vis-à-vis* the recognizing state."[50] On the basis of Kelsen's view of recognition, the Arabs seem justified in arguing that, in as far as they are concerned, the State of Israel does not "legally exist."

The Arab answer to the Israeli *fait accompli* argument runs as follows: The Israelis forgot that before 1948 there was in

Palestine a different *fait accompli;* the population of Palestine was then mostly Arab; and, at least until World War II, there was very little hope that the Zionists might succeed in creating the Jewish state. This *fait accompli* was not important to the Zionists and it did not deter them from pursuing their goal; it is strange that the Zionists should accuse the Arabs of being dreamers when they were the ones who dreamt for centuries of a "return" to Palestine and dreamt for more than fifty years of establishing the Israeli state. If Jews can dream for so long, why can't the Arabs dream for a few years; after all, the Palestinian Arabs still remember their homes in Palestine, and 1,500,000 of them are displaced persons.

History, argues the Arab, is a series of *faits accomplis.* If it were not, life would have stood still, and there would have been no history, or very little of it. One *fait accompli* replaces another, which is a way of saying that a *fait accompli* exists only between one historical change and another. The Zionists upset the pre-1948 *fait accompli.* It is now the Arabs' turn to upset the *fait accompli* that came after. If the Arab task seems impossible at this time in history, it is because the Arab world is in a state of transition. In the future, the situation will change, the task will be easier to accomplish, and the world will no longer see the Arab as "unrealistic."

In reality, the *fait accompli* argument is the argument of the winner in a competition. In other words, it is the argument of the strong. The argument also contributes to the comfort of third parties who supported the winner or who benefit from the new situation. Also, third parties who are afraid to be drawn into a second competition usually accept the outcome of the first, or a peaceful settlement of the issues separating the main parties. This may explain why there is a great deal of agreement among the nations of the world on the right of Israel to exist as a state.

The Arabs do not recognize the legal status of the Israeli *fait accompli* argument. A wrong, they argue, can never be right. If other nations are willing to ignore the wrong, it is because the wrong did not affect them. However, since the wrong had direct and detrimental effects upon the Arabs, it is not possible for the Arabs to accept it or submit to its outcome.

The Persecution Issue. Fundamental to the Zionist argument is the idea that the creation of a Jewish state is the only solution to the problem of persecution of Jews. This was the main assumption upon which Theodor Herzl, the founder of the Zionist movement, based his arguments in his famous book, *The Jewish State.*

No doubt there is a causal relationship between Jewish persecution and the establishment of the State of Israel in 1948. Had it not been for Hitler's massacre of Jews during World War II, there would probably be no State of Israel today; there would have been no broad international support to create the state. Persecution was a factor in two respects. First, it created guilt feelings among the people of the Western world and developed a Western desire and willingness to do something for the Jews.[51] Secondly, it caused Jews initially apathetic to the idea of a Jewish state to support the idea, and it caused Jews opposed to it to reduce sharply their opposition. The Zionists benefited from both these developments, and they exploited them effectively.

Nor has the creation of Israel solved the persecution problem. Most Jews still live in the Diaspora and discrimination against many of them continues. However, Israel does provide the uncomfortable Western Jew with the alternative of a second country. Should his life become oppressed, he can go to Israel and automatically become a citizen. Persecution has caused many Jews to distrust the Gentile world. Even Jews who live in liberal countries such as the United States do not exclude the possibility of future mistreatment. The Zionists exploit this distrust and fear. Fear of anti-Semitism has for some Jews become an element in their relationship to Israel.

The Arabs have their own views regarding the various implications of Jewish persecution. They argue that, as a people, they were not the persecutors of Jews. Their treatment of Jews had been good until at least the turn of the century, when Zionism began to advocate the establishment of a Jewish state in Palestine. Even in the twentieth century, their conflict with the Jews was confined to what was necessary to protect Arab rights. Furthermore, Arabs insist they are not anti-Jewish, but anti-Zionist and anti-Israeli. The idea that Israel should be a country for all Jews is abhorrent to the Palestinian Arab. He argues that he lost his home to make room for a European Jew he did not persecute.

Arabs also suspect the motives of the West in helping the Zionists. They argue that the anti-Semitic Western world helped the Jews establish Israel in order to get rid of them, whereas decency required the Western peoples to accommodate the Jews in their own countries. Some Arabs argue that it would have been more honest if the West had given the Jews a "slice of Germany" rather than expect the Arabs to give up their homes to the victims of German atrocities.[52]

The Arabs also claim that the Zionists exploited the persecution issue to achieve their ends. The charge of anti-Semitism has been used to silence opposition to Zionism and to Israel. They claim that many scholars, journalists, government officials, politicians, and businessmen who would have supported the Arab point of view were afraid to express their sentiments for fear of being called anti-Semitic.[53]

Some Arab intellectuals claim that fear of being called anti-Semitic has prevented a better Western understanding of the Arab point of view. As a result, public opinion in the Western world is either misinformed or is simply ignorant of the facts. Arabs do admit that their non-Western culture has been a difficulty in presenting their case to the Western world. However, were it not for this fear of being called anti-Semitic there would be enough Western writers and journalists to explain the Arab point of view to their own peoples. After all, it is to the advantage of the Western countries to understand the problem, since the Middle Eastern conflict affects their own interests and could very well affect the future of world peace.

The Majority Argument. The Arabs argue that Palestine belonged to them because they were the majority of its population before the establishment of Israel. The Zionists, on the other hand, argue that Palestine was not a sovereign state, and therefore, the Arabs had no legitimate claim to it.

Thus while the Arabs argued that people had rights regardless of the status of the territory, the Zionists argued that the status of the country determined the rights of its people. The Arabs spoke of self-determination as a legal and moral right and the Zionists spoke mainly of international "commitments" as the more important. Both argued in terms of international law and morality. Generally, however, what the Zionists called international law the Arabs called international politics.

Not only did the Zionists ignore the majority argument of the Arabs, there is evidence that they underestimated the fact that Palestine had Arabs. Even Herzl ignored this problem. In *The Jewish State* he laid down the foundation of the Jewish state without addressing himself to the problem of how to deal with the non-Jewish population of the territory in which the state was to be established. He planned immigration to, and colonization of, the territory without once mentioning the indigenous population. Either Herzl assumed the territory had no population at all or he was not concerned with the problem.[54]

Zionist literature assumed that the Palestinian Arab, perhaps like the red Indian of the American continent, was too backward to be important and that his opposition to Zionism would be limited.[55] Events proved the Zionists wrong. The Arabs are unlike the red Indians: they cannot be permanently subdued because there are just too many of them; they have contributed to world civilization and are quite capable of resuming, in the long run, their historical role as civilizers. In other words, although the Arabs can be defeated, they will not disappear.

Had the Zionists given greater consideration to the fact that Palestine did have an Arab majority whose opposition to outsiders was natural, the conflict between them and the Arabs would have been less sharp. In this connection, the nationality of the Arabs had very little to do with their attitude toward Zionism. It is doubtful if their attitude would have been any different if they themselves were French and the Zionists were English. Had the Zionists assumed that Arab negative attitudes toward them were natural, Zionist methods, as well as aims, might have been different.

The Zionists were rigid in their relations with the Arabs, whom they considered to be their inferiors.[56] But they were highly flexible in dealing with public opinion in other countries. In the international arena, they did not underscore their real aims. They spoke of their desire to help the Arabs, at least in the area of economic development. They adopted gradualism as their guiding principle. Third parties saw them as realistic men who wanted to solve immediate problems, problems that all agreed were pressing and serious.

In the next chapter we shall see how the arguments, issues, and attitudes relating to the Palestine problem interacted to produce wars. As we shall see, the wars solved nothing; if they did anything, they complicated the Palestine problem even more: new arguments, new issues, and new attitudes developed as a result. And the future remains very uncertain.

Chapter 6

The First Two Wars

Between 1948 and 1967, the Arabs and the Israelis fought three wars. The Israelis won all three; and, except in the second (1956), they enlarged Israel's territory as a result.

Many intricate questions were at issue in each of the three wars. Some were legal; others relate to security; still others were moral questions. Whatever the immediate causes of the conflicts, all of them had their basis in one event: the establishment of the State of Israel.

It is a mistake to think of these wars as ethnic or religious in character. Jews and Arabs are not natural enemies, and before Zionism the two peoples got along for centuries. Had there been no Zionism, they would be living in relative peace today. From the Arab point of view at least, these wars are called the Arab-Israeli wars, to indicate that they were fought over the question of Israeli statehood and not because of an inherent animosity between the two peoples. (In other words, these wars are not Arab-Jewish wars.) The only period to which this designation does not apply is the few months before May 15, 1948, when the war was really a civil conflict between the Palestinian Arabs and the Zionist movement.

THE 1948 WAR

The Palestinian Arabs look upon the first war as a war of dispersion or expulsion, because it lost them their homes in

Palestine and denied them their right to self-determination. The Zionists call it the war of independence because it won them the establishment or the "reestablishment" of their Jewish state. Whatever name one chooses, both Arabs and Jews are right about the facts: the 1948 war brought about both the establishment of Israel and the dispersion (and displacement) of the Palestinian Arabs.

The Civil War. Fighting began immediately after partition (November 29, 1947). One of the questions often asked is who started the 1948 war. The Zionists accuse the Arabs, arguing that the Arabs rejected the UN partition resolution and were determined to prevent its "implementation." [1] They themselves could not have started the war, say the Zionists, because they accepted the resolution.

On the other hand, the Arabs claim the war was started by the Zionist Jews, who knew that they could defeat the Arabs and who recognized the opportunity to enlarge the territory of the Jewish state before May 14, 1948, the date which the Zionists had fixed for the establishment of their state. After all, the Arabs argue, although the Zionists did declare their acceptance of the UN resolution, they were also on record as complaining that the territory assigned to the Jewish state was inadequate.

The facts are difficult to determine. No doubt both sides had strong motivations to start the war. However, the Arabs certainly did not start the war simply by rejecting the UN resolution. Nor did the Zionists start it by complaining about inadequate territory. The point is that determining the validity of the arguments about who was motivated to start the war does not answer the question about who did start it. (Who actually attacked first in significant force?)

In the period before May 15, 1948, the battles were fought between the Haganah as the main Jewish force and the Arab Liberation Army aided by armed Arab civilians. The Haganah was better disciplined and better organized than the Arab forces. It was officered by competent men—many of whom had fought in World War II. In contrast, the Arab Liberation Army, which consisted of volunteers from Palestine and the Arab countries, was poorly trained and equipped. Its leader, Fawzi al-Kaukji, had earned a reputation as a courageous guerrilla leader during the 1936 Arab Palestine rebellion, but his abilities were not equal to the task of leading the Arab forces in the more advanced warfare of 1948. The armed civilians who were part of the Arab forces were more of a liability than an asset. Although some of their leaders, like Abdul Qadir al-Husaini, were courageous and dedicated, the rank and file lacked even the most rudimentary military training. They fought with small arms, very often defective, which they purchased themselves at high prices.

Before any fighting started, the Zionist leaders had already planned for the anticipated war. These plans were not limited to the "implementation" of the UN resolution, or even to frustrating Arab efforts to prevent the creation of Israel. They were designed to push out the boundaries of the Jewish state at the expense of the Arabs. This point is clear in the writing of many Zionists and Israelis. Ben-Gurion, for instance, declared: "Nothing a tottering [British] administration could do stopped us from reaching our goal on May 14, 1948, in a state made larger and Jewish by the Haganah." [2] The Zionist leaders needed only an excuse to execute their plan; and by going to war unprepared, the Palestinian Arabs played right into their hands. But in a way, the Arabs had no real alternative. Partition, they strongly believed, was wrong. For them, then, the choice was between accepting a permanent wrong and risking a defeat that would at least voice their claims. They could not foresee that more defeats would follow later in new wars and that Israel would enlarge its territory even more than it did in 1948. Had they predicted these developments they would probably have accepted the UN resolution. Such a decision would have forced Israel to choose between two alternatives: openly start the war and push out the boundaries of Israel, or be prepared to accept a future in which the possibility that the Arabs might become a majority in the Jewish state could be ruled out.

During the war, the Zionist leaders mercilessly exploited Arab weaknesses. Methodically, their troops set out to conquer town after town and village after village. By May 15, 1948, these troops had already incorporated into the Jewish state territories not assigned it by the UN resolution.[3]

The civil war period itself resulted in the displacement of about 300,000 Palestinian Arabs. Still more territory was to be conquered and more Palestinian Arabs displaced after the war entered its second stage, on May 15, 1948. This was the day after Zionist leaders had declared officially the establishment of Israel and the day that the Arab regular armies entered the war.

The Widening of the War. With the beginning of April, 1948, the Zionists had turned from primarily defensive to mainly offensive tactics.[4] Anxious to formalize their gains and face the world with a *fait accompli*, the Zionist leaders declared, on May 14, the establishment of Israel, in spite of the UN resolution's anticipation that this should not take place before June 15. The following day, the regular armies of seven Arab states entered Palestine—at the same time the last British troops left the country.

The Arab countries justified their action in terms of "establishing security and order" and restoring "peace . . . and law" in Palestine.[5] The Israelis argued that the Arab states were committing "aggression" against a legally constituted state, Israel.[6]

In reality, the Arab governments did not decide to enter Palestine until late in April, 1948. In part they were motivated by the fact that the Palestinian Arabs had lost the war and by the fact that the Israelis had occupied territories not assigned them by the UN resolution. More important, perhaps, was the nightmare of having to care for thousands of displaced

Palestinian Arabs. Finally, the feeling of kinship with the Palestinian Arabs was also a significant factor.

One can argue that it was Israeli excesses and ambition that brought the Arab regular armies into Palestine. Had the Israelis confined their gains to the control of territories assigned them by the UN, and had they allowed the Palestinian Arabs to return home, the Arab armies might have stayed out of Palestine. (The Arab decision to enter the war came after Israeli troops occupied areas outside the Jewish state's UN-assigned boundaries.) Possibly too, such a gesture by the Israelis might have softened Arab bitterness at the creation of a Jewish state in what they considered their homeland. Restraint on the part of Israel could have been seen as evidence of a real desire for friendship.

Instead, Israel's excessive ambition caused the civil war to become a regional war. Preoccupation with her historic "mission," the realization of a great dream, caused her to forget that her geographic position as an island in an Arab "ocean" necessitated Arab friendship. Later, the same problem would create a potential international war. Israel's responsibility in these developments relates to her military superiority vis-à-vis the Arab countries. It is an axiom of life and experience that peace and war depend more upon the strong than upon the weak.

From an Arab point of view, the involvement of the Arab armies in the Palestinian war was not illegal, first because Israel herself was not a legal entity and secondly because the Arab states were invited to intervene by the Arab Higher Committee, which represented the people of Palestine. Of course, the Israelis contend that they were a legally constituted state. Further, they argue that the territories which Israel won in 1948 had become part of their "national" territory.

This latter part of Israel's argument seems to support a thesis that war makes territory "fair game." A by-product of this thesis is that there is no obligation to return people or territory to their prewar legal condition.

The "fair game" thesis, if accepted, should be conceded to both parties in the conflict, not to just one party. If it is all right for Israel to annex Arab territory and displace her population, why isn't it all right for the Arabs to do the same? The fact that Arab leaders used harsher language ("Throw the Jews into the sea") to express their position while the Israelis used softer words, although harder actions, is a matter only of differences in expression and style. By acting sternly and speaking softly, the Israelis were obviously "smarter" than the Arabs.

As an alternative to peace, the fair-game theory is very dangerous. It means that the Arab-Israeli conflict has a cumulative nature, i.e., it becomes more complex and the chances of peace diminish after each war. In the long run, the theory is detrimental to the Israelis, although so far they have gained from it. While the Arabs have plenty of territory and can survive their defeats, the Israelis have very little of it and cannot afford even a single defeat.

It is unfortunate that Israel did not take advantage of her victory in 1948 to offer a withdrawal to the UN partition boundaries in return for Arab friendship, or at least acceptance. An opportunity for peace, for Israel and the Middle East, was lost.[7] (This problem recurs after the 1967 war.)

Thus the 1948 war revealed Zionist weakness as well as Zionist strength. It proved that the Zionists were militarily stronger, better organized, more modern, better united, more advanced, and more progressive than the Arabs. But it also demonstrated that they were shortsighted and fanatic. They could not envision a future with the Arabs, whom they considered inferior. They could see only their glory, the miracle that was Israel. By degrading the Arabs, the Zionists made the mistake that could one day be fatal: they made their national glory synonymous with Arab humiliation. Israeli victories give Israel immense pride, and Arab defeats give the Arabs a profound sense of shame. To recover their dignity, the Arabs must defeat the Israelis; and Israel, in order to preserve her glory, and indeed to maintain herself as a state, must keep the Arabs down. This is the most tragic aspect of the Arab-Israeli conflict.

The tragedy could have been avoided, or at least an attempt to avoid the tragedy could have been made, if Zionist leaders had considered Arab reaction to the event of the establishment of Israel to be understandable. After all, the Jews who displaced the Palestine Arabs were immigrants from other countries, and they displaced Arabs for whom Palestine was their birthplace. Consequently, regardless of the legal question of whose Palestine was, Arab reaction to the establishment of Israel was normal. Had the Zionist leaders seen the problem in that way their attitude after the 1948 war might have been different. They would have accepted the return of the Palestinian Arab to his home and their own return to the boundaries prescribed by the UN resolution. This price would have been worth paying in return for permanent peace and Arab goodwill.

A second alternative for Israel was latent in the Arabs' real ability to carry out their threats. The 1948 war, and later the 1956 and 1967 wars, showed the tremendous disparity between Arab and Israeli military strength; this means that the survival of Israel has never been a real issue. Israel's complaints about the Arab threat to destroy her are valid only in the sense that the Arabs do not recognize her, and that, until 1967, the Arabs wished they could dislodge Israel as a state. But, in terms of reality and capability, both Israel and the Arab leaders knew that Israel had superior arms and the Arabs could not accomplish their aims.

But, for propaganda purposes, after the 1967 war, Israel succeeded in presenting herself to other countries as the underdog; Israel did this so well that she was able to obtain whatever sympathies third-party cultures had for the defeated and, *at the same time,* the admiration they had for the victorious. The actual losers in the 1948 war could not even play the role of the defeated in order to be recognized at least as a party in the conflict. They were mostly ignored as if they were not part of the contest.

The 1948 war had the important effect of confusing the conflict's main, or primary, issue—namely, whether the Jews, a minority in Palestine, had the right to establish a *Jewish* state there. When the war began, this was clearly understood to be the issue, linked with the related question of whether the United Nations, more particularly the General Assembly, had the legal authority to partition Palestine.

After the war, secondary issues developed, and the main issue was lost. In fact, the main issue was treated as decided, since the secondary issues took the Israeli state for granted. These included Israel's boundaries, her "right" of free passage through the Suez Canal and the Gulf of Aqaba, and Arab "raids." Even the Arab refugee problem, a very serious problem, had difficulty being recognized as an issue. Obviously it was never in the interest of Israel to acknowledge the main issue, and Israeli propaganda stressed those issues that assured her legal right to existence. Consciously or otherwise, third parties accepted this situation in their effort to find a solution to the Arab-Israeli conflict. Since after the war the Arabs continued to see the conflict in terms of its primary issue, third-party solutions were irrelevant, negotiations were extremely difficult, and the conflict seemed insoluble.

Arab Defeat. Many factors contributed to the Arab defeat in 1948. First, the Arab countries were not ready for a war. Some of them, like Syria, Lebanon, and Jordan, had obtained their independence only recently. As sovereign states, these three countries were only a few years older than Israel. Also, some Arab countries were independent only on paper. Jordan, Egypt, and Iraq were still occupied and dominated by Britain, with whom they had important treaty obligations. Jordan's army was headed by a British general and most of the technical officers were also British. This, plus the fact that the government had no adequate sources of revenue, put Britain in control of both Jordan's finances and its military. Naturally, the nation's foreign relations were also dominated by the British.

Secondly, Arab troops were outnumbered. Contrary to what many people think, the Arab states had a little less than half as many soldiers as Israel had fighting in the 1948 war.[8] (Probably, the error was in the expectation that the smaller and less populous country, Israel, would have the smaller army.) Then, in addition to their numerical inferiority, the Arab armies relied on European countries for ammunition and equipment. These countries were unwilling to support them against Israel, and showed no sympathy with their cause. While the war was going on, Britain withdrew her commissioned officers serving with the Jordanian army. The British commander wrote later that the effect of this event resulted in virtual paralysis of Jordan's forces.[9] Most of the British officers had technical skills which Jordan could not replace from among her own troops.

The Israeli army, on the other hand, was in a sense non–Middle Eastern, and therefore, little affected by the problems of underdeveloped cultures. Its leaders and many of its soldiers came from European and other non–Middle Eastern countries. Zionist writer Harry Sacher asserts that "18 percent of the Army was composed of volunteers from fifty-two countries."[10] The percentage is much higher if we consider the fact that most Israelis were not born in Israel or Palestine.

Early in the war, when the problem of shortage in military equipment and ammunition affected both sides, the Arab armies did well. However, on June 11, 1948, the UN Security Council declared a truce, and Israel was able to take advantage of it by purchasing arms from Communist Czechoslovakia, violating the UN resolution, which forbade both sides from altering their military situations. According to a British Zionist writer, "a regular airlift" of arms and ammunition operated between Prague and Palestine. Arms purchases were greatly enhanced by the American Jews' "generous supply of dollars."[11]

The Arab countries also ignored the UN resolution and attempted to increase their strength. They failed, however, be-

cause their traditional suppliers, Britain and France, were reluctant to help.[12] Consequently, at the end of the four-week
truce, Israel emerged stronger. Ironically, it was Communist
assistance to Israel and British reluctance to support the Arabs
that probably saved Israel from a possible defeat.[13] Israel was
oddly fortunate to have on her side the two great rivals of the
cold war, the Soviet Union and the United States.

Another weakness of the Arab armies was their lack of
strong common leadership. Although King Abdullah of Jordan
was the supreme commander of the Arab forces, his leadership
was more nominal than real. He had no military qualifications,
and his interest in the whole affair was more political than
military. Furthermore, he had personal ambitions which were
more important to him than the Palestine adventure. He hoped
to enlarge his kingdom not only by obtaining Palestinian territory but by someday gaining control of Syria. Also, he believed his ambitions were reconcilable with those of the Zionists. In the 1948 war, therefore, Abdullah was a reluctant
participant.

Lack of common leadership resulted in lack of coordination.
In fact the Arab leaders were especially suspicious of one another, and they competed for control of Palestinian territory.
Their commanders argued over who should get what of Palestine and where each army should be or should not be. In addition, the Egyptian and Jordanian heads of state were competing for greater prestige in the Arab world, perhaps not
realizing that their quarrels, because they contributed to Israel's victory, would ultimately weaken their positions in their
own countries. (In 1951, Abdullah was assassinated by a Palestinian, and in 1952 King Farouk lost his throne as the result
of an army coup.)

Obviously, the Arabs faced Israel disunited. Disunity characterized not only their military and political relations but
also their attitudes toward Palestine, the country they were
trying to save from Zionist-Jewish absorption. For them it was
unfortunate that the war with Israel took place at a time when

Arab nationalism was still politically immature. They looked upon Palestine legalistically, as a separate state and not as part of Arab "national" territory. Reflecting the division of the Arab world into a number of sovereign and semisovereign states, this attitude was understandable. But it meant that the Arab countries considered the battle as one of assistance to their "brothers," whereas the Israelis saw it as a fight for survival.[14] Psychologically, Arab incentive during the war would have been greater if the Arab countries' nationalistic feelings had been strong enough to consider Palestine their "own."

But the problem of Arab unity has been exaggerated by the Israelis, the Western countries, and the Arabs themselves. In a sense it was only because the technological gap between the Israelis and the Arabs was wide that Arab disunity became an important factor in the war's outcome. Had the Israeli and Arab levels of technology been even, the Arabs would not have had to act jointly. Egypt or Syria alone might have successfully challenged the Israelis.

True, in 1948, and later in 1967, Arab unity would have increased the quantity of the Arab effort against Israel but it would not have made a *real* difference in the quality of that effort, which is the crucial element in the winning of *modern* wars. Quantity is significant only where it can offset the quality gap between enemies. For the Arabs, unfortunately, their technical backwardness demanded a great quantitative effort if they were to win. Disunity made this effort impossible.

Moreover, their very (technical) backwardness made unity unlikely. Unity requires national consciousness, which is difficult to create in areas which are not relatively developed. A certain level of technological advancement was necessary for the achievement of a durable unity among the Arabs,[15] and so the Arabs were caught in a vicious circle.

In 1948 the Arab sense of defeat gave the Arabs greater awareness of the need for technological progress. Western influence had made this point clear, but the Arab-Israeli conflict elevated the awareness to a sense of emergency.[16] However, technological advancement required time. Furthermore, it was complicated by another by-product of the Arab-Israeli conflict: the need felt by Arab nationalists for radical political change. Radical political changes meant internal turmoil and political instability, which are inimical to economic and technical progress. Thus, although defeat made the Arab nationalists aware of the necessity of development, it also made them aware of the necessity for political change, which, if brought about in an erratic revolutionary fashion, would hinder development.[17] Thus a second vicious circle existed to handicap the Arab peoples.

THE AFTERMATH OF THE 1948 WAR

The 1948 war had two major effects on Palestine. One involved territory, the other, people, and both had long-range implications.

Effect on Territory. The Israel that emerged from the 1948 war was a much larger country than the UN had authorized. The partition resolution had given the Jewish state about 5,600 square miles of the 10,000 square-mile Palestinian territory.[18] During the war, Israel acquired an additional 2,140 square miles, almost half the territory originally allotted by the UN for the Arab state. The remainder of the territory allotted for the Arab state, which never came into existence, passed under Jordanian or Egyptian control. Of this territory, 2,200 square miles, known as the west bank, were later incorporated by Jordan, by a decision of a parliament in which the people of the area were represented. A 28-mile-long strip of land, extending along the Mediterranean coast and known as the Gaza Strip, was administered by Egypt as a Palestinian territory with a special status that did not incorporate it into Egypt.

Of course, the Arabs did not accept Israel's territorial gains as legitimate. Whether the various armistice agreements be-

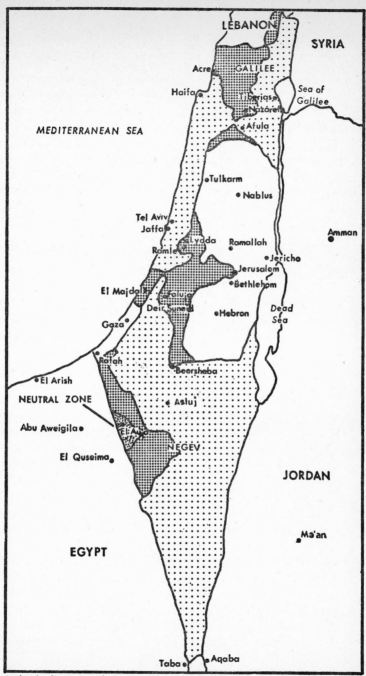

Light shading—Jewish State under UN partition
Dark shading—Area occupied by Israel during the 1948 war

ISRAEL IN 1949

tween Israel and the Arab countries, concluded between March and July, 1949, constituted a permanent peace agreement was the subject of long debate, involving the parties themselves and specialists in international law. The Arabs argued that armistice agreements neither constitute permanent peace agreements nor establish permanent rights. Rather, said the Arabs, they are transitional instruments establishing commitments to suspend military hostilities in anticipation of a final resolution of claims. Only a peace treaty can establish permanent rights. (A peace treaty between Israel and the Arab countries has never been concluded.)

Scholars agree with the Arab point of view on the legal status of armistice agreements and the difference between this type of agreement and peace treaties. The author of a standard textbook reflects a popular position among scholars when he wrote: "Suspension of hostilities must be differentiated from termination of war. The latter restores the status of peace but the former merely halts—sometimes only very temporarily— military action and does not necessarily carry with it the legal implication of termination of war." [19] However, in rare instances, armistice agreements such as the 1918 Armistice Agreement between the Allies and Germany, contain provisions making the resumption of hostilities impossible.[20] The armistice agreements between Israel and the Arab countries conform to the traditional, rather than the exceptional, type. They clearly state that "no provision . . . shall in any way prejudice the rights, claims and positions of either Party hereto in the ultimate peaceful settlement of the Palestine question, the provisions of this Agreement being dictated exclusively by military, and not by political, considerations." [21]

Israel, on the other hand, argued that the armistice agreements established permanent boundaries, in spite of the fact that these agreements contained specific provisions to the contrary. For instance, the first paragraph of Article V of the Israeli-Syrian General Armistice Agreement states: "It is emphasized that . . . arrangements for the Armistice Demarcation Line between the Israeli and Syrian armed forces . . . are not to be interpreted as having any relation whatsoever to ultimate territorial arrangements affecting the two Parties to this Agreement." Also, the same article states: "The Armistice Demarcation Line . . . [has] been defined with a view toward separating the armed forces of the two Parties . . . without prejudice to the ultimate settlement."

Israel considered that the Arab territory which she gained as a result of the war had become an integral part of the sovereign Israeli state and was not negotiable in any final settlement of the conflict. According to Israeli official sources, the armistice boundaries were international boundaries that could not be adjusted without the consent of Israel. The implication is that even the UN, which partitioned Palestine and made possible the creation of the Jewish state, did not have the authority to deal with the boundary issue. Furthermore, Israel claimed that the UN partition resolution no longer existed because it was annulled by the Arab "invasion" of Israel.[22]

Israel also argued that the armistice agreements ended the war and established peace. Later it used this argument to support its claim to the right of passage through the Suez Canal and the Gulf of Aqaba. For Israel, the armistice agreements were equivalent to "non-aggression pacts." [23]

Since Israel was the winner of the war and had acquired new territory, the argument that the armistice ended the war was very much consistent with Israel's interests, in spite of her difficulties with respect to international law. Furthermore, the argument was very useful for Israeli propaganda outside the Middle East. It made the Arabs look like warmongers and the Israelis like angels of peace.

For the Arabs, however, acceptance of the armistice as a permanent peace meant accepting the territorial losses sustained during the war as permanent also. Their rejection of this enabled the Zionist-Israeli propagandists to formulate in the Western world an Arab image of warmonger and Jew-hater.

However, the most astonishing aspect of Israel's territorial gains is that some of them were made during the second truce, which Israel had agreed to and the United Nations had ordered. These gains included the Negev area (October and December, 1948), western Galilee (October, 1948), and a number of Arab villages near the Lebanese border. Clearly, Israel's conquest of these areas was in violation of international law and of the UN resolutions establishing the truce. Moreover, Israel refused to withdraw from these areas in spite of UN orders requiring withdrawal.

Even after she had signed an armistice agreement with Egypt (February, 1949), and while she was negotiating with the other Arab countries for similar agreements, Israel made one more territorial gain. In March, 1949, she seized the remaining Negev area north of the Gulf of Aqaba.

In many instances, the conquests were, according to the UN mediator, Count Folke Bernadotte, accompanied by "large-scale looting" and "instances of destruction of villages without military necessity." [24]

Effect on People. The 1948 Arab-Israeli war resulted in an enormous Arab refugee problem. By May 15, 1948, about 300,000 Palestinian Arabs had been made homeless. And the more territorial gains Israel made, the more Palestinian Arabs became refugees. Some of them lost their homes during the second truce as a result of Israel's military conquests in the Negev, western Galilee, and south of Lebanon.[25] Others became refugees after the conclusion of the armistice agreements of 1949.[26] All in all, the number of Palestinian Arabs uprooted as a result of the first Arab-Israeli war was over 800,000.[27] After the war, these refugees waited in the neighboring Arab countries to return to their homes in Israel.

The cause of the refugee problem is an intricate question for which the Arabs and the Israelis have different answers. The Israelis contend that the refugees were not forced to leave; that their departure was urged by the Arab leaders in order to

discredit Israel in the eyes of the world. They add that the solution of the problem is the responsibility of the Arab countries
because the war was the outcome of Arab aggression against
Israel.

The Arabs maintain that the refugees were deliberately ex-
pelled by Israel in order to leave room for the Jewish immigrants whose admission into Israel had been anticipated and
planned for by the Jewish state. Zionist leaders, the Arabs
claim, had prodded extremist Jewish groups (the Irgun and
the Stern Gang) to commit atrocities against innocent civilians
with the object of terrifying the population into fleeing for
safety. In April, 1948, for instance, the Israelis massacred the
entire population of a small Arab village called Deir Yaseen including women and children. The incident was later admitted
by the leader of the Irgun, the group that was responsible for
the massacre.[28]

The truth of the matter is that some refugees left voluntarily,
while others were forced to leave. For instance, the departure
from the city of Haifa of many Arabs was not forced by the
Israelis. On the other hand, about 50,000 Arab inhabitants of
the Lydda and Ramleh areas were forced out by the Israelis.
The same was true of the 30,000 Arabs from the Negev area.[29]
There is no evidence for the Israeli claim that Arab leaders
encouraged the Palestinian Arabs to leave their homes. On the
contrary, there is evidence that Arab leaders did not urge departure.[30] Also, there seems to be some substance in the Arab
claim that Zionist leaders urged Jews outside Israel to come
to Israel to effect a *fait accompli* that could be used to deny
the Arab refugees an opportunity to return to their homes.[31]

But how the Arabs left their homes is immaterial. There is
nothing unusual about a civilian population leaving a battle
area for safety.[32] It happens in every war. The essential fact
is that, after they had become refugees, Israel would not allow
their return.

Of course, the Israelis argue that the refugees have no right
to return because they "abandoned" their homes. However, in

international law, abandonment of territorial right requires—
in addition to physical abandonment—the failure over a period
of time to make claim to the territory. And the Palestinian
Arabs never ceased to claim their right to return home. Furthermore, they made their claim clear by Fedayeen "attacks,"
which Israelis call "raids" and "terrorist activities," although
they themselves resorted to terrorist activities before the first
Palestine war.

The UN has recognized the legal right of the refugee to
repatriation or compensation. The same organization which in
1947 voted to create the Jewish state voted a year later to
solve the refugee problem by repatriation or compensation.[33]
The UN continued, by formal resolution, to press this obligation upon Israel every year from 1948 to 1966.

The Israelis also argue that the return of the Arab refugees
would be a security risk that their government cannot afford
taking. In the years following the end of the war, Israelis
pointed out that the refugees were taught to hate Jews and
this made the security problem greater than before.

Israel's security argument is understood in the Western
world and has received support from individuals who appreciate power and interest more than morality and peace. But
the Israeli argument, although very appealing to pragmatists,
ignores certain factors and exaggerates others. It ignores the
fact that Israel rejected, in 1948, a UN demand for the repatriation of the Arab refugees—before any program to teach
them to hate Jews was instituted. Nor was Israel on record as
having accepted the principle of repatriation while posing the
difficulty of security. Had she accepted the principle at the
same time she raised the question of security, one would have
understood her position to be sincerely motivated.

Also, the question concerning the return of the refugees is
not an isolated question: it is related to the larger question of
permanent peace. Accordingly, if the return of the refugees
should be tied to a peace agreement guaranteed by other
parties, the problem of security becomes less relevant, and the

refugee problem should look less insurmountable. As long as the arrangement guarantees state security, the repatriation should raise no objections on these grounds.

The refugee issue is also a moral issue. The Palestinian Arabs cannot understand how Israel can admit thousands of Jews from other countries every year, Jews who were not born in that part of the world, many of whom have never seen Israel before, while they, who were born in Palestine, are denied the right to return home. What moral consistency, they ask, justifies the fact that they cannot return to Jaffa or Haifa while a Russian or an American Jew can live in these cities in houses the exiled Arabs built? There is plenty of room in Israel for both the Israelis and the Palestinian Arabs. And the evidence that this is true is Israel's own admission of the fact. On various occasions, Israeli leaders have declared that Israel is the home of all Jews and urged that Jews in the Diaspora should "return" to their "homeland." [34] In addition, Israeli law gives Jews outside Israel the unlimited right to immigrate to Israel and become citizens of that country.[35]

Admittedly one might point to the difficulty or even the impracticality of returning to the refugees their old properties after years of Jewish occupancy. Perhaps socialism might eliminate the problem of *private ownership* (i.e., the question of who gets what in Palestine) and raise instead the less difficult question of *use* of property. The answer to the latter question would require the state to provide the returning Palestinians with adequate housing facilities and equal economic opportunities. Under socialism, the ownership titles to all property, whether Jewish or Arab, would have to be surrendered to the state. And socialism, one should keep in mind, should be acceptable to Arabs and Jews because the system is familiar to both. The ruling party in Israel and perhaps most Israelis are ideologically socialistic. On the other hand, socialism is the ideology of many Palestinians, and it is the official doctrine of Syria, Iraq, Egypt, Algeria, and Libya. On the basis of current Middle Eastern ideological trends, it seems reasonable to predict that in the future socialism will be the region's dominant system.

In a socialist democratic state, Arabs and Jews can pull together in the interest of the state. True, the more advanced Jewish population would naturally dominate the economy, but if Jews are to be true to socialist principles, such domination would be only a form of trust to be used for the benefit of all. It would be a form of supervision necessitated by superior know-how rather than an exploitive system motivated by extreme self-interest.

If this seems utopian, it is because it relies on the good sense of Jews and Arabs and assumes that man is more good than bad. But this reliance and this assumption are the key to peace and better life. Without them we need not be concerned about the Arab-Israeli conflict, about human life (Jewish and Arab), and about the future of world peace.

But if socialism is not acceptable to one or the other side, then another equitable formula could be worked out. The international community including the Arab states, Israel, and the big powers, should assist, financially and otherwise, in this great humanitarian problem. Whatever the cost of their effort, it cannot be more than the cost of Arab-Israeli wars, especially considering the price in human suffering.

But is Israel's security argument the real reason for her rejection of repatriation? The primary reason why Israel takes an uncompromising position on the refugee question is that repatriation would ultimately undermine the Jewish character of the state. And the Jewishness of the state is what the Israelis insist should not be jeopardized. It is the all-important element in Israel's political and social existence.

THE 1956 SUEZ WAR

In a previous chapter, the political circumstances surrounding the construction of the Suez Canal were explained. Briefly, the important elements are the following: (1) Egypt paid about 72 percent of the total cost of the construction of the canal in return for 15 percent of the net profit from the operation of the canal. (2) Two irresponsible rulers of Egypt, Said and Ismail, had to borrow large amounts of money from Europeans for the construction of the canal and other projects. (3) The European creditors charged exorbitant rates of interest on Egyptian loans; and when Egypt procrastinated in making payments, these creditors pressured their governments to intervene in their behalf. (4) In the late 1870's, France and Britain took over the Egyptian treasury to ensure the payment of Egypt's debts. (5) A few years later France and Britain decided to occupy Egypt; but when the occupation did finally take place in 1882 a change of government prevented France from participating in the occupation.

History nearly repeated itself in 1956. Britain and France again decided to attack Egypt, which had become independent in 1922. The circumstances leading to the decision were different but they too involved the canal. Thus Mohammed Ali's prediction that the construction of the canal might ultimately cause Egypt to fall under foreign domination was substantiated by subsequent events in both the nineteenth century and the twentieth century. However, in 1956 the Anglo-French attempt did not succeed.

The Canal Crisis. The Suez Canal crisis began on July 26, 1956, the day President Nasser announced the nationalization of the Suez Canal Company.[36] The event was associated with Egypt's reaction to the American Government's decision to withdraw its offer to help finance the Aswan High Dam, a project which Nasser considered to be of great importance.

The Aswan Dam project was conceived before Nasser came to power. Egyptians had been sold on the idea that the project was essential to the economic prosperity of the country. Many thought that without the dam Egypt was doomed to a future of misery. Although the Farouk regime talked a lot about the project it did very little to realize it. When Nasser came to power he found the project on paper and on the hearts of millions of Egyptians, but nothing more than that. Having decided that the project was essential and economically sound, he was, unlike his predecessor's regime, determined to do something about it.

It was predicted that the Aswan Dam would increase Egypt's arable land by 25 percent—about two million acres. In addition, it was expected to increase the electric power of Egypt tenfold, thereby allowing for the development of industry. Initially, the United States agreed that the benefits to Egypt were real and she agreed in principle to help financially in the fulfillment of the project. The United States was to give Egypt $56 million. Britain offered $14 million, and the World Bank offered a loan of $200 million.

On July 19, 1956, the United States withdrew the offer.[37] Then Britain and the World Bank followed suit. (Because the United States holds a large number of the World Bank's shares her influence in the bank is strong. She appoints a permanent member to the bank's board of executive directors; and presidents of the bank have so far been Americans.) In its official statement, the U.S. State Department claimed that "the ability of Egypt to devote adequate resources to assure the project's success has become more uncertain than at the time the offer was made." However, this cannot be accepted as the real reason for the withdrawal of the offer. Nor can we accept Nasser's argument that nationalization of the Suez Canal Company was necessary to provide revenue to match up the loss of funds resulting from the withdrawn offers. More fundamental motives were at work in the crisis.

On the American side, Secretary of State John Foster Dulles was irritated by Nasser's policy of cooperation with the Soviet Union. Nasser's opposition to the Baghdad Pact (1955), his acceptance of arms from (Communist) Czechoslovakia (1955), his recognition of Communist China (May, 1956), and his drifting toward the camp of nonaligned nations, all influenced Dulles' attitude.

On the Egyptian side, Nasser's strong desire to assert Egyptian independence and sovereignty by limiting foreign influence and interference was the principal reason for his decision to nationalize the Suez Canal Company. Like many of his contemporaries among middle-class Egyptians, Nasser was fully aware of the history of foreign dominance in Egypt, and since his childhood days he had yearned for the time when Egypt could be the master of her destiny. It was natural for him, as a revolutionary leader, to attempt the elimination of all vestiges of foreign hegemony. He had just succeeded in ending the British occupation: the last British soldier had left in mid-June, 1956.[38] The Suez Canal was symbolic of what the Egyptians called "European imperialism at its worst," and for Nasser it was time that Egypt asserted her authority over her whole territory, including the canal.[39]

Of course, the nationalization of the Suez Canal Company had its greatest effect not on the United States or the Soviet Union, for whom the canal had very little economic significance, but on Britain and France, who considered the canal vital to their international trade. For instance, in 1955 British shipping through the canal accounted for 28.3 percent of the total canal tonnage. In the same year, the portions of Britain's national supply of oil, rubber, and wool that went through the canal were 56, 85, and 70 percent respectively. For France, the proportions for the same products were 47, 76, and 70 percent.[40]

Furthermore, the majority of the Canal Company's shares were owned by French citizens and the British government.[41] In 1955, about $39 million went to all shareholders and, of course, France and Britain received most of it.[42]

In addition, the canal was significant to other countries. "One seventh of all cargoes in world-wide international trade" went through the canal in the few years before the crisis began. Two thirds of Suez cargoes involved oil products going from the Middle East to western Europe. In the year 1955–1956, an average of forty ships a day went through the canal. It was estimated that if the canal were to be closed to traffic, western Europe would have to pay out about half a billion dollars every year in additional transportation costs because of the necessity of going around Africa.[43]

Clearly, however, the Suez Canal held more significance for Egypt than for any other country. Politically, it had always been linked to foreign influence on, and domination of, Egypt. In the 1870's, Britain and France took control of Egypt's treasury, largely as a result of pressures exerted upon them by Egypt's European creditors. In 1882, this indirect control became direct: British troops occupied Egypt. Thereafter, until June, 1956, the British argued that their military presence in Egypt was necessitated by the Suez Canal. Therefore, Egyptian independence was synonymous with Egyptian control over the canal.

Economically, too, the canal is important to Egypt. However, in spite of the important fact that the canal is situated entirely in Egyptian territory, Egypt was not receiving a fair share of the income from the canal. In other words, the "legal" share that Egypt received was not enough. There is a moral issue related to the situation of a country that contributed most of the money and all of the labor to an enterprise whose profits went mostly to others. Before 1956, the canal's annual income averaged about $100 million, a large amount for a small and poor country such as Egypt. Had Egypt received a fair share of this amount, she would have benefited from it. Consequently, legality notwithstanding, the financial aspects of the Suez Canal operation reflected foreign disregard for the moral rights of Egypt.

Being related to her independence as a country, Egypt's political interest in the canal outweighed her own and other countries' economic interests in it. Political reasons, not economic ones, were behind Nasser's move to nationalize the canal.

The violent Anglo-French reaction to Nasser's nationalization decision was also mainly political. True, Britain and France were concerned that Egypt might not be able to run the canal efficiently because she was "backward." But their strongest feelings lay elsewhere. With France, Egypt's moral and material support for the Algerian revolution was the main sore point. Prior to the Anglo-French invasion of Egypt, French propaganda pictured Nasser as "the Hitler of the Nile." The slogan was very appealing to the Israeli propagandists, who were glad to feed the French with more ammunition.

With Britain, pride was a factor. The conservative government of Anthony Eden was disturbed by the declining British influence in the Middle East and sensitive about the gradual dissolution of the British colonial empire. Britain had very little control over decolonization trends and that was frustrating for a government which, although sufficiently pragmatic, was nostalgic about "the good old days" of British power and glory.

In Britain there was the additional factor of Eden's intense distaste for Nasser. Eden saw Nasser as a defiant and arrogant demagogue, and he was so obsessed with Nasser that he became determined to "teach him a lesson." [44]

The Invasion. European reaction to the nationalization of the Suez Canal Company was strong. However, under American pressure Britain was restrained from immediately using force against Egypt. Consequently, a short period followed in which diplomacy, military preparation, and pressure preceded the invasion of Egypt by France, Britain, and Israel. In order to embarrass Nasser by demonstrating his inability to run the canal, the Canal Company withdrew its Western pilots. To pressure Nasser into making concessions the British government blocked all Egyptian accounts in the United Kingdom and began mobilizing troops in the eastern Mediterranean area.

On the diplomatic front, negotiations were conducted to find a solution to the problem. On August 16, 1956, an international conference of twenty-two nations met in London and proposed the creation of an international board consisting of eighteen nations plus Egypt to operate and develop the canal. A committee of five, chaired by the prime minister of Australia was dispatched to Cairo to persuade Nasser to accept the conference's proposal. But Nasser refused.

Another attempt was made in September of 1956, at the urging of the United States, which had developed a new plan. This plan proposed the establishment of a Suez Canal Users' Association, to be composed of maritime nations using the canal, which would operate the canal and yield revenues in excess of cost to Egypt. It was not very different from the first one, but Britain and France hoped that the prestige of the United States would unite the user nations against Nasser. More important, Britain and France thought that if Nasser rejected the plan the United States would be willing to support some action against Egypt. They were disappointed, however. Secretary of State Dulles made statements to the effect that the United States would not consider the use of force should Nasser reject the plan.

It became clear that a gap existed between the positions of the United States and her European allies on the question of the canal. In addition, the concept of international control of the canal could not obtain the approval of the UN Security Council. In October a resolution embodying this concept was vetoed by the Soviet Union.

Eden became impatient with the turn of events. In spite of the withdrawal of the Western pilots, Nasser was running the canal efficiently. This meant that there would be no question about the Suez Canal remaining open to traffic even though it was not internationally controlled.

Also, Britain was urged by France to take a more forceful position. Although it is not clear what secret diplomacy contributed to the crisis, France, Britain, and Israel were in collusion in the adventure, which soon proved to be tragic.[45]

Israel's interest in the adventure was obvious. She hoped to force the Suez Canal open to Israeli shipping, which had been kept out by Egypt. She had always considered Nasser to be the strongest Arab enemy and she too was therefore eager to "teach him a lesson." The Arabs claimed Israel had territorial ambitions and that this was her real motive. Israel claimed that her survival was at stake and that *fedayeen* raids and Egypt's interference in Israeli shipping through the Suez Canal and the Gulf of Aqaba were major factors in her decision to attack Egypt.

Israel invaded Egypt on October 29, 1956. In a very short time Israel approached the canal. The next day, Britain and France sent Israel and Egypt an ultimatum: cease fire and move ten miles away from the canal. Israel said she would consent if Egypt obeyed. Egypt thought the whole affair was ridiculous: to retire she would have to withdraw beyond the "canal territory" and leave open many miles of her own territory. Why should she withdraw, when she was the one who had been attacked? On the same day as the ultimatum, October 30, Britain and France vetoed a United States–sponsored resolution in the Security Council calling on Israel to withdraw from Egyptian territory and requesting all UN members to "refrain from the use of force or threat of force." [46]

The Soviet Union attempted to use the Security Council machinery to force Israeli withdrawal.[47] But the Soviet attempt, as well as that of the United States, was frustrated by the Anglo-French veto. The Soviet Union also proposed a joint U.S.-Soviet force under Article 42 of the UN Charter, but the United States opposed the idea.[48] Outside the UN, the Soviet Union threatened to intervene on behalf of Egypt. And it appeared the crisis was getting out of hand.

On October 31 the British bombed Egyptian airfields. The next day the Security Council invoked the "Uniting for Peace" procedure to call the General Assembly for an emergency meeting. And on the third day the Assembly adopted a resolution urging a cease-fire and the withdrawal of all forces behind the armistice boundaries.[49] On the fourth day (November 3), the Council adopted a Canadian resolution establishing an international force "to secure and supervise the cessation of hostilities." [50]

On November 5, Anglo-French forces invaded Egypt and

occupied Port Said and Port Fuad. In a short time they were able to penetrate inland thirty miles along the canal. World public opinion seemed outraged by the event and on November 7, 1956, the UN General Assembly voted a resolution calling on Israel, Britain, and France to withdraw their forces from Egypt. Only Israel voted against the resolution while Britain and France abstained.[51] British internal politics were such that Eden's government was in serious trouble.[52] Of course, American pressure, world public opinion, and Soviet threats all played their part in the political retreat of Britain and France.

The political retreat was followed by the military evacuation of Egypt. Britain and France withdrew their last contingents on December 27, 1956. However, the Israelis procrastinated. Ben-Gurion argued that the Suez war made the armistice boundaries "dead and buried." [53] The implication was that Israel's boundaries would change as a result of the war. Soon, however, he began to condition withdrawal by effective international guarantees of Israel's "security." President Eisenhower insisted that a nation should not reap the fruits of its aggression and, therefore, although he was sympathetic to the Israeli case, he considered that Israel's withdrawal from Egypt should come first.

Israel had to yield to American pressure. By January 22, 1957, Israeli troops were withdrawn from the Sinai peninsula. Two areas were still under Israeli control: the Gaza Strip and Sharm el-Sheikh on the Gulf of Aqaba. Ben-Gurion wanted "civilian" control of the Strip and guarantees of free passage through the Gulf before withdrawing.[54] However, greater American pressure induced Israel to withdraw from these two areas as well. In March, the withdrawal was complete and the situation in the Middle East returned to where it was before the war.

The Arguments. The Suez problem can be seen as a case where two former colonial powers (Britain and France) could not adjust to the fact that colonialism was on its way out and that former colonies were eager to redress past grievances in order to assert their independence and sovereign rights. Before we can delve into the legal arguments of the parties involved, a few comments about the diplomatic behavior of states and about international law in general are necessary.

Some aspects of international law are patently unjust by the standards set in most national legal systems. This is because international law has largely reflected the interests of strong states. Thus, for instance, a treaty, which in essence is a contract between states, is considered legally valid even though one party has been coerced into signing it. Peace treaties often fall into this category. Also, a treaty could obligate a state even though that state did not exist at the time the treaty was made. It is only necessary that the treaty be signed by the state which had legal sovereignty over the territory and population of the as-yet-unestablished state. Thus, under international law, treaties signed by the Ottoman state on behalf of Egypt were considered binding on Egypt after Egypt became independent. In fact, independent Egypt was obligated to honor Ottoman contracts (treaties) after the Ottoman empire had ceased to exist.

Also, some treaties are not limited by time, and the obligations they impose upon the parties are likewise unlimited. The world could change, states disappear, new states appear, strong states become weak and weak states become strong; but, basically, the obligations remain and the treaties are valid. This situation has caused many problems for the contemporary world, which is very different from the world at the time the treaties were signed. The arbitrariness and the unreasonableness of these aspects of international law sometimes contribute to war between states.

There is need to modify international law to eliminate such arbitrary and outmoded elements. Municipal (i.e., internal, national) law could provide useful guidelines, at least in some instances, in achieving this objective. This law, for instance, provides an element of fairness in the making of contracts. Thus, a contract is usually not binding on a party that was forced to agree to its terms. (And there are other instances in which civil contracts can be dissolved for reasons which normally cannot justify the dissolution of a treaty.)

In the Suez crisis, the international law that related to the problem embodied some of the defects and weaknesses discussed in the previous paragraphs. Mainly, four old documents were relevant: An 1888 treaty, which provided for the internationalization of the canal; an 1854 concession relating to the construction of the canal made by the viceroy of Egypt to Ferdinand de Lesseps; an 1856 document modifying the 1854 concession; and an 1866 agreement between the viceroy and the Suez Canal Company (ratified by the Ottoman head of state) which, *inter alia,* approved the articles of the Company.[55]

In spite of the weaknesses of international law from the standpoint of common justice these documents were accepted by all the parties involved in the Suez crisis. Our analysis was intended to make the reader aware of some of the difficulties which can result from these weaknesses. We are not trying to refute the validity or relevance of the documents, but to question the basis on which they stand. Let us now explain the legal arguments of the conflicting parties, to see how international law can be used by states to defend their policies and actions.

The Anglo-French argument concentrated on the effect of nationalization on the right of nations to use the canal without restriction by Egypt. Britain and France were concerned mainly with the long-run implications of the nationalization decision. They had little interest in Israel's immediate difficulties.[56] Israel's main argument was that Egypt's exclusion of Israeli shipping was illegal, but this was a problem that had arisen before nationalization of the canal. The fact that the three countries cooperated in the invasion of Egypt did not mean that they had the same reasons for attacking Egypt. One thing they had in common, however, was their hatred of Nasser.

Egypt's main argument was that the nationalization act was legal because the Suez Canal Company was Egyptian,[57] a fact that had been recognized by the British before the Mixed Court in 1939.[58] The Egyptian character of the company is explicit in articles 9, 10, 11, and 16 of the 1866 agreement, referred to above. Egypt also argued that, since the Company was Egyptian, there was no question about the right of Egypt as a sovereign state to nationalize the Company. International law permits nationalization, provided compensation is paid. The nationalization decree promised compensation to share-holders on the basis of the value of the share on the Paris stock market on the day preceding nationalization. (In 1958, an agreement on compensation was reached between Egypt and the Company and in 1963 Egypt made the last payment to the Company.)

At the beginning, Britain preferred to take "issue with Nasser on the broader international grounds" rather than plunging into "legal quibbles about the rights of the Egyptian Government to nationalize what is technically an Egyptian company." [59] Gradually, however, Britain developed her case. She was slow in doing so mainly because of U.S. concern about the impact of the case on the Panama Canal. The United States was opposed to either nationalization *or* inter-nationalization of the Panama Canal, and was afraid that an incorrect legal argument might set a precedent that would jeopardize her control.[60] Another difficulty for Britain was that a legal argument had to be developed out of a political situation. Britain could not object to nationalization itself be-cause she herself had nationalized many of her private com-panies. She needed a legal argument that would avoid directly challenging the international legality of nationalization.

The legal basis finally chosen argued that the Suez Canal Company had an international character of its own and an international (treaty) responsibility. The argument was based on the fact that the Company's concession was tied to the 1888 treaty, which guaranteed to all nations at all times freedom of passage through the canal. The link between the concession and the 1888 treaty was argued to be the preamble of the 1888 treaty, which stated that the contracting parties wished "to complete the system" begun by the 1866 agreement (which approved the concessions of 1854 and 1856). Dulles argued that since the concession was linked to the treaty, Egypt's nationalization of the Company violated the treaty.

The thrust of this argument is that under the 1888 treaty only the Suez Canal Company could legitimately operate the canal, since only the Company was vested with the legal obligation to ensure freedom of navigation. Consequently, Nasser could not nationalize the Company without violating the treaty.

The weakness of the argument is that the link between the treaty and the concession (upon which depends the international character of the case) is extremely vague, even if we accept the view that the preamble of a treaty is an integral part of the treaty. To imply from the vague connection that only the Canal Company could ensure freedom of navigation stretches the point a little bit too far.

Another weakness is that although the treaty had no time limit the concession did. Under article 16 of the 1856 document "the term of the Company's existence is fixed at 99 years." [61] Although the Company's term was renewable, Egypt was not obligated to renew it. This raises an important question: if the treaty is to be indefinite and therefore the freedom of navigation is to be permanent, how can this be reconciled with the fact that the Company (allegedly responsible for ensuring freedom of navigation) is limited to a ninety-nine-year term? In other words, how can the freedom of navigation be permanent while the authority to ensure it is not?

Furthermore, it is clear that article 9 of the 1888 treaty gives the responsibility of enforcing the treaty to the Egyptian government. This would include enforcing the freedom of navigation guaranteed by the treaty. This article would appear to contradict the argument that responsibility for freedom of navigation was vested with the Canal Company. And it is important to remember that the nationalization decree did not deny Egypt's obligations under the 1888 treaty.

With regard to Israel's involvement in the Suez controversy, her legal arguments ran as follows: by not allowing Israeli shipping through the canal, Egypt violated the first article of the 1888 treaty, which stipulated clearly that "the Suez Maritime Canal shall always be free and open, in time of war as in time of peace, to every vessel of commerce or of war, without distinction of flag." Egypt also violated, said Israel, a 1951 UN Security Council resolution which "ordered" Egypt to terminate the restrictions on the passage of international commercial shipping and goods through the Suez Canal wherever bound, and to cease all interference with such shipping.[62] Thirdly, Israel argued that by barring Israeli shipping Egypt also violated article II of the 1949 Israeli-Egyptian Armistice Agreement, which prohibited "any warlike or hostile act by either party." Finally, Israel asserted that Egypt had blockaded the canal and had therefore violated another part of the first article of the 1888 treaty, which said that "the Canal shall never be subject to the exercise of the right of blockade."

Egypt took issue with Israel's charge that she had violated the 1888 treaty, arguing that although the treaty guaranteed freedom of navigation to all nations, it also authorized Egypt to take measures "to assure . . . the defense of Egypt and the maintenance of public order." [63] Since the Suez Canal is an integral part of Egypt as recognized by articles 9, 10, and 13 of the 1888 treaty, article 8 of the 1936 Anglo-Egyptian Treaty of Alliance, and article 8 of the 1954 Anglo-Egyptian treaty, Egypt has the right to bar Israeli shipping as a defense measure against her enemy.

Clearly, in considering the legal arguments of Israel and Egypt we must conclude that the 1888 treaty has conflicting provisions. It requires (under article 1) freedom of passage in time of war and peace, permits Egypt (under article 10) to take measures for the country's security, and proceeds (under article 11) to deny Egypt measures that would interfere with "the free use of the Canal." The conflict between articles 1 and 10 should baffle the most reputable specialists in international law. Frederick L. Schuman, who is sympathetic to Israel's point of view, admits that "even the most subtle of lawyers would have difficulty reconciling" the two articles in question.[64] Consequently, Israel could not derive rights from an inconsistent, or at least ambiguous, treaty. On the other hand, Egypt's sovereignty over the canal is recognized by instruments other than the 1888 treaty (articles 9, 10, and 11, of the 1866 document, for instance). Therefore Egypt can, if she chooses, bar a state which she considers to be her enemy from shipping through the canal.

In this connection Egypt has another argument. In both World War I and World War II, Britain, then occupying Egypt, barred German ships from passing through the canal. Now that Egypt is independent and no longer dominated by Britain, Egypt's interference with her enemy's shipping may be objectionable to the Western world and especially to Britain, but it is certainly not inconsistent with the precedent established by Britain herself.

As to the Israeli argument that a state of war did not exist between the two countries and that, therefore, Egypt violated the armistice agreement by barring Israeli shipping, Egypt replied that the armistice agreement is not a peace treaty and that a state of war between the two countries did exist.

And here again Egypt seems to be on firm legal grounds. Because war is the outcome of disagreement, the absence of subsequent agreement on the issues that caused the conflict originally indicates that war continued to characterize their relations. Moreover, since 1948 the two countries have been involved in reprisals and counter reprisals so often that it is wishful thinking to suggest that they were at peace with each other at any point during this time. Yet it is understandable that Israel and Egypt would argue the opposites on this question. For Israel, peace would allow her to retain her gains from the 1948 war. For Egypt, the assertion of a state of war is an important way of indicating her unwillingness to recognize as permanent the Arab losses in the 1948 war.

Whatever the merits of the different legal arguments, international shipping through the canal was not negatively affected by the nationalization of the canal. In fact, in the period following the invasion and before the 1967 Arab-Israeli war that resulted in the closing of the canal, Egypt ran the canal more efficiently than the defunct Suez Canal Company had done.[65] More ships and more cargo went through the waterway per day than when the canal was run by the Company. And Egypt was planning to widen the canal to allow still more traffic.

In conclusion, the Suez invasion was a wasteful effort for the invaders, because it did not achieve its objectives. And it was an unnecessary adventure as well: Egypt's control of the canal improved upon the canal's previous situation and made clear the fact that international control was not indispensable for the efficient management of the canal.

Chapter 7

The 1967 War
and the Ultimate Chances of Peace

We have already discussed, in connection with the 1948 war, the differences in perspective between the Arabs and Israel. After 1956 the Arabs continued to see the conflict in terms of the pre-1948 issues. To them, the right of Israel to exist as a state and the repossession of their lands by exiled Palestinian Arabs were still undecided questions in an undecided war. The Israelis, on the other hand, looked upon such Arab concerns as dead issues. They saw as fixed and final the existence of the State of Israel and the dispossession of the Palestinian Arabs. To the Israelis, both issues had been settled in 1948; and that war was over.

This fundamental difference in outlook affected the behavior of both parties in the years between 1956 and 1967. The Arabs resorted to occasional border attacks to keep alive their pre-1948 claims. The Israelis denounced these attacks as illegal aggression during peacetime. (To them the Arab attacks were a "new" war.) They resorted to massive reprisals to "discourage" the Arabs.

Meanwhile, the countries of the Western world were more inclined to sympathize with Israel's position. Perhaps they, as third parties, found it easier to forget the "old facts" of the pre-1948 situation—which were advocated, after all, by the losing party.

These attitudes are certainly among the root causes of the 1967 war, but there are other attitudes which we must understand before discussing the war's immediate causes.

The Years Between the Wars. Two very important factors in the Arab-Israeli dilemma are the Arabs' feeling of injustice and Israel's feeling of being trapped. These two factors were major causes in the Arab-Israeli war of 1967. We have earlier explained the Arab view that the establishment of Israel had resulted in a major injustice to the Palestinian Arabs. The fact that a large number of these Palestinians had lived in refugee camps since 1948 was a reminder to all Arabs that the injustice has not been redressed.

Israel's consistent and persistent refusal to obey UN resolutions on repatriation meant that Israel did not *recognize* the right of the Palestinian Arabs to return to their homes in what was Palestine and is now Israel. Consequently, the Arabs refused to *recognize* the State of Israel. Because Israel is surrounded, except for her western borders, by Arab territory, Arab nonrecognition of Israel contributed to Israel's feeling of being trapped.

This feeling became a factor in the deteriorating condition of Arab-Israel relations. And it grew until it developed into an Israeli phobia that caused the Zionist state to overreact whenever the Arabs did something to register their feeling of injustice. Israel's overreaction to occasional Arab raids was in part a manifestation of her feeling of being trapped. In spite of the fact that the Arabs were militarily no match for her, Israel tended to exaggerate Arab capabilities and intentions: she treated them as if they were militarily strong. But there were other manifestations of Israel's feeling of being trapped. In 1956, Israel attempted to open the Suez Canal by force, and in 1967, when Nasser closed the Gulf of Aqaba, she went to war to open it. In both cases, Israel reacted like a person with claustrophobia: she could not stand being confined.

Even before the Suez and the Aqaba incidents, Israel had refused to respect the sanctity of the demilitarized zones and no-man's-lands. The territories in question were intended to provide buffer zones between the belligerents. In 1948 the UN rejected Israel's claim that the demilitarized zones were part of her sovereign territory.[1] In 1953 the United States suspended economic aid to Israel and insisted that Israel obey the orders of the chairman of the Mixed Armistice Commission to stop work on a canal project in the demilitarized zone between her and Syria.[2] Violations also took place in the no-man's-land in the Jerusalem area. In 1953, Israel drove out the Arabs of the al-Auja demilitarized zone separating Egyptian and Israeli territories and established a kibbutz. In 1954 the Mixed Armistice Commission ruled that the kibbutz "was organized as a unit of the Israeli armed forces" and therefore violated the armistice agreement.[3] By 1955 the zone was under the complete control of Israel. All these incidents are further manifestations of Israel's feeling of being trapped, a feeling that caused her to violate UN orders and international law.

And in defying the United Nations, Israel had on occasions resorted to force to enforce her illegal policies. On the other hand, the Arabs have often manifested their desire to submit Arab-Israeli issues to adjudication procedures. In 1947, they urged members of the UN to let the World Court give an opinion on the question of UN competence to "enforce or recommend the enforcement of . . . any plan of partition." Their proposal lost by one vote.[4] In 1957, Egypt accepted the compulsory jurisdiction of the World Court and expressed willingness to submit the Suez Canal issue to the Court. And earlier she had declared her willingness to let the international court decide the issue relating to the Gulf of Aqaba.[5] In all these situations, Israel showed no interest in involving the World Court. An opinion from the World Court on each of these critical issues would have ended all legal arguments and might have contributed greatly to the deescalation of the Arab-Israeli conflict.

In fact, Israel's attitude toward the UN, the organization that helped "create" the State of Israel, has been poor. The implication of this attitude is clear: it has left unrestrained the deteriorating condition of Arab-Israeli relations. In 1956,

Israel refused to allow the UN Emergency Force to be stationed on her side of the Egyptian-Israeli border. Egypt accepted. On May 18, 1967, when UN Secretary-General U Thant complied with Nasser's request that he withdraw the UN Emergency Force from Egyptian territory on the grounds that denial of the request would violate Egyptian sovereignty, Israel criticized the Secretary-General for yielding to Nasser's demands. In fact, after the withdrawal of UNEF from the Egyptian side of the border, U Thant asked Israel to allow the same force to move to her side; but Israel refused.[6] Thus, while one might view Nasser's request to withdraw the UN force to be unwise and foolish, we should also consider Israel's refusal to station the same force on her territory to be equally foolish and unwise. Had Israel cooperated with the Secretary-General on this matter it is possible that the June war would have been averted.

Increased Border Clashes and Arab Fear of Israeli Attack. In the six months preceding the June, 1967, war, border incidents increased sharply. Lebanon, Jordan, and Egypt attempted to curb these incidents, but unsuccessfully. As leader of the Arab world, Egypt was forced to follow a dual policy: while attempting to curb the incidents, she publicly approved them. Nasser's image as an Arab hero required him to give moral support to the Palestinian cause, although as head of state he knew Egypt was weaker than Israel, and should not encourage a confrontation. However, at times he could not control the situation, especially when events threatened his leadership role and hero image.

The increase in border incidents was largely the product of Syria's challenge to Nasser's leadership of the Arab world. Syria was under the control of the Baath party, which believed in the unification of the Arab states. After 1961, when the union between Syria and Egypt was disrupted, the Baath party leaders argued that they, not Nasser, were the true Arab nationalists. In 1967 they began an anti-Nasser campaign, accusing him of being "soft" on Israel. They went so far as to imply that Nasser was "playing a game" with the Palestinian issue and that he had never been serious about regaining Arab rights in Palestine. In the period preceding the war, Syria was the only Arab country that materially supported Arab "commando" incursions into Israel. In fact, the Syrian armed forces were themselves involved in the border incidents with Israel. The extent and activism of their involvement was designed—by the Syrians—to support their argument that Nasser was "soft."

The climax of this Syrian-Egyptian rivalry was reached on May 8, 1967, when Syria informed Nasser that Israel was planning an all-out war against her (Syria). This was the test case for Syria's claim that Nasser was "soft" on Israel. Should Nasser ignore the information about an impending Israeli attack on Syria, his reputation as the trusted leader of Arab nationalism would suffer and the Baath party might win the political battle against him. But for Nasser to act on this important information he needed more evidence that it was serious and correct. Even if he were to act in support of Syria, his action should be limited to a show of force short of open confrontation with Israel. After all, he was quite aware of Israel's military superiority and the danger that would come to Egypt from an open confrontation with her enemy. (Nasser's awareness of Israel's military superiority and his intention to avoid a confrontation with her were confirmed in the reports of Charles Yost, James Reston, and UN Secretary-General U Thant.)[7]

From an Egyptian point of view, the evidence was strong. It was provided in part by the Soviet Union, which warned Egypt that Israel was planning a swift blow at Syria to be delivered at the end of May, 1967.

Israeli statements and behavior also gave credence to Syria's claim of an impending attack. Israeli leaders publicly threatened an all-out war if Syria did not stop border incidents. By May 12, there were indications that Israel had reached the decision that force "may be the only way to curtail increasing terrorism" on the Syrian front.[8] And on May 14, Prime Minister Levi Eshkol said Israel would "choose when, where, and how to reply to the attacker." [9]

Then, a few days before the war, Eshkol reshuffled his cabinet to include Moshe Dayan as minister of defense. Dayan had been the hero of the Suez war of 1956 and he was known to be tough and uncompromising; and the Arabs interpreted the event to mean that Israel was expecting, or preparing, a new war.

There was another factor making credible the possibility of Israeli attack. The Arabs knew that the Israelis were aware of their weaknesses. Through her efficient intelligence Israel knew that she could win the war. Israel had little doubt that she would be able to obtain new territories, open the Suez Canal and the Gulf of Aqaba, and, more important, bring down both Nasser in Egypt and the Baath regime in Syria.

In sum, the Arabs interpreted the events preceding the war in the following manner: Israel planned to attack Syria and force her to take precautionary measures (such as seeking the help of the other Arab countries and mobilizing her armed forces). Then Israel would cry out that the Arabs were planning an attack against her as "evidenced" by these Arab activities and use this as a pretext to wage war against the Arabs.

Economic and Other Domestic Causes. Another cause contributing to the June, 1967, war was the fact that the countries involved had domestic problems—problems that forced national leaders to be more aggressive on external issues. In a sense both Eshkol and Nasser were the prisoners of circumstances. Neither wished to fight, but both were influenced by events beyond their control.

Before the war both countries were experiencing serious economic and political problems. In Egypt there was inflation, unemployment, bureaucratic inefficiency, and dissatisfaction by certain social groups with the military regime. Nasser's socialist program had run into serious difficulties, and there were people who complained and urged reform. Although Nasser himself was honest and serious, many of the military officers in charge of the socialist program were not. These officers were involved in nepotism and they used their positions for personal gain and to increase their political and social influence. In 1967 many Egyptians, especially the educated, complained that corrupt practices in the bureaucracy were similar to the old practices of the Farouk regime. Consequently, the domestic situation, along with the problem involving Syria's bid for Arab leadership, forced Nasser to seek a dramatic way to save his hero image. Since domestic reforms were usually slow in yielding results, the Arab-Israeli issue seemed just the issue he needed to relieve himself from domestic pressures. Nasser might have hoped to win this issue in the same way he won the Suez Canal issue eleven years earlier.

In Israel the unemployment rate was at its highest level since 1948. People were complaining of high taxes and there was a general feeling that Eshkol was not a strong leader. Furthermore, the rate of Jewish immigration to Israel was declining and a large number of Israelis were leaving the country to find better economic opportunities elsewhere. For a state whose Zionist raison d'être was to be the home of all Jews, these latter developments were very disturbing.

There was also a struggle for power going on just before the war, and Israel's decision to transform the border clashes into a full-scale war was directly related to that struggle. Since Ben-Gurion's retirement in 1963, Eshkol had been trying unsuccessfully to fill the old man's shoes. Ben-Gurion was unique. His image as the father of his country enabled him to employ authoritarian political methods without much opposition. In 1965, Ben-Gurion came out of retirement to oppose Eshkol in the parliamentary election. Although he failed to wrest the leadership from Eshkol, he nevertheless continued to attack him. Israel's economic problems seemed to indicate that Ben-Gurion's charge that Eshkol was not a strong leader might be valid. Moshe Dayan, who in the 1965 elections had joined the Ben-Gurion opposition, manipulated the events preceding the war. He charged that Eshkol was not capable to respond to Arab "threats" and that the prime minister was risking Israel's security. Consequently, Eshkol felt he had to do something to prove that he was in charge and that his domestic political enemies were wrong in accusing him of being "soft" on the Arabs. At any rate, the domestic situation of Israel was an important element in the background of the causes that precipitated the June war.

The Closing of the Gulf of Aqaba. As mentioned earlier, Nasser felt compelled to do something about domestic pressures and Syria's challenge to his leadership of the Arab world. At the same time, Nasser did not want a direct confrontation with Israel. What he needed was a dramatic issue that he could exploit politically and win without risking a military defeat. In other words, he wanted a repetition of his Suez Canal victory minus, perhaps, the unhappy military activity that went with that victory.

The Gulf of Aqaba was such an issue. If Nasser could close it to Israeli shipping and get away with it, he would have won a victory similar to that of the Suez Canal. However, he wrongly assumed that the issue could be confined to political fighting with Israel and that no military activity would follow. As it happened, the issue relating to the closing of the Gulf enabled Israel to transform the issue of border clashes to an all-out war that had greater local and international implications than anyone could imagine at the time.

Did Egypt have the legal right to close the Gulf of Aqaba to Israeli shipping? As in the Suez problem, both Egypt and Israel advanced legal arguments to support their positions on the Gulf controversy. Of course, Israel argued that Egyptian "blockade" of the Gulf was contrary to international law, which considers the Gulf international.

According to Israel's interpretation, the Gulf is to be considered international for several reasons: (1) Geography requires it, since the Gulf is bound by the territories of four sovereign states: Saudi Arabia, Jordan, Israel, and Egypt.[10] (2) The Gulf is connected through the Straits of Tiran to an international waterway, the Red Sea.[11] (3) Many sovereign states, including the United States, recognized it as international. (4) It was so confirmed by Article 15 of the 1958 Geneva Convention on the Territorial Sea and the Contiguous Zone.

Egypt's argument for her right to close the Gulf to Israeli shipping consists of the following elements: (1) Israel occupied the port of Eilat on the Gulf after she signed the 1949 armistice agreement with Egypt and, accordingly, her geographic position in the Gulf was illegal and in violation of many UN resolutions relating directly or indirectly to it. (2) The international law which Israel relies on refers to the rights of states "in time of peace" and requires that passage be "innocent." Since a technical state of war existed between Egypt and Israel, because they had not signed a peace treaty, Israel is not entitled to rights under that law. (3) The Gulf is a *mare clausum* ("closed sea"), "subject to absolute Arab sovereignty" because "the only navigable entrance, which, itself, is within Arab territory, does not exceed 500 metres." [12] (4) Egypt did not sign, and therefore is not bound by, the 1958 Geneva Convention, which Israel cites in her argument. Also, the convention, even if accepted, applies only "in time of peace."

THE PROBLEMS OF PEACE

The 1967 war resulted in an astounding victory for Israel and a humiliating defeat for the Arabs. Israel occupied Arab territories almost three times her size, including the remaining part of Palestine (the West Bank and the Gaza Strip), the Syrian Golan Heights, and the Egyptian Sinai Peninsula.

The war also resulted in more refugees. Some were Syrians

(about 100,000) and Egyptians (about 50,000); but they were mostly Palestinian Arabs.

If we consider the total number of Palestinian refugees from the 1948 and 1967 wars, the 1970 figures would indicate there were 1,425,219 such refugees.[13] All of them live on subsidies from the United Nations, which amounts to about $30 per refugee per year.[14]

The war cost Israel 679 dead and 2,563 wounded. It cost the Arabs 20,000 dead and an unknown number of wounded— in addition to heavy losses in arms and weapons, which had been provided mostly by the Soviet Union. For all its cost the war solved nothing, and added to the already complex conflict. The belligerents remained as far apart as ever. In this section we will attempt an analysis of the main difficulties of resolving the conflict between Israel and the Arabs, with the hope that a better understanding of these problems may strengthen future efforts for a peaceful settlement of the conflict.

A Multiplicity of Parties. "Too many cooks spoil the broth," states a familiar proverb. In the Arab-Israeli controversy, the broth of peace is being stirred by ten cooks: Israel, seven Arab countries, the United States, and the Soviet Union. Occasionally assistant cooks are also involved, including Arab countries such as Tunisia and non-Middle Eastern countries such as Britain, France, and Yugoslavia.

The problem of peace is further complicated by the fact that the cooks are not sure of their recipes. They do not have a unified approach to peace and are uncertain about their aims. In Israel both the government and the people are divided over what to do about the state's territorial gains. Some Israelis want to expand Israel's territory even further, perhaps into eastern Jordan and southern Lebanon, to include Biblical Jewish territories and to establish a more viable economic base for the state; others want to return the oc- cupied territories, except Jerusalem, to the Arabs; still others would retain the Syrian Golan Heights and Jerusalem while returning the remaining occupied territories.

The Arab side is also divided. Egypt and Syria want all the occupied territories back. Jordan is willing to recognize the State of Israel and to allow "minor" adjustments in the pre-June, 1967, boundaries. She might also accept a new regime for Jerusalem, one that will not leave the holy city entirely in the hands of the Israelis. But the situation in Jordan is complicated by the fact that the majority of her population are Palestinians, most of whom oppose their government's position. For them, the most important issue is whether they will be able to return to their homes in Israel, possibly under a state that is neither Arab nor Jewish but "Palestinian."

The 1967 war also reintroduced the Palestinian Arabs as an active party in the conflict. The Arab-Israeli conflict began with the Palestinians as a main party and later developed to exclude them entirely even as an interested party. Thus one of the ironies of the Arab-Israeli controversy is that the people who lost most in the conflict are not represented in the peace discussions. This is partly the result of Israel's policies of ignoring the primary issues of the controversy and of obscuring the role of the Palestinian Arabs by emphasizing the role of the outside Arab states. In the latter policy the Israelis were helped by the Arab states' adoption of the Palestinian Arabs' cause as their own. Thus they tended to replace the Palestinian Arabs in the minds of others. Of course, the Palestinian Arabs contributed to their own situation. Instead of speaking and acting on their own behalf between 1948 and 1967, they relied on the Arab states to secure their rights and safeguard their interests.

In fact, the Palestinian Arabs voluntarily surrendered to the Arab states their rightful responsibility and role in the conflict. It was the failure of the Palestinian Arabs in the 1948 civil war that brought the Arab armies into the battle with Israel. The failure of the Arab armies in the 1948 Arab-Israeli war

caused the Palestinians to believe that their rights could not
be secured except by modernized and enlarged regular Arab
armies. And after 1948 they practically sat waiting for the
Arab armies to enlarge and modernize. Nor did the 1956 Suez
war change their outlook. Egypt's military failure was explained to them in terms of the overwhelming forces of imperialism and the great military superiority of the invaders.

But the 1967 war drastically changed the Palestinian outlook on the military situation. The astounding victory of Israel
and the astonishing "easy" defeat of the Arab armies made it
clear that even with Soviet assistance the Arab armies could
not challenge Israel. This realization called for a change in
strategy by the Palestinian Arabs, indeed it required a change
in their whole outlook toward Israel.

The Palestinian Arabs concluded that their relinquishment
of responsibility for their fate had been a tragic mistake. Since
they were the reason for, as well as the victim of, the conflict,
they should have remained in the front lines of the confrontation.

They also concluded that guerrilla warfare would be more
effective against Israel than the open warfare attempted so
far. This conclusion was at least partly the result of the
Palestinian Arabs' new awareness of their own and the Arab
states' "backwardness." Israel was so technologically advanced,
they decided, that it would be almost impossible for the Arab
armies to win a modern war against her. Guerrilla warfare was
more attuned to the circumstances of a less-developed people,
and although its goal could not be the occupation of Israel—a
goal associated with regular army operations—guerrilla tactics
could weaken the social-economic structure of the enemy state
to the point of vulnerability.

Thus only after 1967 did the Palestinian guerrillas become
active. As a result of their conspicuous presence on Israel's
borders, the possibility of including them in the peace efforts
was discussed, especially in the Western world. Ironically,
very few people had considered the Palestinian Arabs for

consultation on peace when these Palestinians were quiet and relatively peaceful, despite the fact that the Arab-Israeli conflict primarily related to their own destiny. When the Palestinians took up arms and showed determination, a willingness at least to consider their inclusion in the peace talks was demonstrated in official and nonofficial Western reports. Can the world recognize right without might? This is the age-old question that the Palestinian experience posed. The question was manifested in another way when in 1970 the Palestinian guerrillas were quieted by King Hussein's Bedouin troops and the possibility of their inclusion in the peace talks diminished as a result.

Divisions over the approach to peace characterized the Palestinians just as they do the other parties in the Arab-Israeli conflict. Some want a Palestinian state to replace the Zionist state and to include Jews and Arabs. Others think this solution is impossible because Israel would not accept it, and these prefer a Palestinian Arab state to be established outside the 1948 boundaries of Israel. Still others would like to remain as part of the state of Jordan.

Perhaps the most revealing element in the positions of the different Arab parties is that the most radical policies are pursued by Iraq, Algeria, and Libya, states that have no borders with Israel. These seemingly hypocritical states are the least affected by the conflict. Their radicalism is the outcome of the physical distance from Israel, which enables them to see the conflict in moralistic terms to a greater extent than do the other Arab states. The contiguity of the latter with the enemy has inserted a degree of pragmatism into their approach to peace.

But radicalism has also characterized the policies of one Arab state that borders on Israel. Until recently, Syria was probably the most difficult Arab state on the question of settlement. Her attitude was the product of historical circumstances. Before World War I, Palestine was generally considered part of Syria, at least geographically and historically, if not politically. The Syrians never forgot their loss of Palestine resulting from the highly controversial policies of the European powers and the Zionists. Although early in 1971, Syria became less radical (she supported the Egyptian position), this new attitude is probably not permanent. More likely it reflects a phase in the process of changes in the power structure.

Nor are the policies of the Soviet Union and the United States toward the question of war and peace in the Middle East clear. Although there is strong evidence that the two superpowers are not interested in a military confrontation over the Middle East, they still disagree on the solution to the Arab-Israeli conflict. The Soviet Union is limited by its investments in the military organizations of many Arab countries, and the United States is limited by Zionist-Jewish pressure and electoral politics within her own borders. Although their identification with one side or the other in the Middle East has not been complete, these two powers support their clients in a very substantial way. Accordingly, their peace efforts are limited by the complexities of the policies of their clients and by their own indirect involvement.

The Military Gap. Peace between belligerents is obtainable in several ways. One, of course, is for one side to overcome the other, after which peace terms are dictated by the victorious party. In the Arab-Israeli confrontation, however, Israeli victories did not result in complete Israeli control of the Arabs. For this to happen, Israel would have to occupy all Arab territory, an impossibility, since even if Israel has the power to achieve occupation initially, she does not have the population to manage such an occupation. She would overextend herself, and at least make herself vulnerable to guerrilla warfare in the cities. Consequently, the possibility of peace through the total defeat of the Arabs does not exist.

For the Arabs to impose peace terms on Israel they must meet a different test. Although the Arabs do not have the population and logistical problems of the Israelis, they also lack the necessary technology. Nor will they have such a technology for some time. Therefore, peace through Arab defeat of Israel is also impossible (at least in the foreseeable future).

Another opportunity for achieving peace occurs when each of the belligerent parties has a real interest in a negotiated compromise. This opportunity only arises, however, when the relative military strengths of the opposing parties is nearly equal: where there is no "military gap." In the Arab-Israeli conflict a very large gap exists between the military strengths of Israel and the Arabs. Consequently, negotiations can only favor Israel, who is militarily much superior and therefore has a much better bargaining position. For many years the Arabs recognized this dilemma and, therefore, refused to negotiate with Israel. They believed that since they had not been completely defeated, they should wait to improve their bargaining position. Although their policy was unpopular outside the Middle East, it was nevertheless justifiable from the point of view of the weaker (but not totally defeated) side.

Although before 1967 Israel talked a lot about peace, her talk was mostly propaganda and the Arab refusal to negotiate with her made this propaganda very effective. However, after 1967 it became clear that Israel was no longer enthusiastic about a settlement. She refused total withdrawal from Arab territories in return for a peace treaty and Arab recognition of her existence as a state. The reason has already been mentioned: the party with a superior military force will refuse to offer acceptable terms to the weaker party. In other words, Israel did not want peace badly enough to offer acceptable terms to the Arabs.

The problem of the military gap is probably the strongest obstacle to the peaceful settlement of the Arab-Israeli conflict. The problem is aggravated by the erroneous assumption by the United States that a balance of power exists in the Middle East. By giving Israel more weapons, the United States had widened the military gap. Soviet military aid to the Arabs has not significantly affected the military gap. The reason is that Soviet aid for the Arabs had very little qualitative effect on Arab strength. (The Arabs simply need time to be able to use Soviet weapons, while the Israelis can put American weapons into effective use very quickly.)

Ironically, the Palestinian guerrillas could increase the chances of peace in the Middle East. They could do this by offsetting Israel's military superiority and thus introducing a certain parity between the parties at the bargaining table. Their contribution would be largely psychological, of course; but it could be potent. The guerrillas have the ability to make life miserable in Israel, and thus to lower national morale— perhaps enough to induce greater concessions than could otherwise be expected, in view of Israel's military superiority. At the same time the guerrilla activity would raise Arab self-confidence and belief in the effectiveness of negotiation.

It is doubtful if the Palestinian guerrillas alone can cause the Israeli state to disappear. Certainly, only in the long run could they actually threaten to do so—by weakening Israel economically and psychologically and by affecting immigration.

In the short run, however, they can force Israel to choose between a safer and happier life and a more dangerous and less happy one. In exerting this pressure, they are actually contributing to peace in two ways: by forcing Israel to make concessions acceptable to the Arabs, and by making the idea of negotiation, at least at a certain point of development, worthy of consideration by both parties.

Big-Power Involvement. As mentioned earlier, the Soviet Union and the United States are not fully identified with the Middle Eastern belligerents. But they support the two opponents in a significant way, and they have contributed to the war's continuation.

The superpowers agree on two things: that Israel should not be conquered, and that they themselves should not fight each other directly. Aside from agreement on these two points, however, the two countries are involved in a dangerous competition for influence in the Middle East. So far, the winner has been the Soviet Union; and today a portion of the Arab world is under Soviet influence.

Ironically, the United States lost influence in the Arab states primarily because of the State of Israel. True, from the 1948 war until about 1954 the Soviet Union supported Israel even more than did the United States. However, she had practically no influence in the Arab world to lose as a result of her support. But when she discovered the opportunity to establish such influence by taking the Arab side, she did so. From then on a general pattern was established. The stronger the Soviet influence with the Arabs became, the greater became American identification with Israel. In time, the positions of the two superpowers became more and more polarized. This polarization is dangerous because just as Nasser and Eshkol were drawn into waging a war in 1967 in spite of their reluctance to do so, the United States and the Soviet Union could also find themselves drawn willy-nilly into a direct confrontation.

To safeguard her security, Israel has encouraged this polarization regionally and internationally. In the Middle East she maintained military superiority as the first and best means of security. However, her overreaction to border incidents helped to polarize the regional situation. In addition, Israel used her excellent propaganda machinery in the Western world to identify the Arabs with Communism and to present the Arab-Israeli conflict as a struggle between democracy and Communism. In this she had some success. During electoral campaigns, American politicians, including President Nixon, spoke of Israeli democracy and the Arab pro-Soviet (pro-Communist) stance, and strong U.S. support for Israel has come from the South, because of the region's anti-Communism.

The polarization of superpower relations in the Middle East will continue and might cause World War III if the Arab-

Israeli conflict is not resolved. The two superpowers should realize that whatever may be the outcome of the Arab-Israeli wars (e.g., Israeli occupation of Cairo, Damascus, and Amman on the one hand, or Arab conquest of Israel and the disappearance of the Zionist state on the other), the world and mankind would be less unhappy with such an event than if World War III were to break out.

If the superpowers could keep this greater danger in mind, they might be able to overcome the polarization in their attitudes and act in favor of a settlement. Surprisingly, their interests are more reconcilable than the interests of the belligerents. The Middle East problem is important for the superpowers, but it does not present them with issues of national territory and national rights as it does to Israel and the Arabs. Both superpowers got along without the Middle East for centuries and they can survive without it. The Middle East is simply not worth a world war.

A compromise solution by the two superpowers is possible. Even should they entertain the thought of military intervention, such intervention should be preceded by an agreement on a solution. Otherwise, intervention is equivalent to World War III.

The danger of World War III comes more from the United States than from the Soviet Union. For one thing, being a pluralistic democracy, the United States is more susceptible to Zionist-Jewish pressure than is the totalitarian Soviet state. The United States might succumb to such pressure and make the grave mistake of confronting the Soviet Union in a war neither side wants. Furthermore, there is ample precedent to indicate that Soviet leaders try harder to stay out of wars than does the United States. In 1939, Stalin signed a pact with Hitler to stay out of World War II, although he was later forced to participate. And during the Korean war and the Indochina war the Soviet Union stayed short of direct involvement. Also, it appears that the Soviet Union is a better loser than the United States. In 1967, the Soviets stayed out of the

Middle East war even though their loss in prestige and money was great. On the other hand, the United States found it difficult to pull out of Indochina and admit her tragic mistake. In case of another Arab-Israeli war, will the United States find it difficult not to intervene when Israel is losing? Also, will the Soviet Union manage not to intervene for a second time?

Intervention by the superpowers even with agreement on a solution is certainly not the best way of handling the Middle Eastern situation. There are enormous difficulties, since any big-power solution will satisfy none of the belligerents. Rather, such a solution will naturally reflect the interests of the United States and the Soviet state more than those of the Arabs or the Israelis. Consequently, it requires the cooperation of the two powers, not only in bringing it about but in maintaining it afterward. Could the United States and the Soviet Union cooperate long enough to do this? Or would they become belligerents themselves as soon as their troops entered the Middle East?

The advantage of joint intervention by the superpowers is temporary peace. However, sooner or later the superpowers will be at each other's throats and the threat of World War III will arise again. This is why it is better to let Israel and the Arabs alone. Eventually their problems will be solved, either through local wars or through some kind of accommodation.

Psychological Obstacles to Peace. Both the Zionists and the extreme Arab nationalists are highly suspicious and distrustful —not only of each other but of any possible third-party mediations.

Past mistreatment of Jews and their persecution in many countries has given contemporary Jewish nationalists (the Zionists) an exaggerated fear that, given the opportunity, non-Jews will always persecute the Jews. A Zionist trusts no one but his kind. Israel's excessive distrust of the United Nations and big-power solutions is a case in point. Even where the

United Nations and big powers might have helped the Israeli cause, Israel has taken a completely negative attitude toward them. In 1967, for instance, if Israel had agreed to the stationing of UN forces on her side of the Egyptian-Israeli border, the war could possibly have been averted.

The fears of the extreme Arab nationalists were caused by the Western colonialism and imperialism of the twentieth century. Arab extremists tend to blame the Western world for all the ills of the Arab world. An aversion to things foreign has developed in the political culture of these extremists. Although most Arab nationalists are not extremists, the few who are create so much fuss in Arab politics that they are often conspicuous.

There is no denying that both the Jews and the Arabs have endured a great deal of pain and unhappiness. The histories of the two peoples provide the evidence very clearly. Nor can we deny that at present discrimination against the Jews exists and imperialistic interference in Arab affairs persists. But the Zionists and Arab extremists have allowed their fears and suspicions, however correctly based on history, to distort their picture of current reality. And this has helped disrupt peace efforts.

The Zionist lumps the Arabs with all other non-Jews—as potential religious and racial persecutors. This he does despite the fact that the Arabs and the Jews historically got along well together. This view adds an "anti-Semitic" dimension to the conflict, and anti-Semitism is not negotiable, whereas the wars and territorial conflicts might be. On the other hand, the Arab extremists have lumped the Israelis into the general category of "foreigner," an inflammatory concept that does not recognize the fact that many Jews are not foreign. A number have family histories going back hundreds of years in Palestine. And even among more recent immigrants, their sons and daughters have been born in Israel, so that the native Israelis will soon be a majority. Moderate Arabs, including the leadership of the Palestinian guerrillas, have reconciled

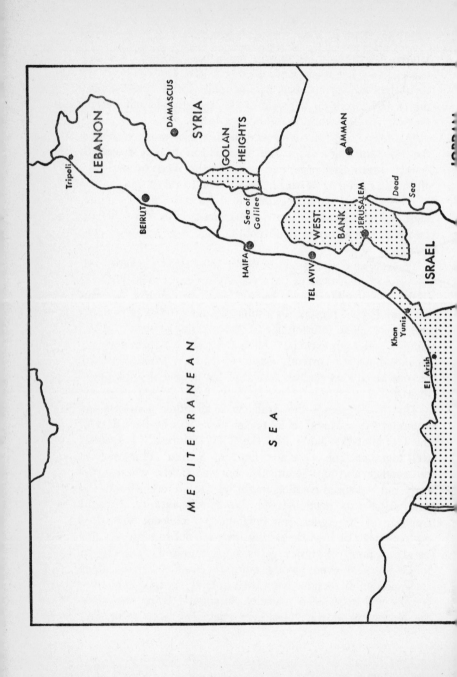

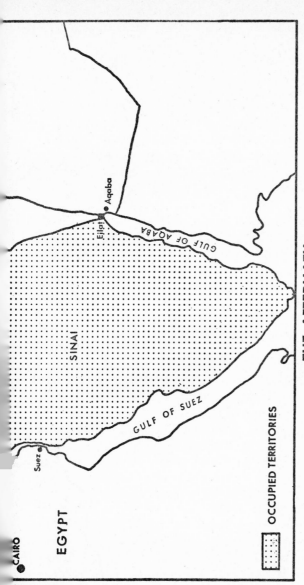

THE AFTERMATH
OF THE 1967 ARAB–ISRAELI WAR

OCCUPIED TERRITORIES

themselves to the fact that Israelis born in Israel have birth rights, but the extremists continue to see all as foreign invaders.

Another psychological factor has been historical: European prohibitions against Jewish ownership of land. This has created a psychological need among Jews, an important factor in their effort to establish a Jewish state. And it was also a factor in Israel's procrastination and reluctance to return Arab lands conquered in the 1967 war. (Not only did this psychological need create Jewish desire for territory, it affected the Israelis' handling of agriculture as well. They did an excellent job in an occupation, i.e., farming, which they knew very little about.)

To the Zionist, land and Jewish nationhood go together. (In this sense, land meant national territory.) Consequently, the Zionists will accept no peaceful settlement of the conflict that does not recognize the Jewish character of the State of Israel. How one reconciles the right of the Palestinian Arabs to return to their homes and this Zionist desire is a problem of the first magnitude. Israel clearly will not accept the repatriation of the Palestinian Arabs, because this would eventually undermine the state's Jewishness. And the Palestinian Arabs, who see their dilemma mainly in moral terms, will insist on returning. They will resist an arrangement that would permit the repatriation of a percentage of them. For them a moral right cannot be divided or compromised.

The struggle is also influenced by the Jewish psychological fear of loss of identity, partly through assimilation—a fear that has not affected the Arabs. Consequently, the Zionist considers the existence of Israel to be the stamp of Jewish identity; the survival of Jews depends on the survival of Israel as a state. This is why many Israelis consider the Arab-Israeli conflict as one that involves their very survival. Even when they win a war with the Arabs they emerge fearful, complaining that they are being threatened by those whom they have just defeated. It is doubtful if there is in modern history another example in which the winner feels threatened by the loser.[15]

THE PALESTINIAN GUERRILLAS

Although Palestinian guerrillas operated against Israel before the 1967 war, they did not become a movement until after that major event. They were largely the product of the psychological vacuum created by the almost total disintegration of Arab armed forces. The war shattered Arab morale to the point where people felt helpless and saw the future to be hopeless. The political situation in Jordan was so desperate that a small group of dedicated Palestinians were able in a short time to organize a relatively large group of unsophisticated guerrillas and to give them limited military training and political education.

The Karameh battle of March, 1968, the first major confrontation between the guerrillas and the Israeli army, was a landmark in the short history of the Palestinian resistance movement. In that battle the guerrillas fought house-to-house, causing heavy casualties among Israeli troops, who had difficulties drawing back into Israel. The result was almost incredible: for the first time since the 1948 war the Israelis met a determined group of Arab fighters, and were forced to fight every inch of the way. The battle demonstrated that Palestinians could fight Israelis better than other Arabs for the obvious reason that the Palestinians had stronger motivation to fight Israelis than other Arabs had. They had a greater stake in the battle for Palestine.

Karameh strengthened the guerrilla movement. In the aftermath of the battle the Arab masses looked to the guerrillas for leadership and guidance, financial contributions poured in from Arab governments and from private sources, and the guerrilla leadership had to cope with the sudden need for rapid growth.

The Jordanian Experience. By 1970 the Palestinian guerrillas had become a formidable political force in Jordan, indeed a state within a state. King Hussein saw them as a serious threat to his regime. In spite of assurances by the leadership of al-Fatah, the largest guerrilla group, that the movement had no intention of capturing power in Jordan, the king continued to see them as rivals in a power struggle, rivals who would ultimately replace his government and run him out of the country. And so in September, 1970, he made up his mind to have a showdown with the guerrillas.

The leadership of the guerrillas claimed that the American CIA and Israeli intelligence conspired with Hussein to bring about the downfall of the Palestinian resistance movement. A member of the Jordanian cabinet that preceded the debacle told the author that he and the prime minister suspected that something was being "cooked up" at the royal palace during the few days before the battles. He said "there were too many Americans around the palace" and that he had very little doubt about American involvement in the guerrilla tragedy.

Of course, the Israelis made no secret of their concern about events in Jordan, and when the Syrians intervened on the side of the guerrillas, Israel was prepared to force the withdrawal of Syrian troops. These troops did, as a matter of fact, under persuasion from the Soviet Union, withdraw before Israel acted. In any case, Israel made clear her intention to save Hussein. How much and what kind of actual assistance the Israelis gave Hussein remains unknown, but circumstantial evidence seems to argue that Hussein, Israel, and the United States were in collusion.

Hussein won his battles largely because of faults in the strategy and political assumptions of the leadership of al-Fatah. Arafat, the head of al-Fatah, wrongly assumed that co-existence with Hussein's regime was possible, not realizing that kings and guerrillas seldom go together. This was a fatal mistake for which Arafat was clearly responsible, a mistake that cost the Palestinian movement dearly, not only in terms of men and equipment but also in terms of its future credibility with the masses. Consequently, the defeat of the guerrillas in 1970 destroyed what the Karameh battle had built up since 1968.

The Lebanese Experience. The guerrillas left Jordan to reorganize in Lebanon, the only place where they could do this without submitting to the complete control of the host government. Lebanon's army was too small and weak to resist the guerrillas' determination to establish themselves in the country. Its population was heterogeneous and therefore highly susceptible to divisions over emotional questions such as the one involving the Palestinians. It was feared that a civil war could erupt if the government tried to curb guerrilla activities. Finally, there were Palestinian refugees and affluent Palestinians already in Lebanon, and they welcomed the "transfer" of the guerrillas from Jordan to Lebanon.

In Lebanon the guerrillas were aided by liberal and leftist groups who had ideological interests in their revolutionary work. Educated native Palestinian Arabs, especially from Europe and the United States, converged on Beirut to lend a hand to the movement. Even non-Arabs visited the area either out of curiosity or to test their own revolutionary theories. Some came to join the struggle.

There was no doubt that Beirut had become the center of revolutionary work in the Middle East. The intellectual atmosphere of the city was filled with dialogues, ideological questions, and revolutionary theories of all kinds. The Palestinians organized two important research centers for the study of Palestinian subjects. One of them, the Institute for Palestinian Studies, published a large number of new books by well-known authors, issued pamphlets on matters of interest for Palestinians, and translated Arab documents into many languages. It maintains a library and runs a school for teaching the Hebrew language. The work of the Institute is sophisticated enough to impress scholars from other countries, a few of whom had come to Beirut to do work on their research projects.

The leadership of the guerrillas, especially that of al-Fatah, listened very little, however, to the Beirut intellectuals, and a wide gap separated the guerrilla leaders and the intellectual elite that surrounded the movement. True, the intellectuals were not themselves united on an approach to the Palestine dilemma; many of them were amateurs flirting with old revolutionary theories and paying little attention to the realities of the Palestinian struggle.

Nevertheless, the guerrillas needed an intellectual elite to aid them in much of their political and ideological works; yet it is obvious that they have not effectively used this important resource to their advantage. In fact, some guerrilla leaders have shown much reluctance to cooperate with the intellectual elite.

It was clear that the prestige of the guerrillas declined after the Jordanian tragedy. Only a bigger Karameh battle could have saved their reputation and revitalized people's enthusiasm for them; but another Karameh was not forthcoming. The movement had first to cope with internal problems relating to leadership, ideology, and political strategy.

These problems were difficult to solve. Consequently, the Palestinian movement continued to weaken; and its prestige continued to decline. Occasional attacks against Israeli interests kept the movement in the news and raised the prospect that it might after all survive. The attacks also had the effect of reminding the world that the *potential* of the Palestinian movement was much greater than was generally believed. Israeli retaliations, however, forced the Lebanese government to question the logic and rationale of guerrilla operations. Tension mounted while government and guerrillas discussed the issue of the limits of their legitimate authorities.

The Lebanese government supported the Palestinian cause but argued that Lebanon alone could not take up the Israeli challenge. Guerrilla operations, said the government, could only invite Israeli retaliations and therefore destruction to Lebanon. The guerrillas argued that the Lebanese government is as hypocritical as other Arab governments: it supported the cause but did very little for it.

Briefly, these were the arguments that precipitated the showdown of May, 1973, between the Lebanese government and the Palestinian guerrillas. Of course, Israel's raid on Beirut during the preceding month contributed heavily to the crisis. In that operation the Israelis were able to reach downtown Beirut undetected and kill three top leaders of the guerrillas. The manner by which the Israelis achieved their objective (checking into hotels, riding taxicabs and withdrawing by helicopters and boats) indicated that Lebanese security was ridiculously weak. However, the Israeli raid also proved that the guerrillas were equally unprepared. In fact, the Israelis were able to return to their bases with documents stolen from guerrilla files. These documents contained the names of guerrilla comrades in the west bank territory, Gaza, and Israel itself.

The result of the Lebanese showdown was much less certain than the results of its Jordanian counterpart. Neither the government nor the guerrillas won. On May 17 a secret agreement between the two warring parties was signed. Whatever the terms of this agreement were, however, the issue concerning the exact nature of guerrilla–government relations remained unresolved, at least for the time being.

The Need for a Sanctuary. The Palestinian movement after this continued to experience serious difficulties. The first and foremost of these was the problem of establishing a sanctuary. The guerrillas needed territory for refuge and to use as a base for operations against Israel. This sanctuary would be controlled either by them or by a government that identified with them in deeds as well as in words.

The problem of the sanctuary is in a sense identical with the problem of guerrilla–government (Arab) relations; and the guerrillas have not been able to solve either problem. There are only two solutions: either the guerrillas control an Arab government or allow themselves to be controlled by an Arab government. The latter alternative cannot guarantee their effectiveness unless the controlling Arab government is fully identified with their cause. Had Arafat realized this in Jordan, he would have made the decision to act against Hussein before the king had a chance to act against the guerrillas. There was a strong possibility that he might have won.

In Lebanon the problem is different. Although geographically Lebanon "qualifies" as a guerrilla sanctuary, the diversity of its population makes it difficult for the guerrillas to control it. A prolonged civil war might be the outcome of guerrilla attempts to dominate the government, and this also would be the probable outcome of a government attempt to control the guerrillas. In Lebanon the guerrillas could neither be completely free nor completely controlled.

Thus the guerrillas need a sanctuary outside Lebanon. More democratic than other Arab countries, Lebanon can offer the Palestinians certain advantages that they cannot have elsewhere. They can make it their "intellectual" and cultural center and launch from it their propaganda war. More important, Lebanon can serve them in difficult times, when they find themselves without other Arab friends. During such times they can organize quietly in Lebanon, but they cannot use its territory to launch attacks against Israel.

It is not unusual for "movements" to be born in Lebanon, but they rarely "live" there. And if they attempt to do so, they either disintegrate and die out or unconsciously evolve into something else. This was the fate of the Syrian Nationalist Party. Born in Lebanon, the party came very close to succeeding in Syria. Later, it was forced to "return" to Lebanon where in time it became an ordinary Lebanese party, no longer a "movement." Should the Palestinian movement decide to stay in Lebanon, it might eventually meet a similar fate.

The guerrillas have at least two other choices: either attempt to go back to Jordan or turn Syria into a real sanctuary. The first choice would require a successful coup by Jordanian officers loyal to the guerrillas. The second would be easier to accomplish. In Syria the guerrillas would have to submit temporarily to control by the Syrian government, become part of its armed forces, and later find an opportunity to participate in a pro-guerrilla Syrian coup. In either case, the guerrillas would have to make sure the coup would produce no local heroes who could later compete with them. For the sake of their cause, any hero should be from their ranks or someone on whom they can rely.

Of course, guerrilla success in controlling an Arab government would almost certainly bring the Israelis into action. If Israel were tempted to capture more Arab territory, the new situation would have other repercussions. Arabs who were previously moderate or apathetic would be radicalized. The governments of Kuwait and Saudi Arabia would become insecure when the people ceased to support them. These two countries would then be in the same circumstance as Egypt, Syria, and Iraq. Turkey and Iran might fear internal pressures also, and their governments, especially Turkey's government, would be uncomfortable with a "big power" (Israel) in their region, even though this big power was pro-Western.

The extension of Israeli territory at the expense of neighboring Arab countries would ultimately result in the formation of a greater *Arab* guerrilla movement. It would also confront Israel with the problem of managing a large Arab population. In other words, further Israeli victories might not benefit Israel. Such victories would only increase Arab bitterness and bring about more radical anti-Western regimes in the area.

Finally, to accomplish their aims, the guerrillas need a way to organize underground guerrilla units in territories occupied by Israel and in Israel itself. They have attempted this in the past but not very successfully. The reason for their failure has been the feeling of the people that the military situation is hopeless. But in the Gaza Strip, the guerrillas were able to operate almost daily. However, even there the struggle had to slow down, mainly because many of the local leaders were killed and because the central leadership, in Lebanon, became preoccupied with its own problems.

If the guerrillas could establish themselves in the west bank territory and revitalize their work in the Gaza Strip, they would be able to change the character of the struggle: Israel would be forced to make concessions to the Arabs. This could not very well happen unless conditions in occupied territories change. The people's low morale could scarcely be raised without some guerrilla successes in a series of isolated battles with the Israelis. Above all, the guerrillas would have to establish credibility with the people and this they could not do without solving their internal problems and presenting the people with a competent leadership, one they could trust.

The Problem of Strategy. From the beginning, the type of warfare that the Palestinian movement has used in its military activity has been based on the strategy of guerrilla warfare. In principle, this strategy is workable. Its objective is to tire out the enemy and force him to abandon his aims. In the case of the Palestinian movement, the leaders hope that eventually they will succeed in weakening Israel to the point where Arab armies could conquer it. Again, theoretically, this strategy is sound. Perhaps one could modify it to provide for the possibility of serious negotiations taking place at the end of a long struggle in which the guerrillas show some strength against the State of Israel. Negotiations become possible only when both warring parties abandon *some* of their aims, and this would happen only when the Palestinian guerrillas were able to continue the struggle over a long period of time.

The Palestinian guerrillas, however, have not yet understood what is really required in guerrilla warfare. They have put out a great deal of literature on the subject; but they have, in fact, applied very little of it. Part of their problem has been that they have identified only one enemy, Israel, not realizing, or ignoring, the fact that there are other "enemies." Actually the Arab governments have prevented them from doing serious fighting with Israel. Experience, especially in Jordan, has shown clearly that the Arab "enemy" can be more ruthless than Israel. That enemy did not hesitate to use modern weaponry to destroy the Palestinian movement. The Arab "enemy" has fought the Palestinian guerrillas much harder than he fights Israeli troops. Since the 1968 war, Lebanon, for instance, has refrained from occasional engagement with Israeli troops, but did not hesitate to use its airplanes, tanks, and artillery against the Palestinian guerrillas.

It is evident that, if it is to succeed, the Palestinian movement will have to be prepared, in terms of training, type of weaponry, as well as tactics, to deal with both enemies. Guerrilla tactics might be effective when used against Israel, but they are apt to be ineffective in open warfare against Arab armies. In Israel the guerrillas can use hit-and-run tactics, but in Arab countries they cannot do this because there their objective is to "hold" territory to establish a sanctuary.

The Palestinian guerrillas have brought themselves damage politically and physically, first in Jordan, and then in Lebanon, by appearing conspicuously in the cities, especially in the capitals. There are four reasons why this practice has been detrimental. First, it has given the impression that the guerrillas were more interested in power than they were in their military objectives. Secondly, it has caused people to complain that the guerrillas have come to appreciate city life and to be corrupted by it. Thirdly, it has brought complaints that the guerrillas are "showing off" when they should be serious. Finally, it has stirred up fear that their presence in cities jeopardized the safety of large numbers of civilians. All these negative results were evident in Jordan before 1970 and in Lebanon during the May, 1973, crisis.

Friendly critics point out that the guerrillas would be well advised to adopt a policy of staying out of Arab cities. Of course, cities can be used for the intellectual-cultural activities of the guerrilla movement, but only individuals involved in these activities need to live there. In order to effect a withdrawal of guerrillas from the cities, their leadership could explore the possibility of moving refugee camps out of urban centers. Refugees provide personnel for the movement and they would be more readily available in places close to training camps. There their families can be protected by the guerrillas.

In Israel and the occupied territories, guerrilla strategy is most effective when based on *urban* warfare. Generally, the Middle East is not an ideal place for guerrilla warfare, because of the lack of thick forests. That problem could be minimized if operations were limited to urban centers. This would give the guerrillas three advantages. First, they could cause the greatest physical damage to the enemy. Secondly, they could produce the maximum psychological effect on people. And, thirdly, after "hitting," they could "run" by getting lost in the crowds.

The task of battling with Israel will never be easy. The Israelis have a sophisticated security system and are highly advanced technologically. Any sensitive person must hope that conflict will not continue indefinitely, for war is terrible to both sides. But, realistically, the achievement of a solution will require that the Arabs show strength to close, or at least to narrow, the gap between them and the Israelis. Only then can there be hope for a negotiated settlement, one that will allow both parties to attain their humane goals.

Future Prospects. The future of the guerrillas is not apt to include their total disintegration and disappearance. As long as there are displaced Palestinians, there will be armed Palestinians attempting to redress the wrong done to them. These Palestinians will either be independent or part of an Arab country's anti-Israel effort. Such a country will have to be as radical and revolutionary as the Palestinian movement itself.

Otherwise, the Palestinian movement will not accept Arab government control and will attempt to operate independently.

The growth of Arab nationalism will strengthen the Palestinian movement, although such a movement will have to be more Arab than Palestinian. However, Arab national aspirations cannot be divorced or separated from Palestinian aspirations.

The economic integration of Palestinians with other Arab countries will not cause the Palestinian problem to disappear. Those who believe in an economic approach to the Arab-Israeli conflict seem to assume that an improvement in the economic standards of Palestinians will result in a reduction of their political aspiration and, therefore, their desire to continue the conflict with Israel. But such an approach is mistaken. Nationalism increases with economic affluence and power. Palestinian influence on Arab politics (compare Jewish influence on Western countries) will ensure that Arab countries will develop political ideologies and policies favorable to Palestinians.

The Arab people have been going through a peculiar experience, one characterized by cynicism and apathy toward politics and leaders. Military coups and countercoups have tired them out. A succession of leaders who talked a lot and did very little caused them to lose hope in the future. "Why another leader?" and "We tried them all and none of them did anything" seem to describe their feelings. This probably accounts for the survival of weak leaders like Sadat of Egypt, Assad of Syria, and Bakr of Iraq.

But this condition is deceptive and cannot go on forever. No people can accept a static condition for very long, especially a people with too many problems. Sooner or later they will rise again, and the world will witness another Arab revolution no less forceful than the revolution of the Chinese people. Whether it will be a revolution the Western world would like is a different matter. One thing is certain: it will be a revolution the Western world must deal with.

Chapter 8

The United States
and the Arabs

In the post-World War II years the United States lost a great deal of influence in the Arab world. Her support of the Zionists on the Palestine question and later her support of the State of Israel were the major reasons.

THE AMERICAN IMAGE
BEFORE WORLD WAR II

In the period between the two world wars American prestige in the Arab world was very high. Immediately after World War I, the Arabs of Syria (including Palestine) and Iraq expressed their preference for the United States, rather than Britain or France, as the power to have tutelage over their affairs. This was reported by the King-Crane Commission, whose work we discussed in an earlier chapter:

They [the people of Syria] declared that their choice was due to knowledge of America's record; the unselfish aims with which she had come to the War [World War I]; the faith in her felt by multitudes of Syrians who had been in America; the spirit revealed in American educational institutions in Syria, especially the College in Bairut, with its well-known and constant encouragement of Syrian national sentiment; their belief that America had no territorial or colonial ambitions, and would willingly withdraw when the Syrian State was well established as her treatment both of Cuba and the Philippines seemed to them to illustrate; her genuinely democratic spirit; and her ample resources.[1]

At that time, the American image in the Arab world was that of a noncolonialist, fair-minded, democratic, and free country. The United States was then a champion of national self-determination, and this principle appealed to the Arab peoples, who had hoped it would enable them to obtain independence.

President Wilson contributed to this image, because of his idealistic approach to international politics. The Arabs hoped that the American President might rescue them from European intervention and greed for territory in the Middle East.[2] Even the fact that Wilson was sympathetic to the Balfour Declaration and to Zionist aspirations did not disturb the Arabs. At the time, they did not understand the full implications of the Declaration. Later, however, they realized that the Zionist interpretation of the document was contrary to their interests, and they opposed it with all its implications.

Another reason for Arab high regard for the United States was that American involvement in the Arab Middle East was largely nonpolitical—mostly economic, cultural, and religious. What little political activity there was resulted from the efforts of the few American Jews who were dedicated to the aims and programs of the Zionist movement.[3] It was reflected in Congress more than in the executive branch, because the constituencies of congressmen were much smaller than that of the President. In the smaller constituencies significant concentrations of Jewish voters were possible. Even this influence was small, however, because the Zionists were a small minority among American Jews.

American political involvement in the Middle East was further limited by the country's isolationism. There was no public support for an activist policy toward the Arab world or any other region. Nor was there an experienced foreign policy cadre able to formulate a dynamic foreign policy. Public apathy and ignorance of world affairs, therefore, coupled with governmental inexperience in international dealings, effectively kept the United States out of the Middle East and elsewhere.

Also, the nature of the political process imposed further limitations: the frequent necessity of appealing to voters and the large number of elected officials meant that the United States was unable to look too far ahead and plan accordingly. Matters of the national interest were often overshadowed by the politics of elections.

American interests in the Middle East, therefore, were private interests. They involved the American government only to the extent of assisting private enterprises in securing oil concessions in Saudi Arabia and the Persian Gulf areas. Politically, the United States was content to leave responsibility (and the blame) with Britain, trusting Britain to safeguard, or at least not jeopardize, her interests. As for the British, as long as American interests were nonpolitical, limited, and not threatening, Britain was willing to leave them unchallenged.

Had there been no historical and cultural ties between Britain and the United States to bind them together in friendship, American interests in the Middle East would have been in jeopardy. And America would have had to protect her interests by political involvement or by the formulation of a military policy for the Middle East.

Another factor contributing to the relative security of American interests in the Middle East is the fact that the United States was not then a world power. Consequently, the need to balance interests with commitments, which Walter Lippmann associates with the positions of big powers,[4] was not crucial in the case of the United States. In other words, the absence of a concrete American policy toward the Middle East was not detrimental to American interests in the region. Nor was the fact that these interests "overtook us, so to speak, without prior warning" was significant.[5] However, when after World War

II the United States assumed the position of a world power, these problems became more relevant and more serious.

THE NATURE OF AMERICAN INTERESTS IN THE MIDDLE EAST

The interests of the United States in the Middle East were mainly cultural, including religious, educational, and humanitarian activities. More recently, American interests became more diversified to include economic and strategic interests.

Cultural Interests. American missionary work in the Middle East dates back to 1820. But the religious aspects of these activities were never really effective. The Middle East was itself an exporter of religions, and it resisted the importation of new ones. Consequently, American religious groups turned their interest to education, finding there an efficient facility for reaching the people. And it is in this area that the Americans were successful and effective.

Several important schools were founded. In 1866 the Syrian Protestant College was established in Beirut. After 1920 this school was known as the American University. Today it is one of the best institutions of higher education in the Middle East, if not the best. A number of other types of schools were also established, some of them in non-Arab countries such as Turkey and Iran. But perhaps the second-best-known American institution is the American University in Cairo. Although less known and not as good as the one in Beirut, it is nevertheless an important university and potentially an outstanding institution.

American educational facilities in the Middle East made three important contributions to the region itself and to Arab-American relations. The first was purely educational: thousands of Arabs received a good-quality education. They were trained in a large variety of fields, from medicine to history, languages, and art. The second contribution was cultural. The American schools were an important Westernizing element. No one can speak of Westernization and modernization without giving credit to the contribution of the American schools in transforming Middle Eastern society. Many Arabs in all walks of life, especially in politics, were influenced by American education and, therefore, American ideas. In fact, the political elites of the Fertile Crescent countries and Egypt are largely Western-educated.

The third contribution was a by-product of the second. By creating a good image for America in the Middle East—and later by providing the only serious effort to prevent its decline —the American schools played an indirect but important political role. At the same time that the United States is having difficulties with the Arabs, mainly as a consequence of her support of Israel, the American universities in Beirut and Cairo are able to maintain fairly good relations with both the people and the governments—because the universities have always been sympathetic to Arab aspirations. For instance, after the 1967 Arab-Israeli war the American community in Beirut, including the staff of the American university and their families, became indignant and frustrated at the way the American government handled the Middle East crisis. They organized various groups for the main purpose of helping the Arabs communicate with the American people. A few publications came out of these groups. For instance, *The Middle East Newsletter,* put out by Americans for Justice in the Middle East and published in Beirut, finds its way to the mailboxes of many individuals in the United States.

Therefore, America's educational institutions in the Middle East did for America what its policies could not do. So good were the relations between the American institutions and the Arab peoples that President Nasser expressed particular pleasure at President Kennedy's choice of John S. Badeau as the American Ambassador to Cairo. Badeau had been the president of the American University in Cairo. The short period of his tenure as ambassador was probably the best period in American-Egyptian relations since these relations began to deteriorate. And this was partly due to Badeau's ability to comprehend the Egyptians.

Indeed, one of the few things that the United States can do today to offset the ill effects of political differences on Arab-American relations is to encourage and increase the educational efforts of private American organizations. By financing, directly or indirectly, American education in the region, the United States can limit Soviet attempts at cultural penetration. This would not be sufficient to stop Soviet political influence and military penetration of the Middle East, but it might help make such influence difficult to maintain in the long run. The Soviet Union has gradually increased her political influence since the mid-1950's, but she has not buttressed this influence by positive cultural ties with the region. As long as this situation continues, Soviet penetration has less of a chance to become permanent.

The political elites of the Arab world understand the West better than they can understand the Soviet Union. This is true even of the anti-Western Arab leaders, for their anti-Westernism is motivated by purely political considerations. During Nasser's political battles with the United States his daughter was attending the American University in Cairo and later graduated from there.

Economic Interests. In addition to its cultural interests, the United States has established vital economic interests in the Middle East, and the Arab countries are an important part of these interests. The main element in these interests, of course, is oil.

Oil is important to the United States in several ways. First, American companies have invested huge amounts of money in Middle Eastern oil. From 1945 until 1966, $2.85 billion went into the production, transportation, refining, and marketing of Middle Eastern petroleum and petroleum products.[6] By

1973 this amount went up to approximately $4 billion. In 1966 alone the net flow of American investment capital to the Middle East was valued at $121 million.[7] In 1973 it was valued at about $2 billion. Today "the petroleum industry is more profitable in balance of payments terms than the average United States investment abroad."[8] However, this situation is changing, and the U.S. Government in Washington is beginning to worry about the change. More oil will need to be imported—at sharply higher prices. It is predicted that by 1985 the United States will need to import no less than 15 million barrels a day, four times the current need. The cost of this oil might reach the amount of $35 billion. Obviously, more exports will be needed if the United States is to balance this trade.

Thirdly, Middle Eastern oil is also vital to America's European allies and to Japan. It is the major source of their total energy requirements. Thus during the 1967 Arab-Israeli war, when the flow of Arab oil was temporarily halted, Europe was in serious trouble.[9]

What happens to Europe will affect the United States, not only from a security point of view but also economically: "The economies of the United States, Canada, Western Europe, and Japan are interconnected and interdependent in a manner that makes the interest of one nation or group of nations the interest of all."[10]

Fourthly, Middle Eastern oil will become necessary for supplying the future needs of the United States. In the late 1960's, the United States imported only about 19 percent of her needs and most of that came from Latin America: only 3 percent came from the Middle East.[11] In 1971 the percentage of imported oil was 23 percent of which 7 percent came from the Middle East. By 1980 imports are expected to make up 56 percent of the United States oil consumption, two thirds of which will come from the Middle East.

One should keep in mind that Middle Eastern oil output has been increasing at the rate of 10 to 15 percent per year, and that the Arab countries contain about 60 percent of the world's proven reserves. The Chase Manhattan Bank of New York estimates that Middle Eastern crude-oil production will double by 1985, increasing to 40 million barrels a day. Presently, Arab oil production accounts for 90 percent of the exports of the non-Communist world. Unless other forms of inexpensive energy can supplant oil, the United States will need to import Arab oil.

Strategic Interests. Before World War II, the United States was not a world power, and therefore was able to maintain economic and cultural relations with the Arabs without the formulation of a strategic policy concerning them. (Britain, on the other hand, was a world power at that time, and consequently the Middle East was of vital importance to her.) After the war, however, the United States also assumed the role of a world power, and the Arab world became vital to her strategic interests. It will continue to be indispensable to America's strategic interests as long as the American world position and fundamental outlook on world affairs remain the same.

Rivals in the struggle for world power have always been interested in the Middle East. In 1798, Napoleon invaded and occupied Egypt to check British influence there and in the Far East. He attempted to use Egypt as a springboard for his military operations in the neighboring Arab Fertile Crescent. (Both Egypt and the Fertile Crescent were then under Ottoman rule.)

Again during World War II, Germany tried first to infiltrate the Middle East and later invaded it. The infiltration took the form of clandestine activities in Iraq, Iran, Turkey, Egypt, and Palestine. It was clear that Germany was fully aware of the strategic significance of the Middle East. In aspiring to the status of a world power, she saw the desirability of controlling the Middle East. The failure of her infiltration efforts contributed to the failure of the invasion attempt.

The United States became aware of the region's strategic importance during World War II. After the war, the United States openly showed an interest in world leadership. Britain was no longer a first-rate world power, and her interests and commitments in the Middle East began to decline with the decline of her power. This prompted the United States to fill the vacuum.

However, the postwar period was characterized by a de-colonization process. This meant that the old technique of establishing direct political control by military occupation was no longer a feasible means of establishing world leadership. At any rate, this technique ran counter to America's own principles and ideals. Therefore, the United States had to assert leadership through indirect methods short of outright control.

The changing political techniques affected not only the United States but also the Soviet Union, her rival for world leadership. The Soviet Union has always been aware of the strategic importance of the Middle East. Since the time of Peter the Great, she has aspired to have access to the warm-water ports of the Mediterranean and the Persian Gulf. More important, she wished to safeguard her southern borders by establishing influence in the states of the northern tier of the Middle East (Turkey, Iraq, and Iran). During World War II, the Soviet army created a puppet state in northern Iran but had to withdraw as a result of Western pressure and world public opinion. Furthermore, the Soviet Union attempted to exercise some control over the Turkish straits in order to have access to the Mediterranean.

Until the mid-1950's, Soviet efforts to establish a foothold in the Middle East were ineffective. Thus, between World War II and the mid-1950's, the United States had ample opportunity to establish firmly her influence in the Middle East. However, her efforts to do so were damaged by the Arab-Israeli conflict. Mainly because of U.S. support for Israel, U.S. influence in the Arab world declined significantly and a large gap developed between the economic and strategic interests of the United States on the one hand and her political influence on the other. As a world power, the United States is confronted with the problem of balancing her commitments and her interests in the Middle East. These commitments and interests are not at present balanced, and the Soviet Union has benefited from the gap created by the inconsistencies of American policy.

All of the peoples of North Africa and most of the peoples of the eastern Mediterranean are Arabic-speaking. The sheer size of Arab territory plus its strategic location argues for its importance in any major confrontation between the big powers.

However, the strategic importance of the Middle East is no longer limited to its "bridge" function, in which the region served the West mainly as a means to accomplish aims in India and the Far East. Although this function is still important in big-power politics, today the region is also important in its own right. Economic interests, actual and potential, and close proximity to Europe and the Soviet Union have made the Middle East a greater prize than either India or the Far East ever were.

This means that the Middle East has become a potential cause of confrontation between the big powers. It is possible that the next major war could be fought over the area. However, the bridge function would continue to be important, especially in view of China's becoming a world power. But the Middle East would not be very important as a bridge in a Soviet-Chinese confrontation. In a confrontation involving the Western world and China, however, it would be.

This does not mean that the Soviet Union has no basis for an interest in the Middle East. We have already stressed the interest of the Soviet Union in safeguarding her southern borders through control of or influence over the Middle East. It merely means that Soviet interest in the Middle East as a bridge has been exaggerated by Westerners.

The exaggeration is largely caused by Western strategists persisting in old strategical concepts. Since the "bridge" function has been historically of primary importance, it has been difficult to discard it or reevaluate its importance in the short time that the Middle East has been an end, rather than a means, in international politics. For the Soviet Union, the part of the Middle East that really counts is Turkey, Iraq, and Iran. But, of course, she saw an opportunity to establish her influence in Egypt and she took that opportunity, hoping it would make her task easier in the countries of the northern tier. Also, if she could have control of the entire area between the Persian Gulf, the Red Sea, and the Turkish straits, her southern borders would be even more secure than if her control was limited to the northern tier states. The larger territory would also enable her to deny to the Western world the Middle Eastern bridge. Thus, at the same time that she was safeguarding her southern borders, she would be blocking the free access of the Western world to the Far East.

THE EFFECT OF ZIONIST PRESSURE
ON THE UNITED STATES

In the twentieth century, American policy toward the Arabs has been strongly influenced by Zionist-Jewish interests. As a pressure group, the Zionists are well financed and highly organized. Because of this, it is difficult to understand Arab-American relations without understanding Zionist influence on American politics.

Influence and Tactics. The Zionists' influence and propaganda effectiveness is due to their political tactics. One important element in their tactics is to take advantage of American political apathy and alarming ignorance of the realities of the Middle East. An apathetic or indifferent public usually leaves the political arena to interested minorities.[12] As a result, Zionist pressure did not meet with significant counterpressure.[13] The problem of the Arabs, of course, is that they do not have an American constituency to balance Zionist pressure. The Arab-

American population is very small, and, except after 1967, they had very little political organization to counter the pressure of Zionism.[14] In addition, they are not united, and the Arab-Israeli conflict is not significantly related to their voting behavior or politics.

American politicians are pragmatic. Not all who support Israel are necessarily convinced that a pro-Israel policy is the correct one or invariably in the best interests of the United States. But there is little political benefit for them in a pro-Arab position, whereas a pro-Israel position is often beneficial politically. Frequently, the Jewish vote must be considered by politicians running for office. Also, party-minded politicians are concerned about Jewish contributions to campaigns.[15]

In addition to the politicians, businessmen and civic leaders are aware of the importance of good public relations in maintaining their images and furthering their interests. For them to take an anti-Israeli stand, or simply to be critical of Israel, invariably evokes a negative response from Jews and therefore amounts to bad public relations or "bad business."

This invariably negative reaction is partly the result of the fact that many Zionists consider the critics of Israel and Zionism to be anti-Semitic: "Anybody who disagrees with Zionist goals is apt to be branded anti-Semitic." [16] To many Zionists, Israel is a combination of what the Vatican is to Catholics and what France is for Frenchmen. If the critic is Jewish, he is likely to be branded both sacrilegious and unfaithful (if not a traitor). If he is an Arab, he is a "Jew-hater," and lumped with the Nazi Germans.

Especially in the Eastern United States, the Zionists have been very successful in their attempt to influence the mass media. They take advantage of the strong commercial element in American journalism. Newspapers and television must take into account the salability of their papers or programs. Although this does not mean that these media are not free, it does mean that their ability to be objective on certain specific issues is limited by their commercial interests.

The Zionists take advantage of a politically active and dy-

namic Jewish community in the United States. Although the
Jewish community is small, it is strongly interested in the well-
being of Israel; and newspaper and television reports critical
of Israel are not left unanswered. Sometimes a large number
of phone calls, telegrams, and letters protesting the reports
follow such reporting. Newspapers and television stations are
quite sensitive to the protests; and since the pro-Israel response
is not matched by a pro-Arab response, a subtle element enters
the picture: certain truths are agonizing to the media and the
Middle Eastern issue often relates to such truths.

The fact that the Jewish community is concentrated in large
cities such as New York, Los Angeles, Chicago, and Cleveland,
and in large states such as New York, California, and Pennsylvania, enhances its influence on politics as well as on the
mass media. According to the well-known political scientist
Gabriel Almond, "the ultimate pressure exercised by the Jewish minority is in the electoral process. This has been of special
importance in the struggle for control of key states in which
there are large Jewish populations, such as New York." [17] The
New York Jewish community is very powerful because of the
city's importance as a center of mass media, finance, and commerce.

These comments should not be misconstrued. Although more
intense than most other influences, Zionist-Jewish tactics are
not peculiar to the American system. It is simply that the realities of American life give the pro-Israelis the advantage in
the contests for influence. Since the United States is pluralistic
and highly susceptible to minority influences, the American
system gives great advantages to contestants who have a constituency and are well organized. As in any contest, victory
will have more to do with the strength and skills of the players
than with the rights or wrongs of the issue. Unless the pro-
Israelis in the United States are balanced by an organized, active, pro-Arab group, the Arab point of view will continue to
suffer.

Zionist influence is broad. It is not limited to liberals or conservatives but includes both. However, the Zionists use different techniques to reach the two groups. With the liberals, their appeal is based on their minority status as Jews. Since the State of Israel is Jewish and many American Jews identify with it in some way, it is difficult to separate the two. This difficulty, heightened by Zionist propaganda, causes the liberals to treat Israel as if it were an American minority. (The Zionist "contends . . . that Israel and Zionism are one, that the Jew cannot be a good Jew unless he is also a Zionist.")[18] In this connection, the American liberal is simplistic in that he is usually reluctant to investigate the possibility that a minority might be wrong. His liberalism almost appears to be derived from a simple manual of rules which reads, "A liberal is one who sympathizes with minorities." This simplistic, mechanistic view prevents an understanding of the Arab case against Israel.[19]

The Zionists invented slogans and created images for Israel that appealed to the liberal and moderate Americans. Israel was presented as the underdog. "Tiny little Israel" is seen to be surrounded and threatened by "a hundred million Arabs." [20] Few readers or listeners made an effort to distinguish numbers from strength. Three Arab-Israeli wars won by Israel have not been enough to persuade many Americans that militarily Israel is not "tiny" but a giant, the strongest power in the region.

An interesting aspect of the liberal's attitude toward Israel is that when Israel does make an obvious mistake or behaves incorrectly, the liberal treats it as one might treat the misbehavior of a handicapped person. The "handicap" treatment is largely the outcome of American guilt feelings about Jewish persecution. Unfortunately, in the Arab-Israeli conflict, the guilt feelings predetermined the issue in favor of Israel. No substantive inquiry was considered necessary to determine if the Arabs might be right after all.

The liberals are also attracted to the Zionist portrayal of Israel as a democracy. The Zionists argue that the Arabs are authoritarian and their governments are dictatorships, and

from that, somehow, they are able to arrive at the view that
the Arabs cannot be trusted. Only "democratic" Israel is trust-
worthy in the Middle East. Because America is democratic,
she should have interest in other democracies, and it is her
duty to support these democracies.

There is no doubt that Israel is more democratic than the
Arab countries, except perhaps for Lebanon. However, some
liberals make very little effort to question the relationship of
American interests to foreign democracies and dictatorships.
They might find out the United States is not always on the
side of the democratic angels. If she were to follow this rule,
she would have few friends and allies; for, unfortunately, most
of the world is governed by authoritarian regimes. And, of
course, in the contest for world power and leadership, the
United States does not and cannot forgo most of the world
because it is not democratic. In addition, a closer look at Israeli
democracy might disclose an exaggeration in Zionist propaganda. Israeli politics is oligarchic. Since 1948 the country has
been dominated by the same clique that operates within the
Mapai party. Also, the Sephardic (Oriental) Jews have an inferior status in Israel. Although in 1970 they represented over
60 percent of the population, they constitute only 3 percent of
the top government officials and 20 percent of the Knesset, or
parliament. In June, 1971, there was only one Oriental Jew on
the eighteen-man cabinet of Israel. Sixty percent of the Oriental children drop out of high school, and 95 percent of the college students are European Jews.[21]

With American conservatives, Zionist technique is twofold.
It emphasizes American security and Israel's economic achieve-
ments. Zionist propaganda presents the Arab-Israeli conflict as
a battle between Communism and the free world, with the
Arabs, of course, identified with Communism and the Soviet
Union. In order to check Soviet power, therefore, the United
States should side with Israel, which is identified with the free
world. Such a propaganda program, of course, polarizes the
Arab-Israeli conflict and involves the two superpowers. In do-

ing so, it establishes a second safeguard for—as well as a second threat to—Israel's security. Should Israel's own military capability prove insufficient, the second resource, the direct application of American military power, could come into play.

But is Soviet influence really the result of Arab sympathy with Communism? Or is it, rather, the result of the Arab-Israeli conflict itself, of the frustration of the Arabs in their struggle with Israel? There are those who argue that if it were not for the establishment of the State of Israel in 1948, there would be no Soviet influence, or at least not much of it, in the Arab world today. And there are those Americans who see the establishment of Israel as a mistake and consider Israel a "liability" for the United States. Among them is former U.S. Ambassador to Cairo John S. Badeau. He wrote that "in the context of American foreign policy, Israel . . . needs to be viewed as a problem, rather than an asset.." [22] These people are aware that Israel's victories are increasing Soviet influence in the Arab world, a situation that is causing the United States a great deal of trouble.

Israel's economic achievement is appealing to most Americans, but it is of particular interest to conservatives, who see American success in terms of economic achievement. Zionists stress such words as "pioneers," "hardworking," and "aggressive." They assert that the land which became Israel in 1948 was a desert and that the Israelis "made the desert bloom," [23] whereas "lazy" Arabs did not work the land when they had a chance to do so, neglecting it almost completely. From this kind of propaganda, many Americans get a false image of the Palestinian Arab. He is presented as a primitive man, technologically incapable of developing his territory, and indifferent to it as well. He, therefore, did not deserve Palestine, whereas the Israelis deserve it because they "did something with it." Americans who visit Israel are shown "the evidence" and are constantly reminded that "where there is green there was nothing."

While one must acknowledge the fact that Israel is advanced

technologically and that she has contributed to the land, one must consider the following: First, Palestine was not what the Zionists claim it was. The country was, in fact, one of the most advanced areas of the Arab world, and the Palestinian Arabs were, next to the Lebanese, the most progressive Arabs. Like all coastal areas, Palestine was more advanced than the interiors of the Arab world. Those who recall Haifa and Jerusalem before 1948 may remember the clean and nicely built Arab neighborhoods.[24] It is also true that the parts of Palestine that were desert are still desert, a fact acknowledged by Israel.[25]

Second, Israel's economic achievements must be viewed in terms of efforts made by her European-born citizens, and in terms of the large foreign capital invested in development programs, capital never available to the Palestinian Arabs. Also, Israel has been working at development for over twenty years and it is unfair to compare Arab Palestine with Israel more than twenty years later. It is probably more fair to compare the Palestinian Arabs with the Israeli "Oriental" Jews. The cultural backgrounds of these two peoples are similar.

Third, while Israeli achievements are highly publicized, comparable Arab achievements are not. In the decade preceding the 1967 war, Jordan, whose population was largely Palestinian, increased its gross national product and its agricultural output "more rapidly than even Israel." [26] In spite of the fact the Palestinian Arabs are not Western, they have not been lazy.

In the context of economics, Zionist propaganda does not distinguish between the different kinds of Arabs or the different parts of the Arab world. This enables the Zionist to cite examples of extreme poverty, wastefulness, corruption, and "primitive" existence, which might be true of certain parts of the Arab world, and to generalize about all Arabs. The purpose of this propaganda is to undermine the progressive Arabs and their achievements and to help the world forget the hardworking Palestinian Arabs.

Finally, the Zionist economic argument really has no bearing upon the rights and wrongs of the Arab-Israeli controversy. If one accepts this Zionist argument, one should be open about his belief that only the rich, or the advanced, or the capable, should have rights, while the poor or the less advanced should have none.

The deeper probing required for finding the loopholes in the Zionist arguments is done only by a small number of Americans. Most Americans do not probe unless they have a special interest. Consequently, the simplistic approach of the Zionists has been effective.

THE UNITED STATES AND THE PALESTINE QUESTION

United States involvement in the question of Palestine dates mainly from World War II and arises from the problem of the Jewish refugees, victims of Nazi Germany. (As mentioned earlier, Arab-American relations before the war were mostly cultural and economic.) The American position on the Palestine question derived largely from the Zionist view of how the (separate) refugee problem had to be resolved.

During the war, Nazi Germany's brutal treatment of the Jews became an overriding concern of the U.S. Government. The large number of Jewish refugees needing resettlement presented an enormous test of mankind's conscience and capacity for humanitarian work. Unfortunately, this challenge became entangled in politics.

To begin with, it was the Zionists who chose to connect the Jewish refugee problem with the political problem of Palestine. They saw the two problems as inseparable and insisted that the solution of one depended on a solution of the other. They went even farther: in discussions with American policymakers they insisted that the Zionist solution to the problem of Palestine was "essential to the preservation of the [Jewish] race." [27]

Secondly, the United States helped politicize the humani-

tarian problems of the refugees by yielding to Zionist pressure
and by pressuring Britain, which had the responsibility for
Palestine, to accept the Zionist solution to the refugee problem.

Great Britain was caught between the pressures of Zionism
and the U.S. Government and the pressures of her Arab interests and commitments. In the 1939 White Paper, Britain
had committed herself to a Palestinian policy that restricted
Jewish immigration at the same time that it anticipated the
establishment of an independent state in which the Arabs
would continue to constitute a majority of the population. She
also had interests in the other parts of the Arab world. Consequently, she was, during the war, very reluctant to go along
with the United States in anything that could jeopardize her
Arab interests.

As Zionist pressure on America's elected officials intensified,
and as these officials gradually yielded, the gap between the
British and American positions on both the Palestine question
and the refugee problem widened. (In the meantime, the
Arabs complained that the British were being pressured by
the United States into accepting the establishment of a Jewish
state in Palestine.)[28] The British remained firm, however. And
in 1943 they were still "definitely opposed to the establishment
of a Jewish political state in Palestine" and "in favor of a settlement of the issue on the basis of the British White Paper." [29]
The United States was fully aware of this British policy.

The issue played a part in America's electoral politics in
1944, and Roosevelt (and later Truman) tried to pressure the
British into admitting 100,000 Jews into Palestine. Thus when
in September, 1945, the British learned that President Truman
was about to issue a public statement on Palestine, Clement
Attlee, then prime minister of Great Britain, warned the President that such a statement "could not fail to do grievous harm
to relations between our two countries." [30] He also informed
President Truman that the American-Zionist assumption that
the Jewish refugees were interested in Palestine was wrong.
Not all of them wanted to go to Palestine, because they had

not used "the number of certificates [for immigration] which are being made available to them." Attlee saw the Zionist position as more political than humanitarian, saying that the Jews "are insisting upon the complete repudiation of the White Paper . . . regardless of the effect on the situation in the Middle East which this would have." [31]

Attlee objected to the American insistence that the Jews should be given special treatment among the refugees, claiming that such treatment would be "disastrous to the Jews." He said that the Jewish refugees should be treated like all other refugees, with compassion and with awareness of their interests as human beings.[32]

British Prime Minister Attlee pleaded with President Truman for an understanding of Britain's position. He said: "In the case of Palestine we have the Arabs to consider as well as the Jews." He reminded him that "there have been solemn undertakings . . . given by your predecessor, yourself, and by Mr. Churchill, that before we come to a final decision . . . there would be consultation with the Arabs." He again warned President Truman that "it would be very unwise to break these solemn pledges and so set aflame the whole Middle East." [33] Attlee was also aware of the effect of all this upon British relations with the ninety million Muslims of India.

Much of the British effort to persuade the U.S. Government not to push too far its pro-Zionist policy regarding the refugees came from Lord Halifax, the British Ambassador to Washington. This distinguished statesman had the insight to see Palestine as "a terrible legacy." He advised the American secretary of state that "the approach to the problem [of Palestine] in the United States is being most embarrassing to them [the British] and is embittering relations between the two countries at a moment when we ought to be getting closer together in our common interests." He expressed extreme British irritation with the Zionists, who were "using every possible form of intimidation to stop Jews leaving Palestine in order to go back to Europe and to play their part in its reconstruction." [34]

Probably the strongest reaction to American pressure on the British government came from Ernest Bevin, the British foreign secretary. Two events especially irritated him, and on April 27, 1946, he wrote the American secretary of state informing him of these events. In Palestine the Jews were "acquiring large supplies of arms, most of them with money furnished by American Jews." Also, in assisting the British government to fill the Jewish quota for immigration to Palestine, the Jewish Agency selected Jews on the basis of their "military qualities." Bevin bluntly told the United States that the Jews (i.e., Zionists), through their aggressive attitude, were "poisoning relations" between the British and American peoples.[35]

Apparently, American pressure on the British government was so great as to concern and worry some career men in the State Department. The chief of the Division of Near Eastern Affairs was one of them, and he wrote a colleague in the Department, observing that "the present handling of our Palestine policy at the highest levels has already seriously irritated the British and threatens to have even more far-reaching effects upon our relations with the Near Eastern countries." [36]

But British resistance to American pressure had limits. After all, in 1946 Britain desperately needed financial assistance as a result of her losses during the war. She had to have United States help. In the spring of 1946, British opposition began to crumble and the first signs of weakening appeared. Bevin informed the secretary of state that his government would be "prepared to go ahead and permit the immigration of 100,000 Jews." However, he had one condition: Would the United States be willing to share with the British the responsibility for Palestine? Would the United States send troops to Palestine in order to safeguard it against Arab resistance to Jewish immigration?

The United States Government informed the British government that it could not undertake such a task. In the eyes of the British, this was inconsistent and unreasonable: the United States was making heavy demands upon them without sharing in the responsibility. In exasperation, therefore, the British decided to attempt another way out of the dilemma. They began to think seriously of giving up their own responsibility. In 1947, the fragile United Nations, less than two years old, would inherit Britain's responsibility.

The battle over the Jewish refugee problem was a bitter one. The British doubted the sincerity of the American policy makers and thought they were motivated "by domestic political opportunism." [37] Bevin went so far as to state that the American politicians "did not want too many of them [the Jews] in New York." [38] The British were not alone in their criticism. A few high-level American officials were also critical, among them were James Forrestal, Robert Hannegan, and James Byrnes.[39]

In his memoirs, President Truman admits that "the [refugee] issue was embroiled in politics" and that he was under tremendous pressure from the Zionists.[40] In fact, the pressure on him mounted to the point where he was forced to instruct his staff that he was "not to be approached by any more spokesmen for the extreme Zionist cause." On one occasion he was "so disturbed" by Zionist pressure that he had to "put off" seeing Chaim Weizmann, the leader of the World Zionist movement.[41]

Nevertheless, Truman insisted that his motivation was humanitarian: "The fate of the Jewish victims of Hitlerism was a matter of deep personal concern to me." [42] Dean Acheson agrees that President Truman was motivated by "a deep conviction" that the Jewish cause was just. This conviction, Acheson believes, was "in large part implanted by his [Truman's] close friend and former partner, Eddie Jacobson, a passionate Zionist." [43]

However we view the controversy over the Jewish refugee problem, it is clear that the American policy was "based in part—a large part—on a domestic situation," while Britain's policy was "based entirely on a foreign affairs base." Consequently, the two positions were "hard to reconcile." [44]

AMERICAN POLICY AFTER THE
ESTABLISHMENT OF ISRAEL

After World War II, the United States replaced Britain as
the dominant Western power in the Middle East. In the 1950's
the Soviet Union began to compete with the United States for
influence in the region, and in the 1960's the competition became fierce. As a result of the Arab defeat in the 1967 war,
Soviet influence among the Arabs increased to the point where
it became a serious concern to the United States. For the first
time in history, the Soviet Union was able to penetrate the
Arab world and establish a foothold in its midst. Correspond-
ing to this development was a decline in Western influence in
the area and the prospect that whatever remained of Western
influence could vanish completely.

What caused the decline of Western influence and the increase in Soviet influence in the Middle East is an important,
though perplexing, question. One thing is evident: the reasons
for both developments are in many respects related; what
caused the decline in Western influence often operated in
favor of Soviet influence.

In this section we will discuss the problems and limitations
of American policy in the Middle East from the viewpoint of
how these problems contributed to the growing Soviet influence. We will focus on the period from the end of World War
II through the year 1972.

The Problem of the *Status Quo* vs. Revolutionary Change.
Many contemporary Arab states became sovereign either between the two world wars or after World War II. Some of
them, such as the Fertile Crescent states, were created by the
Western powers, particularly France and Britain. They were
created when Arab nationalism was too weak to prevent foreign determination of Arab political destiny. (Later, the Arab
nationalists felt morally justified in their efforts to destroy

Western creations in the Arab world and to replace such creations by a political union based upon an assumption of Arab nationhood.)

After World War II, the United States more or less assumed that the political divisions of the Arab world would be permanent. But at about the same time, Arab nationalism became stronger and began to express its dissatisfaction with the *status quo*, which it considered to be a Western design inconsistent with the real desire of the Arab peoples for unity. This gap between American policy toward the Arab world and the aspirations of the Arab nationalists widened in subsequent years, as the activities of the Arab nationalists intensified and American support of the *status quo* became more rigid.

The Arab nationalists desired unification of the Arab countries but their aim was frustrated by the indigenous governments, which had a vested interest in the political *status quo* (originally established by the Western powers). Obviously, Arab unification would require Arab rulers to sacrifice their power positions, and this they were not willing to do. In the eyes of the Arab nationalists, the "conservative Arab regimes" and the "imperialist" United States shared an interest in the *status quo* and were allies in a common antinationalist cause. In 1958, the nationalists succeeded in temporarily uniting Syria and Egypt to form the United Arab Republic, and in 1971 they began another attempt at unification, this time between Egypt, Syria, and Libya. The 1958 experience was valuable, however. It demonstrated that the obstacles to union included factors other than opposition from "imperialism" and "conservative Arab regimes." Consequently, unification would require more than the neutralization of foreign political interests and the elimination of "conservative" governments.

An equally difficult problem lay with the nationalists themselves, who needed to clarify their confusion about methods and techniques. They had to learn to deal with the fact that opposition to unification could come from Arab nationalist regimes involved in rivalries with other Arab nationalist regimes. This was evident in the Nasser-Kassem rivalry (1958–1963) and in the rivalries between Nasser and the Baath party of Syria and Iraq during the 1960's.

But there is no doubt that most Arab nationalists continued to see as the main obstacles to union the Western powers and the "conservative" Arab regimes, such as those of King Hussein in Jordan and of King Faisal in Saudi Arabia. They argued that the reliance of Hussein and Faisal on the United States increased with the frequency of their attacks upon these regimes, and that these two parties had become allies in their opposition to Arab nationalism.

They cited examples to substantiate their arguments. In 1957, an attempt by a "nationalist" group to overthrow Hussein was frustrated by a U.S. threat of intervention and by actual British intervention. During that episode, the United States rushed her Sixth Fleet to the eastern Mediterranean and announced her readiness to save, by force if necessary, Jordan's integrity and independence. In 1957, also, the United States became concerned about Communist influence in Syria, and an American task force appeared off the Syrian coast. Turkey, an ally of the United States, mobilized her forces along the Syrian borders with the consent of the United States. In 1958, during the civil war in Lebanon, in which the "nationalists" were trying to overthrow the "conservative" pro-Western regime of Camille Chamoun, the United States intervened militarily to save that regime. In 1961, Iraq's attempt to annex Kuwait was checked by the British. In 1970, when the Palestinian guerrillas battled with Hussein and the Syrian army came to assist them, American pressure and Israel's threat of intervention forced the Syrians to withdraw from Jordan. (Nationalists had hoped that the Syrians and the Palestinians would succeed in ousting King Hussein's military regime.)

The Arab nationalists argue that the American Sixth Fleet has become the policeman of the Arab Middle East. They complain that nothing happens in the Middle East without some form of American interference and ask how can they achieve their objectives in the face of American "meddling" in Arab affairs.

Although the events cited by the Arab nationalists did occur, the nationalists' interpretation of them ignores the fact that Western intervention is only one element in a set of highly complicated situations. In Lebanon's civil war, the aims as well as the real identities of the antigovernment groups were not clear. In the case of Kuwait, Kassem was pursuing personal ambitions (or at best Iraqi ambitions) and not the aims of the Arab nationalists. (Nevertheless, Arab nationalists argue that the annexation of Kuwait by Iraq would have reduced the number of Arab states by one.) And in the case of Jordan, the ability of the Syrians and the Palestinians to overthrow Hussein was doubtful. In most of these instances there was no assurance that the success of the "nationalists" would have resulted in mergers of Arab states. Experience had shown that nationalist regimes can be caught in traditional Arab rivalries and themselves become obstacles to union.

Again, while there have been numerous instances of U.S. meddling in Arab affairs, the failure of the 1958 union between Syria and Egypt was caused primarily by Nasser's method of handling Syria and not by U.S. intervention. Also, the union of Egypt, Syria, and Libya attempted in 1971 was not prevented by the United States. These examples are not intended to make light of foreign intervention, but they do argue that Arab unification also suffers from the divisiveness of the Arab nationalists. Perhaps in the future, when Arab nationalism becomes more mature and therefore more cohesive, the responsibility for Arab failures will become clearer.

But there should be no doubt that Western interference has become a problem which the Arab nationalists must be concerned with. Also, it should be clear that Western influence weighs heavily in favor of the *status quo* in the Arab world, mainly because the Arab world that emerged from World War II was shaped in large measure by the Western powers. Also, as long as the Western world, especially the United States, remains favorable to the *status quo*, revolutionary change in the Arab world will almost inevitably express itself in anti-Westernism. Unless the United States wakes up to this reality, the future of the Arab world will inevitably be anti-Western.

It is true that an American policy supporting change is not easy. Arab nationalism is unstable and therefore often inconsistent. But there are numerous opportunities for the expression of American sympathy with the aspirations of the Arab nationalists. In the face of Arab instabilities, American policies will necessarily run into difficulties; but given the right attitudes and motives, such policies will eventually pay high dividends for the United States as well as for the Arabs.

Ironically, the reason why American economic interests in the Arab world have not been ousted is that they have been protected by the Arabs' sense of their own interests. Arabs know, for instance, that an anti-American oil policy would hurt their own interests. Had it not been for this Arab awareness, American interests would have disappeared long ago, for the United States has become her own worst enemy in the Arab world. But how long the Arabs will protect American economic interests depends in part on the future of the Arab-Israeli conflict. Another Arab defeat at the hands of the Israelis might result in the complete destruction of oil installations by an enraged Arab public (lead, perhaps, by the Palestinian guerrillas).[45] It also depends on the development of Arab oil technology. The moment the Arabs can become technologically independent they will begin to nationalize American interests.

This means that a prosperous and advanced Arab world is one with which the United States will have difficulty doing business. Since an advanced Arab world will also be militarily powerful, the United States not only will lose a business partner but will gain a strong enemy. Thus, the American experience with the Chinese people will be repeated with the Arabs. Future Western historians may deplore America's loss of the Arabs and the Chinese, for these two peoples will be very important in world affairs and the loss of their friendship and goodwill can be expected to hurt not only the United States but all of Western civilization.

The Problem of Arab-Israeli Relations. The establishment of Israel has alienated most of the Arab world from the West. The Arabs see Israel as a Western creation and blame the United States and Britain for assisting the Zionist movement in its efforts to establish the Jewish state.

Both the Arab nationalists and those Arabs who favor the *status quo* reject Israel on the grounds that it is a foreign state whose establishment caused the displacement of Arabs. However, the Arab who favors the *status quo* is not bothered by Israel's being a "Western creation," for many of the Arab states are themselves "Western creations." King Hussein, for instance, would have no objection to the Jewish state on these grounds. After all, Jordan was established by Britain and, for a long time, depended on Britain for her continuance as a state. Today, Jordan's reliance on the Western world, especially the United States, is probably greater than Israel's. In fact, her creation had more to do with the West than Israel's creation had. The Arab nationalists, however, do object to Israel as a "Western creation," just as they have rejected the Arab states shaped by Western influence. Thus, Israel's connection with the West, like Jordan's connection with the West, is totally unacceptable to the Arab nationalists.

Even so, the defection of Israel from the Western camp will not make her acceptable to the Arab nationalists, for she would remain foreign to the Arab world (in the sense that most of her 1948 population came from outside Palestine). Thus the withdrawal of American support to Israel will not change Arab relations with Israel. Such a policy would, however, make the United States less objectionable to the Arab nationalists.

The U.S. position, however, is not likely to change much. Therefore the United States must seek a peaceful resolution of the conflict itself. It is true, for example, that American-

Arab relations could markedly improve if the United States totally withdrew her support of Israel. Further, if the United States were to support the Arabs *against* Israel, Soviet influence in the area would weaken considerably. However, because of domestic Zionist-Jewish pressure on the American government, the United States can do neither. Consequently, unless the Arab-Israeli conflict is resolved, Arab-American relations would remain negative. And this is why after 1967 the United States showed some interest in resolving the conflict.

But the United States has been handicapped by her support of one of the main parties in the conflict. The peacemaker is supposed to be impartial, and the United States is not. Also, U.S. peace efforts have been handicapped by two other important factors. First, the United States has ignored the Palestinian Arabs in her negotiations. No *permanent* peace is possible in the Middle East without including the Palestinian Arabs who were the victims of the conflict. If they are not included, the moral issue of the conflict will remain unresolved.

The United States has ignored the Palestinian Arabs for two reasons: their weakness as combatants and Israel's refusal to recognize them as a principal party in the conflict. In 1968, and until September, 1970, when the Palestinian guerrillas were showing strength in Jordan and against Israel, their name was indeed mentioned by the American policymakers as a likely party in the negotiations. However, after Hussein's battle with them and their subsequent weakening, their name ceased to be mentioned. And the possibilities of peace diminished as a result.

The second factor handicapping America's peace efforts is her lack of realization that a true balance of power in the Middle East does not exist and that, as we pointed out earlier, negotiations among unequals cannot succeed. In fact, the difficulty has been compounded by the United States' claim that she has been maintaining a balance of power in the area, when actually Israel has had military supremacy since 1948.

One reason why the United States does not recognize the

imbalance of power is her fear of Soviet influence and military presence on the Arab side. The United States and Israel exaggerate the effect of Soviet aid on Arab military strength. The two "allies" look at the quantity of aid and invariably come to the conclusion that Israel needs more arms to balance aid. Again as we pointed out in Chapter 7, the United States ignores the fact that military power rests more on quality than on quantity, and that the quality of Israel's military organization far exceeds that of the Arabs. The United States fails to assess the balance of power on the basis of the belligerents' ability to use their weapons.

Another reason why the United States does not recognize the imbalance of power is Zionist influence on American policy toward the Arab Middle East. This influence does not determine American policy but it is very strong. It prevents the United States from pursuing a rational policy based on her strategic-economic interests in the region.

Until 1967, the official U.S. position on the Arab-Israeli conflict favored the *status quo,* as did the U.S. policy on Arab affairs. This policy meant that the United States would guarantee and safeguard the territorial integrity of all countries of the Middle East, both the Arab states and Israel. During the Eisenhower administration this position was strictly adhered to. Thus, when Israel occupied the Sinai peninsula in 1956, President Eisenhower insisted on complete Israeli withdrawal. In essence, the policy recognized Israel's territorial gains in the 1948 war and at the same time warned the Arabs not to hope to regain their losses by force and the Israelis not to hope for more territory.

The 1967 war changed American policy. Israel again enlarged her territory at the expense of Jordan, Syria, and Egypt; and the United States did nothing. Instead, she accepted the principle of bargaining, which became the motive behind U.S. efforts to achieve peace in the area. The bargaining was often deadlocked by Israel's reluctance to make adequate concessions to the Arabs, a reluctance largely motivated by her obvious military superiority. Consequently, the net result of America's post-1967 policy was to leave, perhaps reluctantly, the winner with his gains.

The Problem of Soviet Strategy. Soviet strategy in the Arab world is very enlightened, and how to cope with it has become a source of concern for the United States.

Soviet policy can be divided into three stages. The purpose of the first stage was to drive the Western powers out of the Arab world. In this the Soviet Union has been largely successful, presenting herself as an anticolonial power interested in the liberation of the Arab world. American support of the *status quo,* and her identification with the "conservative" Arab regimes, permitted the Soviet Union to pose as a supporter of revolutionary change and build a reputation as a friend of the Arabs and an ally of Arab nationalism. In contrast, the United States was seen as an "imperialist" power and an enemy of the Arabs.

In the Soviet-American propaganda battle, the Soviet Union accused the West of "exploitation" and the Americans accused the Soviets of being "undemocratic," "authoritarian," and "oppressive."

The exploitation theme won over the freedom theme. There are two reasons for this: First, the Arabs had experienced Western "exploitation" and had not experienced Soviet "oppression"; and secondly, Arab cultures have not experienced (modern) democracy. These reasons also account for the failure of American "freedom" propaganda in Asia, Africa, and other parts of the world where people have long been accustomed to authoritarian regimes. To underscore the absence of freedom among peoples who have not experienced it is futile, at least until these people begin to react against their own authoritarian systems. Until then, freedom remains an item hard to export.

In order to ally herself with Arab nationalism, the Soviet Union resorted to the shrewd device of separating her state interest from Communist ideology. In the first stage of her policy planning, the Soviet Union demonstrated no interest in the Communist parties of the Arab world, and tolerated the suppression of these parties by Arab nationalist regimes. Thus, it was possible for Nasser to outlaw the Communist party of Egypt and at the same time to deal amicably with the Soviet Union. Although at times the Soviet leaders showed a little irritation with the Egyptian policy, they did not make an issue of it and did not allow their feelings to influence their own policies.

While the Soviets separated their state goals from their ideological interests, the United States tried to persuade the Arabs that they were actually bound together. In fact, the so-called Eisenhower doctrine (1957), a *status quo* policy, assumed they were the same. It purported to protect Middle Eastern countries threatened by "overt armed aggression from any nation controlled by international Communism."

The Arabs had difficulty understanding the U.S. approach. They repeatedly indicated that their enemy was Zionism and the State of Israel rather than the Soviet Union, and they objected to U.S. insistence on reversing the order of their priorities. They were aware of the danger of Communism, but this danger was less immediate to them than the twin dangers of Zionism and Israel. They responded to warnings about the danger of Soviet influence by asserting that they had no intention of replacing Western imperialism with Soviet imperialism. They would deal with the Soviet state as they would with any other state. If the Soviet Union helped them, they would accept the help but would remain careful not to allow this to destroy their independence. As an example of their ability to handle threats to their independence they cite the period in 1957 when Syria was infiltrated by Communists. Syria's response was to merge with Egypt to stop such infiltration, and the Arabs claim that it was Nasser, not the United States, that saved Syria from Communism. And in 1971 the nationalist regime in the Sudan dealt ruthlessly with the Sudanese Communists. All this is an indication both that the Arabs do not want Communism and that they are able to maintain their independence.

Nevertheless, Soviet long-range planning is implicitly imperialistic. The second stage in the Soviet design was to establish a military presence in the Arab world. The Arab-Israeli conflict was just the pretext for achieving this objective. Arab defeats created the necessity for the Arabs to seek arms from any source. Since the United States could not be pro-Arab because of Zionist-Jewish pressures, the Arabs had no choice but to seek Soviet help. Any state involved in a conflict like the Arab-Israeli conflict would have done the same. In fact, during the 1948 Arab-Israeli war, Israel was the first Middle Eastern country to do so. Moreover, she bought the arms with private American money.

The Soviet Union was foresighted in assessing Arab needs and flexible in switching to the Arab side in the Arab-Israeli conflict. One should recall that in 1947, when the Palestinian question was before the United Nations, the Soviet Union was the most enthusiastic UN supporter of the establishment of a Jewish state in Palestine. And she remained a supporter of that state until the mid-1950's.

It is probable that in that period the Soviets foresaw a situation in which the Arab-Israeli conflict would worsen to the point where it would benefit the Soviet Union. Soviet influence increases where there are problems, and in the Middle East the Arab-Israeli conflict is a problem of the first magnitude. And since it so happened that the United States could not take the Arab side, because of Zionist pressures at home, the Soviet switch to the Arab side was ingenious, for it provided the Soviets with the opportunity to establish a military presence in the area. Since the Arabs were the defeated side, their need for military assistance was much greater than that of Israel. And it was to take much longer to satisfy it, thereby making the Soviet military presence more prolonged.

But why is the Soviet Union interested in a military presence in the Arab world? The answer is simple: the Soviet Union wants to move to the third stage of its Arab policy and strategy, and the third stage is designed to achieve control over the Arab countries. This control is to be in the form, not of nationalist regimes, but of Communist regimes, assisted by the Soviet armed forces.

Only in the third stage of her design will the Soviet Union be interested in local Communist parties. This stage could begin after another Arab defeat at the hands of the Israelis, or after it becomes clear that no peace will be achieved through negotiations. In either situation, the Arab masses will come to the conclusion that the Arab nationalists cannot achieve one of their objectives, which is the restoration of Arab rights in Palestine. It will be a desperate situation, so chaotic that the Soviet Union will be able to offer the Arabs Communism as an alternative. The offer will be accompanied by a *fait accompli:* the Arab Communists will be the only ones politically alive and ready to offer the possibility of reorganization, strong leadership, and a new battle with Israel. The psychological state of the Arabs will be such that their traditional enmity and resistance to Communism will weaken considerably.

Whether the final stage of Soviet strategy will be realized or not remains to be seen. Ironically, by supplying Israel with arms, the United States is helping the Soviet Union to strengthen her military presence in the Arab countries and ultimately to accomplish her political aims in the Arab world. If the United States wishes to complicate Soviet planning in the Arab world, she should act in awareness of the fact that Soviet military aid to the Arabs is less of a threat to Israel than it is to the Arabs.

At any rate, it is quite clear that the first two stages have been successful: today Western political influence is limited to a few Arab countries, and the Soviet military presence in the region is a fact that cannot be denied.

One important question remains unanswered. Why would the Soviet Union not be interested in ideology and in the local Communist parties during the first and second stages of her strategy but become interested in these things during the third stage? It is because in the first stage the Soviet Union would have difficulty building the image of an anticolonial power in alliance with Arab nationalism if she identified with the unpopular local Communist parties. In the second stage, the Soviet Union does not want to jeopardize her important, but limited, military presence in the region by antagonizing the Arab nationalists. Identification with local Communist parties is advantageous only when the nationalist regimes are discredited and weakened to the point where they cannot resist Communism. This point will be reached in an environment of chaos resulting from Arab frustration with the Israeli-Western "alliance."

In the third stage the Soviet Union is interested in control rather than mere influence, which is not necessarily permanent and can be more easily dislodged. However, the mere establishment of Communist regimes in the Middle East is no guarantee of Soviet control, as Soviet experience with Yugoslavia and Red China makes very clear. What the Soviet Union really wants in the Middle East is an "Eastern Europe" type of control, not another Red China. And this cannot be achieved unless preceded or accompanied by Soviet military support.

Conclusion

It is obvious that the limitations on American Middle East policy are great. Zionist and Jewish pressures at home and the American tendency to support the Arab *status quo* have limited U.S. effectiveness in dealing with Soviet influence in the Arab world.

The view that American economic and military support of

Israel is the only way to check Soviet influence in the Middle East is wrong. Continued American support of and partiality toward Israel must result in an eventual confrontation with the Soviet Union. At present this support contributes to polarization of the Arab-Israeli conflict internationally and regionally.

The United States lacks vision in dealing with the Middle East. The first thing American policymakers should remember is that Arab and American interests do not fundamentally conflict. In fact, they coincide on many issues. Both are opposed to Communism and each is useful to the other economically. The United States has economic interests in the Middle East, and the Western world is the largest consumer of Arab oil. The Arabs need Western technology, which they can assimilate better than Soviet technology because they have had more experience with it. Also, the Arab world is an important potential market for American products, a market that will become more important as the Arabs become more urbanized and technically more advanced.

Israel, in contrast, is a liability to the United States because Israel takes from the United States much more than she gives to it, and because American identification with Israel jeopardizes U.S. interests in the Arab world.

However, a shift in the American outlook on the Arab-Israeli conflict does not imply losing sight of the fact that the conflict is harmful to both the Arabs and the Israelis, in terms of human life and in terms of human dignity.

It should be remembered that the Arab-Israeli conflict has dangerous psychological implications for both Arabs and Jews. Humiliation and frustration could force the Arabs to abandon their traditional opposition to Communism. The humanitarian values of Israel's Jewish tradition could give way to militarism. Moreover, continuation of the conflict will ultimately destroy any hope for democracy in the entire Middle East region, including Israel. In fact, these effects can already be seen operating.

The United States must remember that Israel cannot exist forever by force, and that the Palestinian Arabs have a very strong and valid argument, which cannot be ignored simply because Israel exists. These Arabs must be allowed to return to their homes, or no *permanent* peace is possible in the Middle East. As to Israel's interests, the United States should recall that these are not necessarily the same as American interests or Jewish interests, and it is the latter (American and Jewish interests) that the United States should not abandon. Indeed, Jewish interests can be better served by separating them from Israeli interests; and this can be done if the United States becomes less concerned about Israel as a state than about Israel as a people. And in the final analysis it is people, whether Arab or Jewish, who should be the proper concern of statesmanship.

Notes

Chapter 1. ARAB LIFE BEFORE THE EMPIRE

1. It is said that the Arabian peninsula is the place from which all Semites originated. We are not certain whether this theory is correct. However, most scholars seem to support it.

2. One must always keep in mind that Arabia was not a nation-state and that its political organization was basically tribal. Consequently, tribes were either politically autonomous or independent and they had the power to conclude agreements, as do national states in modern times.

3. Muslims frown on the Western use of the words "Mohammedanism" and "Mohammedans" for their religion and for themselves. They insist that God only is the center of their belief, and not Mohammed. Western people use these terms because they refer to the followers of Christ as Christians. According to Christianity, Christ is divine, but in Islam, Mohammed is not. Thus the accurate terms are "Islam" and "Muslims," not "Mohammedanism" and "Mohammedans."

4. Because of the Muslim lunar calendar, the season in which Ramadan falls changes from year to year.

5. Originally, the word *imam* referred to the leader in prayer. Later it was associated with the spiritual and temporal head of Islam, the caliph. Sometimes the word is used to refer to authorities in Islamic theology and law.

Chapter 2. THE ARAB-ISLAMIC EMPIRE

1. John Joseph Saunders, *A History of Medieval Islam* (London: Routledge & Kegan Paul, Ltd., 1965), p. 77.

2. Bernard Lewis, *The Arabs in History* (Harper & Row, Publishers, Inc., Harper Torchbook, 1960), p. 93.

3. Philip K. Hitti, *The Arabs: A Short History,* rev. ed. (Princeton University Press, 1949), p. 115.

4. Thus, after centuries of development, Christianity became as practical as Islam.

5. Carlton J. H. Hayes, Marshall Baldwin, and Charles Woolsey Cole, *History of Europe,* rev. ed., 2 vols. in 1 (The Macmillan Company, 1956), p. 231.

6. The information in this section is derived mostly from two works: Hitti, *The Arabs,* and Rom Landau, *The Arab Contribution to Civilization* (The American Academy of Asian Studies, 1958).

7. Landau, *Arab Contribution,* p. 13.

8. *Ibid.,* p. 19.

9. Alfred Guillaume, *The Legacy of Islam* (London: Oxford University Press, 1931), p. 279.

10. Hitti, *The Arabs,* p. 182.

11. Landau, *The Arab Contribution,* p. 55.

12. Hitti, *The Arabs,* p. 153.

13. Most of the information in this section is derived from Richard W. Southern, *Western Views of Islam in the Middle Ages* (Harvard University Press, 1962).

14. Southern, *Western Views,* p. 14.

15. *Ibid.,* p. 28.

16. *Ibid.,* p. 104.

Chapter 3. DECLINE AND DISASTER IN THE ARAB WORLD

1. Many scholars consider Ibn Khaldun the founder of modern sociology and the greatest Arab historian. In his famous works, he treats history as a science and sets forth principles of sociology and political economy. See Ibn Khaldun, *Muqaddimah: An Introduction to History,* tr. by Franz Rosenthal, 3 vols. (Pantheon Books, Inc., 1958).

2. Francesco Gabrieli, *The Arabs: A Compact History,* tr. by Salvator Attanasio (London: Robert Hale, Ltd., 1963), p. 162.

3. John Marlowe, *A History of Modern Egypt and Anglo-Egyptian Relations, 1800–1953* (Archon Books, 1956), p. 87.

4. See Harry Hopkin's article in *The New Middle East.* Sept., 1969, p. 18.

5. Hopkin, in *The New Middle East*, p. 15.

6. This and the remaining sections of the chapter are based on, and in part reproduced from, my book *Political Systems of the Middle East in the Twentieth Century* (Dodd, Mead & Company, Inc., 1970), pp. 109–117.

7. Hugh J. Schonfield, *The Suez Canal in World Affairs* (Philosophical Library, Inc., 1953), p. 6.

8. Marlowe, *Anglo-Egyptian Relations*, p. 65.

9. Ismail was a very ambitious man. He attempted to obtain credits to finance grandiose schemes, including irrigation projects, the building of schools, and the construction of the Suez Canal. Much of the money he borrowed was wasted and his country was seriously involved in debt. Finally in 1876 he was forced to accept dual French and British management of the Egyptian treasury. In 1878 he attempted to throw off foreign control, but failed. The sultan deposed him the following year.

10. Marlowe, *Anglo-Egyptian Relations*, p. 71.

11. In 1863, when Said died, Egypt's external debt was 3,300,000 Egyptian pounds; in 1876, when the British and the French took over the Egyptian treasury the debt went up to 94,000,000 pounds. The interest on these loans was very high: "On some loans the rate of interest was over 26 percent; indeed, one loan of 9 million pounds was paid over to the Egyptians in defaulted bonds. Typical of the debts contracted was one in 1865 for 3 million pounds. The Egyptians received 2.2 million pounds and had to repay 4.1 million pounds plus various fees and penalties." William R. Polk, *The United States and the Arab World* (Harvard University Press, 1965), p. 91. See also Evelyn B. Cromer, *Modern Egypt* (The Macmillan Company, 1916); and David S. Landes, *Bankers and Pashas: International Finance and Economic Imperialism in Egypt* (Harvard University Press, 1958).

12. The text is in Jacob C. Hurewitz (ed.), *Diplomacy in the Near and Middle East: A Documentary Record (1535–1914)*, 2 vols. (D. Van Nostrand Company, Inc., 1956), Vol. I, p. 210.

13. King Farouk had come of age in 1937, and he was to fall under the influence of a "palace clique," causing Nahas, the

prime minister, great discomfort. Consequently, the old rivalries between the Wafd party and the palace reappeared. In December, 1937, Farouk dismissed Nahas and in his place palace governments ruled Egypt.

Chapter 4. THE WESTERN POWERS DISMEMBER SYRIA AND IRAQ

1. In an attempt to depreciate the significance of British pledges to the Arabs, some writers have portrayed Husein as a naïve and unrealistic leader: "In the interests of the Zionists' thesis the Sharaef's [Husein's] demands have been treated as the wanderings of an old Oriental potentate putting his imagination impulsively onto paper. They were nothing of the sort. They were reiteration of a programme long conceived by all branches of Arabs and now adopted by the Sharaef in conjunction with them." J. M. N. Jeffries, *Palestine: The Reality* (Longmans, Green and Company, Inc., 1939), p. 67.

2. Harry N. Howard, *The Partition of Turkey: A Diplomatic History, 1913–1923* (University of Oklahoma Press, 1931), p. 188.

3. *Ibid.*, p. 190.

4. E. A. Speiser, *The United States and the Near East* (Harvard University Press, 1947), p. 51.

5. For the text of the Sykes-Picot Agreement, see Hurewitz, *Diplomacy in the Near and Middle East,* Vol. II (1914–1956), Document 10.

6. Arnold J. Toynbee and Kenneth P. Kirkwood, *Turkey* (Charles Scribner's Sons, 1927), p. 70.

7. George Lenczowski, *The Middle East in World Affairs* (Cornell University Press, 1962), p. 76.

8. William Spencer, *Political Evolution in the Middle East* (J. B. Lippincott Company, 1962), p. 45.

9. George Antonius, *The Arab Awakening* (G. P. Putnam's Sons, Inc., 1946).

10. See the article by George Kirk, in *Middle Eastern Affairs,* Vol. XIII (1962), pp. 162–173.

11. Hayes, Baldwin, and Cole, *History of Europe,* pp. 131, 137.

12. Landau, *Arab Contribution,* p. 19.

13. Spencer, *Political Evolution,* p. 254.

14. Except for a few minor changes, this section is reproduced from my book *Political Systems of the Middle East in the Twentieth Century,* pp. 215–217.

15. This involved the false arrest and imprisonment of Captain Alfred Dreyfus (1859–1935) by French authorities in 1894. Dreyfus, a French Jew, was exonerated in 1906. The incident caused many Jews to believe that anti-Semitism was for them a fact of life even in the liberal and democratic countries of the West.

16. Marver H. Bernstein, *The Politics of Israel: The First Decade of Statehood* (Princeton University Press, 1957), p. 7.

17. See Theodor Herzl, *The Jewish State: An Attempt at a Modern Solution of the Jewish Question* (American Zionist Emergency Council, 1946).

18. Bernstein, *The Politics of Israel,* p. 8.

19. Israel Zangwill was an English Jew, the author of several books, including *Children of the Ghetto* (1892), *Dreamers of the Ghetto* (1898), *Merely Mary Ann* (1893), *The Melting Pot* (1908), *The Principle of Nationalities* (1917), and *Chosen Peoples* (1918).

20. Text in Hurewitz, *Diplomacy in the Near and Middle East,* Vol. II (1914–1956), p. 25.

21. Thomas Jones, *A Diary with Letters, 1931–1950* (Oxford University Press, 1954), p. 30; see also Leonard Stein, *The Balfour Declaration* (Simon & Schuster, Inc., 1961), p. 45.

22. David Lloyd George, *War Memoirs,* 6 vols. (London: Ivor Nicholson and Watson, Ltd., 1933–1937), Vol. II, p. 50.

23. Howard, *The Partition of Turkey,* p. 198.

24. See the White Paper of June, 1922 (Great Britain, Command Paper 1700).

25. The agreement was concluded in January, 1918. Text in Walter Z. Laqueur (ed.), *The Israel-Arab Reader: A Documentary History of the Middle East Conflict* (Citadel Press, 1969), pp. 18–20.

26. Antonius, *The Arab Awakening,* p. 285.

27. Stein, *The Balfour Declaration,* p. 638. Stein quotes the *Arab Bulletin,* June 18, 1918.

28. Lenczowski, *The Middle East*, p. 88. For more details on this subject, see Harry N. Howard, *The King-Crane Commission: An American Inquiry Into the Middle East* (Beirut: Khayat, 1963).

29. The British and the French refused to allow elections in the territories under their occupation. As a result, the Turkish representation system was used. Jeffries, *Palestine*, p. 282.

30. The principle of self-determination had been accepted by President Wilson in his fourteen-point program for peace declared on January 8, 1918. The twelfth point stated that "the nationalities which are now under Turkish rule should be assured an undoubted security of life and an absolutely unmolested opportunity of autonomous development." The Allied powers were also committed to the principle by the Agreement of November 5, 1918. In addition, the principle had been proclaimed by the Russian Revolution. For details, see Philip Quincy Wright, *Mandates Under the League of Nations* (The University of Chicago Press, 1930), pp. 24–25.

31. As mentioned earlier, the King-Crane Commission had indicated that the people of Syria preferred independence, but if independence was impossible, they wanted the United States or Britain as their guardian. However, the Commission's report was ignored by the Paris Peace Conference and was kept secret until 1922. See Wright, *Mandates*, pp. 44–45.

32. William Yale, *The Near East: A Modern History* (The University of Michigan Press, 1968), p. 317.

33. A political formula for the governing of Lebanon was established in 1943. Known as the National Pact, the formula divided power on the basis of religious identity. Parliamentary seats were distributed between Christians and Muslims according to a ratio of six to five.

34. See Don Peretz, *The Middle East Today* (Holt, Rinehart & Winston, Inc., 1963), pp. 346–348.

35. In 1921, French estimates showed that there were 87,000 Turks out of a total of 220,000.

36. Lenczowski, *The Middle East*, p. 313.

37. According to the 1933 census, there were 89,500 Arabs and 70,800 Turks in the province. Of the Turks 23,500 were Turkish-speaking Armenians. These Armenians were politically

aligned with the Arabs. Stephen Hemsley Longrigg, *Syria and Lebanon Under French Mandate* (Oxford University Press, 1958), pp. 238–239.

38. For more details, see Arnold J. Toynbee and V. M. Boulter, *Survey of International Affairs, 1938* (London: Royal Institute of International Affairs, 1941), pp. 479–492.

39. Longrigg, *Syria and Lebanon,* p. 233.

40. See Royal Institute of International Affairs, *Great Britain and Palestine, 1915–1945* (London: The Institute, 1946), pp. 149–150.

Chapter 5. THE PALESTINE PROBLEM

1. *The Palestine Year Book, 5706–5708* (Zionist Organization of America, 1945), Vol. I, p. 168.

2. Figures on population and immigration are found in Government of Israel, *Statistical Abstract,* 1967, Table D/3; UN Special Committee on Palestine, *Report to the General Assembly* (1947), I, 12; The Palestine Government, *A Survey of Palestine Prepared in December, 1945, and January, 1946, for the Anglo-American Committee of Inquiry* (Jerusalem, 1946–1947), Vol. II, pp. 794 f.

3. From the beginning of the Palestine Mandate, the British government took a census only twice, in 1922 and 1931. Figures relating to other years are official estimates supported by League of Nations and Zionist documents (with negligible differences in the latter sources). In 1922, the official census indicated the presence in Palestine of 83,000 Jewish inhabitants and 660,700 Arabs (Muslim and Christian). The Jewish percentage of the population was less than 11 percent.

4. For text of the White Paper of 1939, see Great Britain, Command Paper 6019; also see Hurewitz, *Diplomacy in the Near and Middle East,* Vol. II, p. 218.

5. As early as 1943, Arab leaders warned the United States that the solution to the Jewish refugee problem should not be at the expense of the Palestinian Arabs. See, for instance, the memorandum from the Egyptian Legation to the Department of State, U.S. Department of State, *Foreign Relations of the United States,* 1943, Vol. IV, p. 766. Many of them suggested

alternatives to Jewish immigration into Palestine. The Egyptian government, for instance, proposed to the U.S. Government that countries of the United Nations should share in the responsibility of settling the Jewish refugees "in proportion to [their] total population." See "Memorandum of Conversation, by the Under Secretary of State," in *Foreign Relations*, 1943, Vol. IV, p. 767.

6. The Arabs were not the first to interpret Western intentions in this light. A slightly different interpretation was offered by Ernest Bevin, the foreign secretary of Great Britain, on June 12, 1946. Addressing the Bournemouth meeting of the Labour Party, he said: "I hope it will not be misunderstood in America if I say, with the purest of motives, that [America's policy regarding Jewish immigration into Palestine] was because they did not want too many of them [the Jews] in New York." *The New York Times*, June 13, 1946; also Dean G. Acheson, *Present at the Creation: My Years in the State Department* (W. W. Norton & Company, Inc., 1969), p. 173.

7. According to official British sources, the total area of Palestine was 26,320,000 Turkish dunums (1 dunum = ¼ acre). Of these the Jews owned only 1,588,000 dunums. The Palestine Government, *Survey of Palestine*, pp. 103, 243. Also UN Doc. A/AC.14/32, Nov. 11, 1947, p. 44. The UN figure on Jewish land ownership is slightly less than the one given by the Palestine (i.e., British) government.

8. Article 22 of the Covenant of the League of Nations.

9. For more details on the mandate system, see my *Political Systems of the Middle East in the Twentieth Century*, pp. 217–219.

10. Jacob C. Hurewitz, *The Struggle for Palestine* (W. W. Norton & Company, Inc., 1950), pp. 29–36.

11. In 1935, a Zionist wrote in his diary: "Herbert Samuel [the British High Commissioner of Palestine] emphasized the need for cooperation with the Arabs and said that the Jews could never make a success of Palestine without taking the Arabs with them. At this point Weizmann winked at me. One might as well expect a ferret to cooperate with a rabbit." Richard Meinertzhagen, *Middle East Diary, 1917–1956* (Thomas Yoseloff, Inc., Publisher, 1959), p. 148.

12. Bernstein, *The Politics of Israel,* p. 19.

13. A descriptive term used by the Palestine Royal Commission of 1937, known as the Peel Commission. See Palestine Royal Commission, *Report* (London: H. M. Stationery Office, 1937) (Great Britain, Command Paper 5479).

14. On the other hand, opportunities for self-government were very limited for the Arabs. Although the British permitted the Arabs to elect municipal councils, these councils had very limited power. For instance, the Arabs had no control over the educational system, which was centralized and British-controlled. And they did not have anything comparable to the Jewish community's administrative and political responsibilities.

15. The text of the agreement is in Hurewitz, *Diplomacy in the Near and Middle East,* Vol. II, pp. 106–111. The Arabs complained that this agreement was unfair. While it mentioned the Jewish community several times and gave it a number of privileges, it referred to the Arabs (who then constituted a 90 percent majority of the population) as "the other sections."

16. *The Palestine Year Book, 5706–5708,* Vol. I, p. 307. Between 1922 and 1929 the functions of the Agency were exercised by the Zionist Organization. This arrangement proved unsatisfactory since it was not acceptable to the non-Zionists who believed in the idea of a national Jewish home but not in the idea of a Jewish state. In 1929, Chaim Wiezmann persuaded his Zionist colleagues who were meeting in Zurich to include in the Jewish Agency representatives of the non-Zionists. He believed that this was necessary in order to obtain greater financial support for the Agency.

17. The British contended that they could not govern Palestine under existing conditions. *The New York Times,* Feb. 13, 1947.

18. The states represented on the committee were Australia, Canada, Czechoslovakia, Guatemala, India, Iran, the Netherlands, Peru, Sweden, Uruguay, and Yugoslavia.

19. However, representatives of Egypt, Iraq, Lebanon, Saudi Arabia, Syria, and Yemen did cooperate with the committee.

20. UN Special Committee on Palestine, Report to General Assembly. General Assembly, 2d Ses., *Official Records,* Supplement No. II, A/364, Add. 1, Sept. 9, 1947, II, pp. 47–64.

21. Chaim Weizmann, *Trial and Error: Autobiography* (Schocken Books Inc., 1966), p. 473.

22. President Truman admitted that he had never experienced such political pressure as he did while the UN was discussing the partition plan. See Harry S. Truman, *Years of Trial and Hope,* Vol. II of *Memoirs,* 2 vols. (The New American Library of World Literature, 1956), p. 186. State Department officials had for some time been aware of Zionist influence on Middle East policy. "It seems true to say that our policy has gradually taken form . . . as the result of pressures that have been applied to us from various directions. We go as far as we can to please the Zionists and other Jews. . . . The main point . . . is that our policy, as it stands, is one of expediency, not one of principle." "Memorandum by the Chief of the Division of Near Eastern Affairs (Merriam) to the Director of the Office of Near Eastern and African Affairs (Henderson)," U.S. Department of State, *Foreign Relations,* 1946, Vol. VII, p. 733.

23. See James Forrestal, *The Forrestal Diaries,* ed. by Walter Millis (The Viking Press, Inc., 1951), p. 341.

24. The Zionists deny such pressure. See Edward Glick, *Latin America and the Palestine Problem* (Theodor Herzl Foundation, 1958), p. 105. They also contend that the Arabs pressured Guatemala and Costa Rica. Jorge García-Granados, *The Birth of Israel: The Drama as I Saw It* (Alfred A. Knopf, Inc., 1948), pp. 263–264. However, there is ample evidence that the United States did pressure Latin American countries as well as other countries. See Chesly Manly, *The UN Record: 10 Fateful Years for America* (Henry Regnery Co., 1955), pp. 49–53; Kermit Roosevelt, "The Partition of Palestine: A Lesson in Pressure Politics," *Middle East Journal,* Vol. II, No. 1 (Jan., 1948), pp. 1–16; and Oscar Kraines, *Government and Politics in Israel* (Houghton Mifflin Company, 1961), p. 3.

25. In reference to the security of the Negev, David Ben-Gurion declared on January 8, 1948, in an address to the Central Committee of Israel's Worker's Party: "Force of arms, not formal resolution will determine the issue." David Ben-Gurion, *Rebirth and Destiny of Israel,* ed. and tr. by Mordekhai Nurock *et al.* (Philosophical Library, Inc., 1954), p. 232. Zionist manipulation was often shrewd and forceful. Weizmann, for

instance, records in his autobiography that when in 1929 he had difficulty arranging an interview with the British Colonial Secretary, Lord Passfield, he "had a conversation at his house with Lady Passfield." In a similar experience with Ramsey MacDonald, the British prime minister, Weizmann sought the help of the prime minister's son, "who was extremely sympathetic to our case." Weizmann, *Trial and Error,* p. 331.

26. A/AC.13/32, General Assembly, 2d Ses., *Official Records,* Ad Hoc Com., pp. 209, 301.

27. UN General Assembly Resolution 181 (II) of Nov. 29, 1947, UN General Assembly, 2d Ses., *Official Records,* Resolutions, Sept. 16–Nov. 29, 1947, A/519, Jan. 8, 1948, pp. 131–150.

28. The negative votes included ten Arab and Muslim states in addition to Greece, Cuba, and India. Among the states that abstained was Britain. (France and the United States voted for partition.)

29. Clyde Eagleton, "Palestine and the Constitutional Law of the United Nations," *American Journal of International Law,* Vol. XLII (1948), pp. 397 ff.; Hans Kelsen, *The Law of the United Nations: A Critical Analysis of Its Fundamental Problems* (Frederick A. Praeger, Inc., 1950), pp. 195 ff.; Leland M. Goodrich and Edward I. Hambro, *Charter of the United Nations: Commentary and Documents* (World Peace Foundation, 1946), p. 47: "The functions of the General Assembly with regard to measures of collective security are limited by Articles 10 and 18 of the Charter to making recommendations to the member states by a two-thirds majority. It is the nature of a recommendation to leave it to the discretion of the addressee whether or not he wishes to follow it." Hans J. Morgenthau, *Politics Among Nations: The Struggle for Power and Peace,* 2d ed. (Alfred Knopf, Inc., 1954), p. 284: "Whatever political or moral force such recommendations of the General Assembly may claim, they are not legally binding." Georg Schwarzenberger, *A Manual of International Law,* 5th ed. (London: Stevens & Sons, Ltd., 1967), p. 289.

30. "The impression was spread by many of our newspapers that the General Assembly had approved a specific blue-print, whereas it had merely accepted a principle. The way in

which this principle might be translated into action had yet to be found." Truman, *Years of Trial and Hope,* Vol. II, p. 187.

31. UN General Assembly, 15th Ses., *Official Records,* Special Political Committee, 209th Meeting, 14.

32. UN General Assembly Resolution 377 (V). There are authorities who do not think that acts of the Assembly under this resolution are binding either. "It [the resolution] does not bind the members of the UN in the same way that comparable action by the Security Council would." H. B. Jacobini, *International Law: A Text,* rev. ed. (The Dorsey Press, Inc., 1968), p. 273.

33. This concern of State Department officials began to develop a few years before the establishment of Israel. The State Department was intensely aware of American interests in the Arab world and the harmful effects of a pro-Zionist American policy on these interests. Some officials foresaw the introduction of Soviet influence in the area even before the Soviet Union had become a superpower and the cold war had begun. In addition, the State Department, on several occasions warned President Roosevelt, and after him President Truman, that the establishment of a Jewish "commonwealth" would set the Middle East aflame. However, purely domestic considerations, Jewish votes and Jewish financial contributions to electoral campaigns, forced the elected officials of the U.S. Government to support many of the aims of Zionism. See U.S. Department of State, *Foreign Relations,* 1944, Vol. V, pp. 623–626, 637, 646, 649; *Foreign Relations,* 1945, Vol. VIII, pp. 712, 748; Forrestal, *Diaries,* p. 365; Norman A. Graebner (ed.), *An Uncertain Tradition: American Secretaries of State in the 20th Century* (McGraw-Hill Book Co., Inc., 1961), pp. 256–258.

34. UN, *Annual Report of the Secretary-General on the Work of the Organization,* July 1, 1947, to June 30, 1948, p. 5.

35. UN, *Annual Report of the Security Council to the General Assembly,* July 16, 1947, to July 15, 1948, p. 78.

36. UN Doc. A/565, General Assembly, 3d Ses., *Official Records,* No. 1, pp. 5, 6, 8, 9. The Arabs interpret this resolution to mean a repeal of the partition resolution. Count Folke Bernadotte, the mediator appointed under the new resolution, con-

sidered himself not bound by the partition resolution. Count Folke Bernadotte, *To Jerusalem,* tr. by Joan Bulman (London: Hodder & Stoughton, Ltd., 1951), p. 33.

37. Replying to this charge, Arab spokesmen point to the fact that the Zionist movement was foreign to Palestine and argue further that without foreign intrusion the State of Israel would have been impossible.

38. For a brief account of the Zionist argument, see *Israel's Struggle for Peace* (New York: Israel Office of Information, 1960), pp. 30–36.

39. American recognition of the State of Israel raised interesting legal questions, because Israel's boundaries were not yet defined with any precision. The United States had been a party to the Montevideo Convention of 1933, which required, among other things, "a defined territory" before a state became "a person of international law." The recognition extended by the United States to the provisional government of Israel was de facto. U.S. Department of State, *Bulletin,* Vol. XVIII, No. 464 (May 23, 1948), p. 673. However, Philip Jessup, the United States representative to the UN, told the Security Council on December 17, 1948, that the United States had recognized, de facto, the provisional government, but that the state itself was recognized de jure. UN, Security Council, 3d Year, *Official Records,* No. 130, 385th Meeting, Dec. 17, 1948. On October 24, 1948, President Truman declared that de jure recognition would be extended when Israel elected a permanent government. *White House Press Release,* Jan. 31, 1949; U.S. Department of State, *Bulletin,* Vol. XX, No. 502 (Feb. 13, 1949), p. 205. Also see discussion and documentation in Herbert Briggs (ed.), *The Law of Nations,* 2d ed. (Appleton-Century-Crofts, 1952), p. 125.

40. Soviet consistency in supporting Zionist claims became subject to various kinds of interpretations. One theory is that the Soviet state predicted trouble in the Middle East as a result of the creation of the Israeli state, and predicted also that such trouble would benefit the Soviet cause.

41. UN General Assembly Resolution No. 273 (III) of May 11, 1949.

42. UN General Assembly Resolution No. 194 (III) of Dec.

11, 1948. Arab spokesmen argue that after her admission to the
UN, Israel failed to live up to the admission resolution.

43. Nadav Safran, *The United States and Israel* (Harvard
University Press, 1963), pp. 72–78. For more details about
Israel's social and cultural divisions, see Leonard J. Fein, *Politics in Israel* (Little, Brown & Company, 1967).

44. *Maariv* (Tel Aviv), Dec. 12, 1969. In Israel the cultural
and social differences of Jews have led to discrimination. See
Newsweek, April 19, 1971, p. 60. *The Jerusalem Post* (weekly
overseas edition), No. 547, April 27, 1971, p. 5; *Maariv* (Tel
Aviv), April 12, 1971.

45. Israel's 1950 Law of Return states that "every Jew has
the right to immigrate to the country [Israel] and enjoy the
same states as Jews born in Israel." See text of the Law in
Laqueur, *The Israel-Arab Reader,* Document 27, p. 128.

46. Zionist leaders consider Israel to be the home of all Jews,
whatever their origin. Ben-Gurion ran into difficulty with some
Jews during his visit to the United States in March, 1967. He
said a Jew was not really a Jew unless he planned to live in
Israel. Earlier, in 1952, Ben-Gurion spoke in defense of the
Nationality Law, which discriminated against the Arabs, and
asserted that Israel "is not only a Jewish state, where the
majority of the population are Jews, but a state for all Jews,
wherever they are, and for every Jew who wants to be
here . . . . This right is inherent in his being a Jew." Ben-Gurion was quoted by Don Peretz, *Israel and the Palestine
Arab* (Washington, D.C.: The Middle East Institute, 1958),
p. 122.

47. In establishing the theoretical basis for the Jewish state,
Theodor Herzl, the founder of the Zionist movement stated:
"We [the Jews] should there [in the Jewish State] form a
portion of a rampart of Europe against Asia, an outpost of
civilization as opposed to barbarism. We should . . . remain in
contact with all Europe, which would have to guarantee our
existence." Theodor Herzl, *The Jewish State,* p. 96.

48. William L. Tung, *International Law in an Organizing
World* (The Thomas Y. Crowell Company, 1968), p. 48; James
L. Brierly, *The Law of Nations,* 6th ed. (Oxford: Clarendon
Press, 1963), pp. 138–139; Charles De Visscher, *Theory and*

Reality in Public International Law, tr. from the French by
P. E. Corbett (Princeton University Press, 1957), p. 239.

49. Hans Kelsen, *Principles of International Law,* 2d ed.
(Holt, Rinehart & Winston, Inc., 1967), p. 392.

50. Hans Kelsen, "Recognition in International Law—Theoretical Observations," in Leo Gross (comp.), *International Law
in the Twentieth Century* (Appleton-Century-Crofts, 1969), p.
589.

51. "The fate of Jewish victims of Hitlerism was a matter of
deep personal concern to me. I have always been disturbed by
the tragedy of people who had been made victims of intol-
erance and fanaticism because of their race, color, or religion. . . . The plight of the victims who had survived the
mad genocide of Hitler's Germany was a challenge to Western
civilization, and as President I undertook to do something
about it." Truman, *Years of Trial and Hope,* Vol. II, p. 158.

52. This argument is consistent with the Islamic "conception
of Justice," which is generally more concerned about the victim than the offender: "Islamic law tries to redress a wrong by
removing its effects upon the victim or by inflicting the same
or an equal situation upon the guilty one." In this connection,
Islam extends "to the limit of practicability, and perhaps beyond it, the early Judaeo-Christian conception that its essence
is reciprocity, that is, equality between the parties." Morroe
Berger, *The Arab World Today* (Doubleday & Company, Inc.,
1964), p. 34. In fact, the argument was used by the king of
Saudi Arabia in response to President Roosevelt's concern
about the Jewish victims of Hitler's policy. The king said, "Give
them and their descendants the choicest lands and homes of the
Germans who had oppressed them." William A. Eddy, *F.D.R.
Meets Ibn Saud* (American Friends of the Middle East, 1954),
p. 34.

53. According to one pro-Arab source, the well-known historian Arnold Toynbee "suffered incredible vituperation and
the smearing label of anti-Semite" for criticizing the Zionists
and Israel. The same source lists the names of other individuals
who were similarly abused by the Zionists. Among them are
Biblical scholar and archaeologist Millar Burrows, of Yale
Divinity School; William Ernest Hocking, of Harvard Uni-

versity; columnist Dorothy Thompson; Henry Gideonse, president of Brooklyn College; Mrs. Willie Snow Ethridge, wife of the publisher of the Louisville *Courier-Journal;* Bayard Dodge, president of the American University in Beirut; and author Vincent Sheean. John N. Booth, "The Moral Case for the Arabs," *The Middle East Newsletter* (Beirut), Sept., 1969, pp. 10–13. According to Ray Vicker, "anybody who disagrees with Zionist goals is apt to be branded anti-Semitic." See his article in *The Wall Street Journal,* Dec. 9, 1968.

54. Herzl did mention the population of the territory in his *Diary.* He says: "We shall try to spirit the penniless population across the border by procuring employment for it in the transit countries, while denying it any employment in our own country." And: "If we move into a region where there are wild animals to which the Jews are not accustomed—big snakes, etc.—I shall use the natives, prior to giving them employment in the transit countries, for the extermination of these animals." Theodor Herzl, *The Complete Diaries of Theodor Herzl,* ed. by Raphael Patai, 5 vols. (The Herzl Press, 1961), Vol. I, pp. 88, 98.

55. On a number of occasions, the Zionists entertained the thought of moving the Palestinian Arabs out of Palestine. In his report of May 5, 1943, Brigadier General Patrick J. Hurley, President Roosevelt's personal representative in the Middle East, stated that "the Zionist organization in Palestine has indicated its commitment to an enlarged program for . . . an eventual transfer of the Arab population from Palestine to Iraq." *Foreign Relations,* 1943, Vol. IV, p. 777.

56. This attitude, which characterized early Zionist relations with the Arabs, is today characteristic of Israeli-Arab relations, according to a recent Time–Louis Harris poll. See *Time,* April 12, 1971.

Chapter 6. THE FIRST TWO WARS

1. For evidence, Zionists rely on a threatening statement made by Husain Khalidi, a member of the Palestine Arab Higher Committee. The statement promised "a holy war" if

the partition resolution was enforced. *The New York Times,* Dec. 1, 1947.

2. Ben-Gurion, *Rebirth and Destiny of Israel,* p. 292.

3. See *The New York Times,* Dec. 21, 1947; Feb. 16, 1948; March 6, 1948; April 4, 1948; April 17, 1948; April 26, 1948; May 1, 1948; May 9, 1948.

4. "Thus, as April began, our War of Independence swung decisively from defense to attack." Ben-Gurion, *Rebirth and Destiny of Israel,* p. 296.

5. UN Doc. A/565, General Assembly, *Official Records,* Supplement No. 1, 1948, p. 9.

6. *Israel's Struggle for Peace,* p. 39.

7. It was not the first time the Zionists had underestimated the importance of Arab goodwill. (As mentioned earlier, this goodwill is required by Israel's geographic position—Israel being a sort of island in an Arab ocean.) Historically, the Zionist movement showed very little recognition of the fact that the Arabs were an important people, with whom Zionist goals would have to be reconciled, since they would be affected most by the fulfillment of these goals.

8. Maxime Rodinson, *Israel and the Arabs* (Penguin Books, 1969), tr. by Michael Perl, p. 39; also *The New York Times,* July 8, 10, 11, 1948.

9. John Bagot Glubb, *A Soldier with the Arabs* (London: Hodder & Stoughton, Ltd., 1957), pp. 135–136.

10. Harry Sacher, *Israel: The Establishment of a State* (London: George Weidfeld & Nicholson, 1952), p. 276.

11. Jon Kimche, *Seven Fallen Pillars: The Middle East* (London: Secker & Warburg, 1950), pp. 249–250.

12. In fact, Britain knew that Israel was secretly obtaining arms from the Communists. Kimche, *Seven Fallen Pillars,* pp. 249–250.

13. Ben-Gurion recognized Communist assistance as "sincere sympathy with Israel's enterprise." State of Israel, *Government Year Book,* 1952, pp. 22–23.

14. One of the Zionist movement's greatest achievements was to inculcate into Jewish life the idea and attitude that without Israel there can be no real Jewish identity. The Zionists also taught the Israeli Jews that failure in "the war of inde-

pendence" would mean their physical annihilation. No doubt Arab rhetoric made this kind of Zionist indoctrination credible.

15. Arab nationalism is largely an urban, middle-class movement. Much of the rural-agricultural population and those of the upper strata who have vested interests in division, such as the kings, the sheikhs, and many politicians, are not sufficiently moved by Arab nationalism.

16. Ironically, Jewish nationalism had the opposite effect upon Jews. It created interest in the past. Thus, the modern Jews are going back in history to discover or to know more about their roots as a people. Witness, for instance, their tremendous interest in archaeological work. In addition, old concepts are becoming attractive among the Zionist Jews. Colonialism, which is something of the past, has adherents among Zionists and Israelis. There is some truth in saying that the Israelis are a "modern" people looking backward and the Arabs are a "backward" people looking forward. Incidentally, both peoples are experiencing visual difficulties.

17. In the Arab world, revolutionary change is introduced by the military regimes, which are themselves rarely consistent or stable. In other parts of the world, revolutionary changes have not resulted in political instability because one revolutionary regime survived long enough to institute the change.

18. Figures on boundaries and territory are taken from Oscar Kraines, *Government and Politics in Israel* (Houghton Mifflin Company, 1961), p. 11. For more details, see A. N. Poliak, "Geopolitics of the Middle East," *Middle Eastern Affairs*, Vol. IV (Aug.–Sept., 1953), pp. 271–277; and Lewis M. Alexander, "The Arab-Israeli Boundary Problem," *World Politics*, Vol. IV (April, 1954), pp. 322–327.

19. H. B. Jacobini, *International Law: A Text*, p. 285. For more details on the subject, see J. B. Moore, *A Digest of International Law* (U.S. Government Printing Office, 1965), Vol. VII, pp. 327–335; Morris Greenspan, *The Modern Law of Land Warfare* (University of California Press, 1959), pp. 385–392.

20. Charles G. Fenwick, *International Law*, 4th ed. (Appleton-Century-Crofts, 1965), p. 753.

21. Article II of the Israel-Syrian General Armistice Agreement, July 20, 1949 (UN Security Council Doc. S/1353). This

article is repeated in one form or another in the other armistice agreements between Israel and the Arab countries.

22. *Israel's Struggle for Peace*, p. 55.

23. *Ibid.*, p. 49.

24. UN Docs. S/1797, Sept. 18, 1950; S/2300, Aug. 1951.

25. *The New York Times*, Oct. 31, Nov. 1, 2, 7, 1948; UN Docs. S/1071, Nov. 6, 1948; S/1122, Jan. 26, 1949; S/1286, March 14, 1949.

26. UN Docs. S/1797, Sept. 18, 1950; S/2300, Aug., 1951.

27. UN General Assembly, *Official Records*, 22d Ses., Supplement No. 13 (A/6713), Table 1, 59.

28. In his autobiography he described the details. Menahem Begin, *The Revolt: The Story of the Irgun*, tr. by Shmuel Katz (Henry Schuman, Inc., 1951), pp. 162–165. Also see Zionist writer Jon Kimche's *Seven Fallen Pillars*, pp. 217–218.

29. *The New York Times*, Oct. 31, Nov. 1, 2, 7, 1948; March 11, 15, 1949.

30. The proof was provided by journalist Erskine B. Childers. He checked all British and American transcriptions of Arab radio broadcasts of 1948, interviewed Arab leaders, and asked the Israeli government for evidence to support their claim that Arab leaders had ordered Palestinians to leave their homes. He could not find evidence to prove the Israeli argument. Instead, he found "repeated monitory records of Arab appeals, and flat orders to the civilians of Palestine to stay put." Erskine B. Childers, "The Other Exodus," *The Spectator*, May 21, 1961.

31. Kenneth W. Bilby, *New Star in the Near East* (Doubleday & Company, Inc., 1950), p. 239.

32. Uri Aunery, an Israeli who fought bravely in the 1948 war, wrote later admitting that "the truth is that it is natural for primitive people to abandon their homes for a few days while their villages are under attack." Aunery, who is currently a member of the Israeli parliament, states that after May 15, 1948, "the eviction of Arab civilians had become an aim of David Ben-Gurion and his government."

33. Paragraph 11 of UN General Assembly Resolution 194 (III) of December 11, 1948, states that "the refugees wishing to return to their homes and live in peace with their neighbours should be permitted to do so at the earliest practicable date,"

and that "compensation should be paid for the property of those choosing not to return and for loss of or damage to property which, under principles of international law or in equity, should be made by the Governments, or authorities responsible."

34. Ben-Gurion was asked if Israel was interested in non-Jewish immigration. He answered that Israel does not need such immigrants and that "what we are interested in are Jews." Peter Grose, "Now that Nasser Is Gone, Ben-Gurion, His Old Foe, Feels Uneasy," *The New York Times,* Oct. 13, 1970.

35. See "The Law of Return" of July 5, 1950, in Laqueur, *The Israel-Arab Reader,* pp. 128–129.

36. U.S. Department of State, *The Suez Canal Problem* (*1956*), pp. 25–30.

37. See U.S. Department of State, *Bulletin,* Vol. XXXV, 1956.

38. There were about 80,000 British soldiers in the Suez Canal area. In July, 1954, Britain and Egypt signed a treaty in which Britain agreed to withdraw within twenty months. The text of the treaty is in Hurewitz, *Diplomacy in the Near and Middle East,* Vol. II, pp. 383–384.

39. There is evidence that Nasser was considering nationalization before the Aswan Dam controversy. Keith Wheelock, *Nasser's New Egypt: A Crirtical Analysis* (Frederick A. Praeger, Inc., 1960), p. 238.

40. Frederick L. Schuman, *International Politics: Anarchy and Order in the World Society,* 7th ed. (McGraw-Hill Book Co., Inc., 1969), p. 366.

41. Originally, the Egyptian government was the second largest shareholder in the Suez Canal Company. In 1874, the Egyptian ruler, Ismail, sold part of Egypt's shares to the British and a few years later the Anglo-French comptrollers of the Egyptian treasury sold the remaining shares, leaving Egypt with no shares and Britain as the second largest shareholder. See John Marlowe, *Anglo-Egyptian Relations, 1800–1953* (London: Cresset Press, Ltd., 1954), pp. 65, 71.

42. Schuman, *International Politics,* p. 365.

43. *Ibid.,* pp. 365–366.

44. Eden's obsession with Nasser has been noted by Anthony

Nutting, Minister of State in the Eden government. Nutting broke a long public silence to reveal some of the unknowns in the Suez crisis. See Nutting, *No End of a Lesson: The Story of Suez* (London: Constable & Co., Ltd., 1967).

45. Israel was mostly in contact with France. Schuman, *International Politics*, p. 377. Also see Terence Robertson, *Crisis: The Inside Story of the Suez Conspiracy* (London: Hutchinson & Co., Ltd., 1965), pp. 108–163; Peter Calvocoressi, "Some Evidence of Collusion," in *Suez Ten Years After*, ed. by Anthony Moncrieff (London: British Broadcasting Corporation, 1967), pp. 83–107.

46. UN Doc. S/3712, Oct. 29. 1956.

47. UN Security Council, *Official Records*, 11th Year, 750th Meeting (Oct. 31, 1956).

48. UN Security Council, *Official Records*, 11th Year, 755th Meeting (Nov. 5, 1956).

49. UN General Assembly, *Official Records*, 1st Emergency Special Session, 562nd Meeting (Nov. 1, 1956).

50. UN Doc. A/3290, Nov. 4, 1956.

51. UN Resolution 1002 (ES-1).

52. For more details, see Nigel Nicolson, *People and Parliament* (London: George Weidenfeld & Nicolson, Ltd., 1958); Frederick S. Northedge, *British Foreign Policy: The Process of Readjustment, 1945–1961* (London: George Allen & Unwin, 1962); Paul Johnson, *The Suez War* (Greenberg, Inc., 1957); Leon D. Epstein, *British Politics in the Suez Crisis* (University of Illinois Press, 1964); Leon D. Epstein, "British M.P.'s and Their Local Parties: The Suez Crisis," *American Political Science Review*, June, 1960, pp. 374–390; Leon D. Epstein, "Partisan Foreign Policy: Britain in the Suez Crisis," *World Politics*, Jan., 1960, pp. 201–224.

53. "Suez and Its Consequences: The Israeli View," *The World Today*, Vol. XIII, No. 4 (April, 1957), p. 158.

54. *Ibid.*, p. 160.

55. For all four documents, see *The Suez Canal Problem* (U.S. Department of State, 1956), pp. 16–20, pp. 1–3, pp. 4–9, pp. 9–16.

56. This is at least true of Britain. Wolfgang Friedman and Lawrence A. Collins, "The Suez Canal Crisis of 1956," in

International Law and Political Crisis: An Analytic Casebook,
ed. by Lawrence Scheinman and David A. Wilkinson (Little,
Brown & Company, 1968), p. 107.

57. The Egyptian argument is contained in Egyptian Ministry of Foreign Affairs, *White Paper on the Nationalization of
the Suez Maritime Canal Company* (1956).

58. On April 12, 1939, the British government stated before
the Mixed Courts of Appeal, while this court was adjudicating
the case known as the Gold Currency Case (decision rendered
on Feb. 24, 1940), that "the Suez Canal Company is a legal
person in accordance with Egyptian law. Its nationality and
character are solely Egyptian." See *White Paper,* p. 59.

59. Eden, Sir Anthony, *Full Circle* [Memoirs] (London:
Cassell & Co., Ltd., 1960), pp. 476–477.

60. Friedman and Collins, "The Suez Canal Crisis of 1956,"
p. 94.

61. The concession would have run out in 1968, twelve years
after the crisis.

62. UN Doc. S/2322 (1951).

63. Article 10 of the 1888 treaty.

64. Schuman, *International Politics,* p. 363.

65. In 1955, 14,666 ships went through the canal; in 1958
and 1966 the figures were 17,842 and 21,250. Total tonnage in
1955 was 115,756,398, while in 1958 and 1966 it was 154,479,000
and 274,250,000. Hugh J. Schonfield, *The Suez Canal in Peace
and War* (University of Miami Press, 1969), pp. 205, 208 f.

Chapter 7. THE 1967 WAR AND THE ULTIMATE
CHANCES OF PEACE

1. United Nations, Security Council, *Official Records,* 433d,
6; *The New York Times,* Dec. 25, 1948.

2. *The New York Times,* Oct. 21, 1953.

3. UN Doc. S/3456, Nov. 3, 1955.

4. UN General Assembly, 2d Ses. *Official Records,* Ad Hoc
Com., 18th Meeting, Oct. 18, 1947, 122.

5. UN Security Council, *Official Records,* 559th, Feb. 15,
1954.

6. UN Doc. A/PV.1527, June 20, 1967, 6.

7. Nasser was reported as saying, "We have no intention of attacking Israel." Charles W. Yost, "The Arab-Israeli War: How It Began," *Foreign Affairs,* Vol. XLVI, No. 2 (Jan., 1968), p. 317. According to James Reston of *The New York Times,* Nasser did not want war because he knew he was not ready for it and Israel knew he was reacting to a Syrian bluff. *The New York Times,* June 4 and 5, 1967. UN Secretary-General U Thant reported to the Security Council that Nasser had assured him he would not attack Israel. UN Docs. S/7896, May 19, 1967; S/7906, May 27. Arab spokesmen in the UN made similar assurances. UN Docs. S/PV.1342, May 24, 31 ff.; S/PV.1345, May 31, 6 ff. Finally, a good reason why Nasser did not want war with Israel is that a large number of his troops were involved in the Yemeni war which, at the time, was in full swing.

8. *The New York Times,* May 13, 1967.

9. *The New York Times,* May 17, 1967.

10. Israel quotes a statement by the well-known authority on international law, Oppenheim, that "all gulfs and bays enclosed by the land of more than one littoral state, however narrow their entrance may be, are non-territorial." Lassa F. L. Oppenheim, *International Law: A Treatise,* 8th ed., 2 vols. (London: Longmans, Green & Company, Ltd., 1955), Vol. I, p. 508. However, the same source (Oppenheim) admits that this rule is "not uncontested."

11. "That states in time of peace have a right to send their warships through Straits used for international navigation between two parts of the high seas without the previous authority of a coastal state, provided that the passage is innocent." The International Court of Justice, *The Corfu Channel Case,* Report 28, 1949.

12. UN General Assembly, 12th Ses., *Official Records,* 697th Plenary Meeting, Oct. 2, 1957, p. 233. Although the United States supported Israel's position in the Gulf controversy, Secretary of State Dulles had recognized the problem to be "a highly complicated question of international law" and that "in one sense of the word the Straits of Tiran are territorial, because they are less than six miles wide." U.S. Department of State, *Bulletin,* Vol. XXXVI, 1957, pp. 482–484.

13. These refugees locate in a number of places: 311,814 in

the Gaza Strip; 272,692 in the west bank; 506,038 in Jordan; 158,217 in Syria; and 175,958 in Lebanon. *Newsweek,* Sept. 21, 1970.

14. Joseph C. Harsch, "The Palestinian Arabs," *The Christian Science Monitor,* Sept. 17, 1970.

15. French fear of Germany might be listed as another example. However, Germany lost World War I and World War II as a result of a larger effort to which France contributed.

Chapter 8. THE UNITED STATES AND THE ARABS

1. George Antonius, *The Arab Awakening,* p. 452. For the text of the recommendations of the King-Crane Commission with regard to Syria-Palestine and Iraq (1919), see *ibid.,* pp. 443–458.

2. Wilson failed to dissuade Britain and France from dividing up the Arab Fertile Crescent into a number of small states economically and politically dependent upon them.

3. Among them was Justice of the Supreme Court Louis Brandeis, who became a Zionist in 1912. As a Jew, Brandeis believed that "to be good Americans, we must be better Jews, and to be better Jews we must become Zionists." Alpheus Thomas Mason, *Brandeis, A Free Man's Life* (The Viking Press, Inc., 1956), p. 446.

4. Walter Lippmann, *U.S. Foreign Policy: Shield of the Republic* (Little, Brown & Company, 1943).

5. E. A. Speiser, *The United States and the Near East,* p. 225.

6. George Lenczowski (ed.), *United States Interests in the Middle East* (American Enterprise Institute, 1968), p. 39.

7. *Ibid.,* p. 39.

8. *Ibid.,* p. 40.

9. Also, the closure of the Suez Canal after the 1967 war had effects upon the price of Middle East oil. It increased the length of the trip from the Middle East to Europe by 70 percent and the cost of oil by $1 billion for the first year only.

10. Lenczowski, *United States Interests,* p. 40.

11. *Time,* Feb. 1 and 15, 1971.

12. "The instability of moods and the typical public indif-

ference to foreign policy in the absence of threat accords disproportionate influence to minority groups." Gabriel A. Almond, *The American People and Foreign Policy* (Harcourt, Brace and Company, Inc., 1950), p. 86.

13. American indifference changes to involvement and activism when a problem or a situation reaches the proportion of danger and threat to the United States. Almond, *The American People,* p. 86. The Vietnam war is an example of such a situation.

14. Morroe Berger, "Americans from the Arab World," in James Kritzeck and R. Bayly Winder (eds.), *The World of Islam* (London: Macmillan and Co., Ltd., 1959), pp. 351–372.

15. Almond, *The American People,* pp. 186–187.

16. Ray Vicker, "Zionism Is Under Attack on Two Fronts," *The Wall Street Journal,* Dec. 9, 1968.

17. Almond, *The American People,* p. 186.

18. Ray Vicker, "Zionism Is Under Attack on Two Fronts." "The activity of Jewish organizations in the postwar period has been primarily directed at getting American support for the establishment of an independent Jewish state in Palestine." Almond, *The American People,* p. 185.

19. It is, however, not characteristic of the ideological liberals, such as socialist groups, and young liberals. These people, including some Jews, have attempted to go deeper into the Arab-Israeli question; and some have become converted to the Arab side of the controversy.

20. As a propaganda slogan, the term "tiny Israel" has been so effective that it has crept into the language of scholars. It is used in such works as Frederick L. Schuman's well-known textbook, *International Politics,* p. 384.

21. *Time,* June 21, 1971, p. 30.

22. John S. Badeau, *The American Approach to the Arab World* (Harper & Row, Publishers, Inc., 1968), p. 27.

23. See, for instance, Robert I. Kahn's article "The Right of the Jews to Israel," reprinted by the Zionist Organization of America in December, 1968, from *The American Zionist.*

24. Historical evidence contradicting this Zionist thesis is found in the works of eyewitnesses such as the English poet George Sandys, *A Relation of a Journey begun An. Dom. 1610;*

William McClure Thompson, *The Land and the Book* (New York, 1859), and others researched by Richard Davis; see his "Making the Desert Bloom," *The Middle East Newsletter* (Beirut), Feb.-March, 1971.

25. See *The Israel Yearbook,* 1960, p. 18.

26. Lenczowski, *United States Interests,* p. 65.

27. "Memorandum of Conversation, by Mr. William L. Parker of the Division of Near Eastern Affairs," March 3, 1943. U.S. Department of State, *Foreign Relations,* 1943, Vol. IV, p. 760.

28. This was reported by Brigadier General Patrick J. Hurley, President Roosevelt's personal representative in the Middle East. See his report dated May 5, 1943, in *Foreign Relations,* 1943, Vol. IV, p. 779.

29. *Ibid.,* p. 780.

30. See Attlee's communiqué of Sept. 14, 1945. *Foreign Relations,* 1945, Vol. VIII, p. 739.

31. *Ibid.*

32. See Attlee's communiqué of Sept. 17, 1945. *Foreign Relations,* 1945, Vol. VIII, p. 740.

33. *Ibid.*

34. See "The British Embassy to the Department of State," *Foreign Relations,* 1945, Vol. VIII, pp. 775 f.

35. See the record of a conversation at the State Department between Bevin and the Secretary of State, April 27, 1946, *Foreign Relations,* 1946, Vol. VII, p. 587.

36. See the "Memorandum by the Chief of the Division of Near Eastern Affairs (Merriam) to the Director of the Office of Near Eastern and African Affairs (Henderson)," Sept. 26, 1945, *Foreign Relations,* 1945, Vol. VIII, pp. 745 ff.

37. Acheson, *Present at the Creation,* p. 169.

38. *The New York Times,* June 13, 1946.

39. Acheson, *Present at the Creation,* p. 169. Also, Francis Williams, *A Prime Minister Remembers: The War and Post-War Memoirs of the Rt. Hon. Earl Attlee* (London: William Heinemann, Ltd., 1961), pp. 185–186.

40. Truman, *Years of Trial and Hope,* Vol. II, p. 185.

41. *Ibid.,* p. 188.

42. *Ibid.,* p. 158.

43. Acheson, *Present at the Creation,* p. 169.

44. Fred L. Israel (ed.), *The War Diary of Breckinridge Long* (University of Nebraska Press, 1966), p. 336.

45. Another possibility is that the Arab governments (or at least some of them) might change their oil policy and cut off the oil supply to Western countries. This could happen if radical (or more radical) regimes succeed to power in these countries. Such regimes might come to the conclusion that since the Arab oil-producing countries, specifically Libya and Kuwait, have huge reserves, the negative effects of a new oil policy would be much greater in the Western world than in the Arab world. Europe has enough oil to keep it going for no more than one to two months. Kuwait and Libya might survive the loss of revenue from oil for much longer, perhaps two to three years.